Red Book Plus: Family Court Essential Materials 2017–2018

LexisNexis®

Published by LexisNexis

LexisNexis
Regus
Terrace Floor
Castlemead
Lower Castle Street
Bristol BS1 3AG

British Library Cataloguing-in-Publication Data

A catalogue record for this book is available from the British Library.

ISBN 978 1 78473 388 9

Typeset by Letterpart Limited, Caterham on the Hill, Surrey CR3 5XL

Printed in Great Britain by Hobbs the Printers Limited, Totton, Hampshire SO40 3WX

Foreword to the First Edition

I am delighted to have been asked to introduce this work, a companion to *The Family Court Practice* ('the Red Book') and a guide to the more common applications in the Family Court. Helpful cross-references to the Red Book appear in each section, with innovative Flowcharts to assist the practitioner at various stages of the application.

This is a refreshing and informative guide which outlines the steps to be taken from start to finish, accompanying those steps with reminders and tips, alerting the practitioner to common pitfalls faced in the legal process and the frequent hurdles placed in the way of the client. Common errors, additional powers of the court, and practical advice which even the more experienced practitioner will find immensely useful (from attending court with copy documents to draft letters of instruction, communication with professionals and lay parties) are presented to the reader clearly and succinctly. One of the many skills which the family lawyer must call upon is the ability to communicate with the court, colleagues and clients and state agencies in a helpful and informed manner, and these tips are innovative and valuable. Assistance of this nature is not found in the major procedural works – there is no room for such matters – and it is enormously valuable, to have such a practical aide memoire at one's elbow.

The opening contents pages are an accessible route to the step-by-step guides which populate this work, referring the practitioner across to the authoritative source material, found within the Red Book, via the now familiar procedural guides.

The fifty pages of annexed guides to applicable tax rates, fostering allowances, 'passport' benefits and the RPI, to name but a few, will be of considerable help to those advising on financial remedies and even child care, as will the narratives on common problems and pitfalls which ensnare unsuspecting applicants.

Dry and impersonal this companion work is not, and I anticipate that it will sit comfortably with the Red Book on the shelves of all family practitioners, just as it will slip easily into the advocate's briefcase on the way to court!

His Honour Judge Anthony Cleary
November 2014

Scope of This Work

Red Book Plus is a reference guide for all Family Court practitioners and judges, providing a portable source of essential materials.

The work combines a wide range of procedural flowcharts with tables, legislation and guidance, complementing *The Family Court Practice* (the Red Book) and *LexisPSL Family*.

CONTENTS

- Flowcharts provide a useful one-page overview, as an aide memoire, for each court procedure (ie applications in respect of Divorce & Dissolution; Children; Domestic Abuse & Forced Marriage; Finance; Enforcement; Appeals), with cross-references to key family law resources
- Core legislation and guidance
- Key cases categorised under clear topic headings
- 2017–18 tables detailing taxation rates/thresholds, social security benefits, and fostering allowances

The law is stated as at 1 October 2017.

CONTENTS

Foreword to the First Edition iii
Scope of This Work v
Contents v

PART I

FLOWCHARTS

Divorce and Dissolution 3
Undefended divorce/civil partnership dissolution 5
Defended divorce/civil partnership dissolution 7
Undefended (judicial) separation 9
Undefended nullity 11
Amending an application for divorce/dissolution 13
Declaration of marital/civil partnership status 15
Staying grant of decree absolute under MCA 1973, s 10A 17
Service of an application for a matrimonial order/civil partnership order outside the jurisdiction 19

Domestic Abuse 21
Application for a non-molestation order under Part IV of the Family Law Act 1996 23
Application for an occupation order under Part IV of the Family Law Act 1996 25
Application for a forced marriage protection order under Part 4A of the Family Law Act 1996 27
Claims under the Protection from Harassment Act 1997 29
Application for variation, extension or discharge of a non-molestation or occupation order under Family Law Act 1996 31

General 33
Service (not of an application for a matrimonial civil partnership order) 35
Service of a document (not an application for a matrimonial order civil partnership order) outside the jurisdiction 37
Applications under Part 18 of the Family Procedure Rules 2010 39

Children 41
Child arrangements orders (Part 1)—pre-proceedings to FHDRA 43
Child arrangements orders (Part 2)—FHDRA to fact finding 45
Child arrangements orders (Part 3)—fact finding to final hearing 47
Parental responsibility orders (Part 1)—pre-proceedings to FHDRA 49
Parental responsibility orders (Part 2)—FHDRA to fact finding hearing 51
Parental responsibility orders (Part 3)—fact finding hearing to final hearing 53
Prohibited steps and specific issue orders (Part 1)—pre-proceedings to FHDRA 55

Prohibited steps and specific issue orders (Part 2)—FHDRA to fact finding hearing 57
Prohibited steps and specific issue orders (Part 3)—fact finding hearing to final hearing 59
Discharge of a parental responsibility order or agreement 61
Enforcement orders and financial compensation orders (child arrangements orders) 63

Financial Provision 65
Application for a financial order (not an interim order) under MCA 1973 or CPA 2004—pre-proceedings to first appointment 67
Applications for a financial order (not an interim order) under MCA 1973 or CPA 2004—first appointment to FDR 69
Application for a financial order (not an interim order) under MCA 1973 or CPA 2004—FDR to final hearing 71
Interim financial orders 73
Variation of a financial order 75
Application after an overseas divorce 77
Application for an injunction 79
Application for a search order (Anton Piller) 81
Contested applications under Trusts of Land and Appointment of Trustees Act 1996, s 14, under CPR 1998, Pt 7 83
Contested applications under Trusts of Land and Appointment of Trustees Act 1996, s 14, under CPR 1998, Pt 8 85
Applications under Schedule 1 to the Children Act 1989 (shortened procedure)—before first hearing 87
Applications under Schedule 1 to the Children Act 1989 (shortened procedure)—after first hearing 89
Variation of a Schedule 1 order 91
Application under MCA 1973, s 10(2)/CPA 2004, s 48(2) 93
Pensions on divorce/dissolution/nullity/(judicial) separation (Part 1)—to first appointment 95
Pensions on divorce/dissolution/nullity/(judicial) separation (Part 2)—first appointment to implementation 97

Appeals 99
Application for judicial review 101
Family Court—appeal from lay justice or district judge level to circuit judge, or from district judge (High Court level) to judge of the High Court (Part 1) 103
Family Court—appeal from lay justice or district judge level to circuit judge, or from district judge (High Court level) to judge of the High Court (Part 2) 105
Family Court—appeal from judge of circuit judge level or a judge of High Court level to the Court of Appeal (Part 1) 107
Family Court—appeal from judge of circuit judge level or a judge of High Court level to the Court of Appeal (Part 2) 109
Applications to set aside a financial remedy order 111
Family Court—appeal from judge of the High Court or from the Court of Appeal to the Supreme Court 113
Family Court—appeal from magistrates to the Family Court under Child Support Act 1991 115

Enforcement 117
Enforcement options (Part 1)—non-monetary issues 119
Enforcement options (Part 2)—monetary issues 121
Obtaining information from the debtor 123
Order for such method of enforcement as the court may consider appropriate 125
Committal for breach of an order or undertaking in the Family Court and High Court—matrimonial and civil partnership financial proceedings 127
Committal and arrest for disobedience of an injunctive order or breach of an undertaking in the High Court, Family Court or County Court 129
Attachment of earnings order 131
Charging order 133
Writ or warrant of delivery 135
Execution against goods—writ or warrant of control 137
Application for a third party debt order 139
Committal by way of judgment summons 141
Means of payment order 143
Writ or warrant of possession of land 145

PART II

KEY LEGISLATION AND GUIDANCE

Matrimonial Causes Act 1973 149
Sections 21A–25D 149

Children Act 1989 163
Sections 1, 2, 4, 8, 12 163

Family Procedure Rules 2010, SI 2010/2955, Part 3 169

Practice Direction 3A - Family Mediation Information and Assessment Meetings (MIAMS) 175

Family Procedure Rules 2010, SI 2010/2955, Part 9 183

Practice Direction 9A – Application for a Financial Remedy 211

Practice Direction 9B – Communication of Information from Financial Remedy Proceedings 219

Practice Direction 27A – Family Proceedings: Court Bundles (Universal Practice to be applied in the High Court and Family Court) 221

Practice Guidance 12 July 2010 – McKenzie Friends (Civil and Family Courts) 227

Practice Guidance 16 January 2014 – Transparency in the Family Courts: Publication of Judgments 231

Practice Guidance 18 January 2017 – Family Court – Duration of Ex Parte (Without Notice) Orders 235

PART III

KEY CASES

Categorised by Topic 239
Applications for leave 239
Applications for leave on notice 239
Arbitration 239
Bankruptcy 239
Capitalisation and variation of periodical payments 239
Child arrangements orders (contact) 240
Determining with whom a child lives 240
Domestic abuse 240
Duty on parents to work together 240
Grandparents 240
Importance of biological parentage 240
Step-parents 241
Child arrangements orders (living arrangements) 241
Importance of biological parentage 241
Companies – treatment 241
Companies – valuation 241
Companies – corporate veil 242
Compensation 242
Conduct 242
Consent orders 242
Contributions 243
Costs 243
Children proceedings 243
Financial 243
General 243
Cost allowances – Schedule 1, Children Act 1989 243
Costs orders – Schedule 1, Children Act 1989 244
Declaration of marital status 244
Departure from CAFCASS report 244
Disclosure 244
Disclosure – children proceedings 244
Duration of the marriage/civil partnership 245
Enforcement of child arrangements orders 245
Expert evidence 245
Expert evidence – children proceedings 245
Fact finding 245
Financial compensation order 245

Habitual residence 245
Human rights 246
Injunctions 246
Finance 246
Anti suit (*Hemain*) 246
Intractable contact 246
Jurisdiction – Forum conveniens 247
Legal services orders 247
Liquid v illiquid assets 247
Lump sums 247
Maintenance pending suit and interim costs (also see Legal service orders above) 247
Marital agreements 248
Non-marriage 248
Non-molestation and occupation orders 248
Parental responsibility 248
Parental responsibility – termination 249
Part III MFPA 1984 249
Pensions 249
Periodical payments – child 249
Periodical payments – spousal 250
Post separation accruals 250
Power to make an order of court's own initiative 250
Pre-marital/inherited wealth 250
Prohibited steps orders 251
Property orders 251
Publicity 251
Relocation 252
Schedule 1, Children Act applications 252
Carer's allowance 252
Scope 252
Gap years 252
Standard of living 252
Separate representation for child 253
Search orders (Anton Piller) 253
Section 7 reports 253
Section 91(14) orders 253
Shared care (prior to child arrangements orders) 253
Specific issue orders 253
Specific issue orders – jurisdiction 254
Standard of living 254
Timetabling 254
TOLATA 1996 applications 254
Transferring residence in light of repeated breaches of orders (prior to child arrangements orders) 255

Trusts 255
Wishes and feelings 255
Without notice applications 255

PART IV

2017–18 TABLES

Income Tax and National Insurance Contributions 259
Income tax allowances 2017/18 259
Income tax bands 2017/18 259
National insurance contributions: 2009–18 259

Other Tax Rates, Limits and Reliefs 261
Capital Gains Tax 261
 Capital gains rate of tax 2017/18 261
 Capital gains annual allowance 2017/18 261
Inheritance Tax 261
 Inheritance tax rates 261
 Taper relief 261
Stamp Duty Land Tax rates and thresholds 262
 SDLT rates for residential property 262

Fostering Allowances 263
 Recommended fostering allowance per week 263
 Tax-free earnings 263
 Tax relief 264

Social Security Benefits 265
Introduction 265
Means-tested benefits 266
 Universal Credit 266
 Income Support and income-based Jobseeker's Allowance 267
 State Pension Credit 269
 Housing Benefit 270
 Tax Credits 271
Benefits for incapacity or limited capability for work 272
 Statutory Sick Pay 272
 Employment and Support Allowance 273
 Incapacity Benefit 274
 Severe Disablement Allowance 275
Benefits for severe disability and carers 276
 Personal Independence Payment: mobility component 276
 Personal Independence Payment: daily living component 276
 Disability Living Allowance: mobility component 277
 Disability Living Allowance: care component 278

Attendance Allowance 279
Carer's Allowance 280
Other benefits 281
Industrial Injuries Disablement Benefit 281
Contribution-based Jobseeker's Allowance 282
Child Benefit 283
Statutory Maternity Pay, Statutory Paternity Pay and Statutory Adoption Pay, Statutory Shared Parental Pay 284
Maternity Allowance 285
Bereavement Support Payment 286
Bereavement Payment 287
Bereavement Allowance 288
Widowed Parent's Allowance 289
Retirement Pension 290

Retail Price Index and Consumer Price Index 291
Retail Price Index 291
Consumer Price Index 292

Interest Rates 293
Bank of England base rates 1999–present 293

PART I

FLOWCHARTS

DIVORCE AND DISSOLUTION

Undefended divorce/civil partnership dissolution

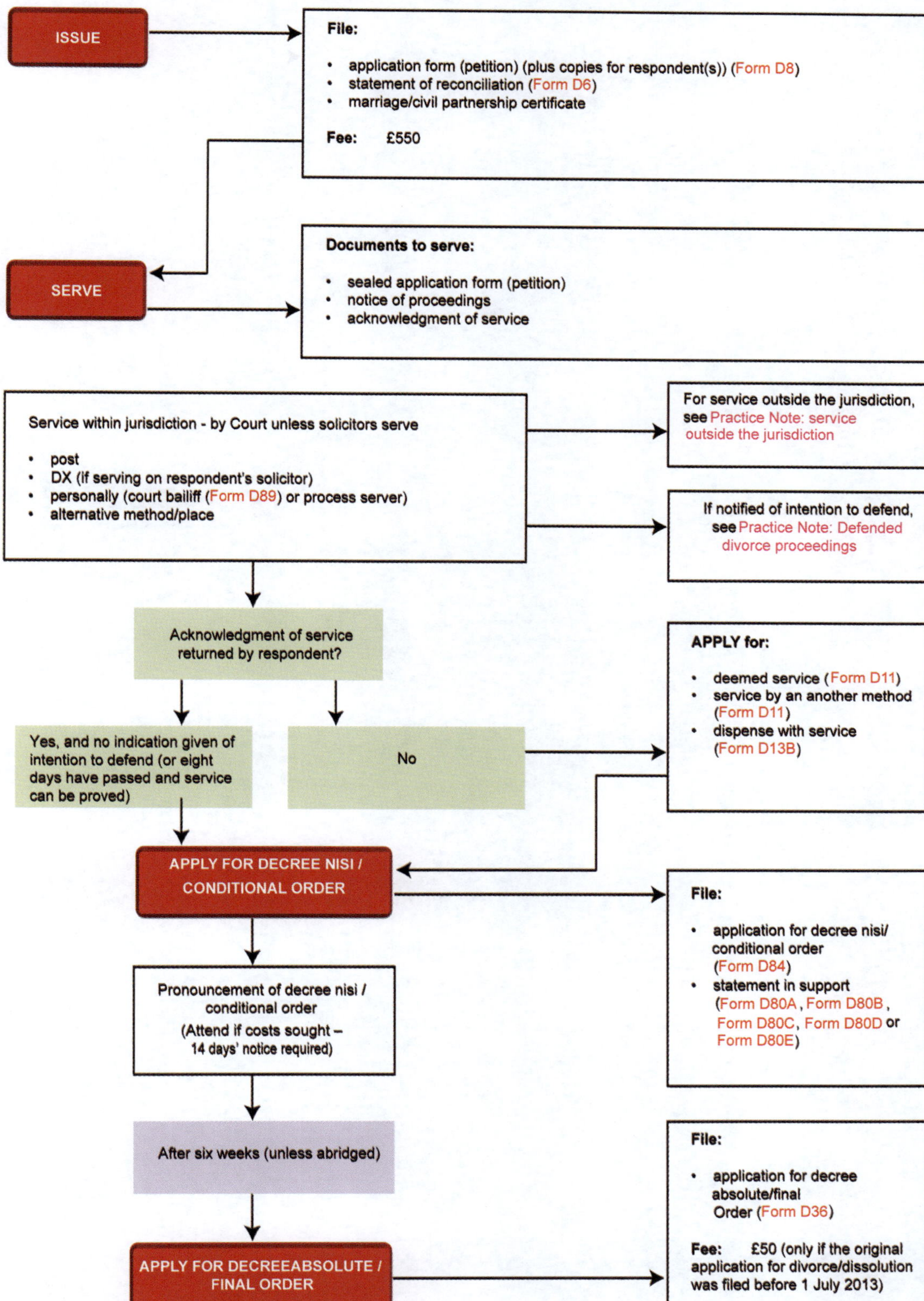

See also Procedural Guide (PG) B2 in Family Court Practice (The Red Book)

Defended divorce/civil partnership dissolution

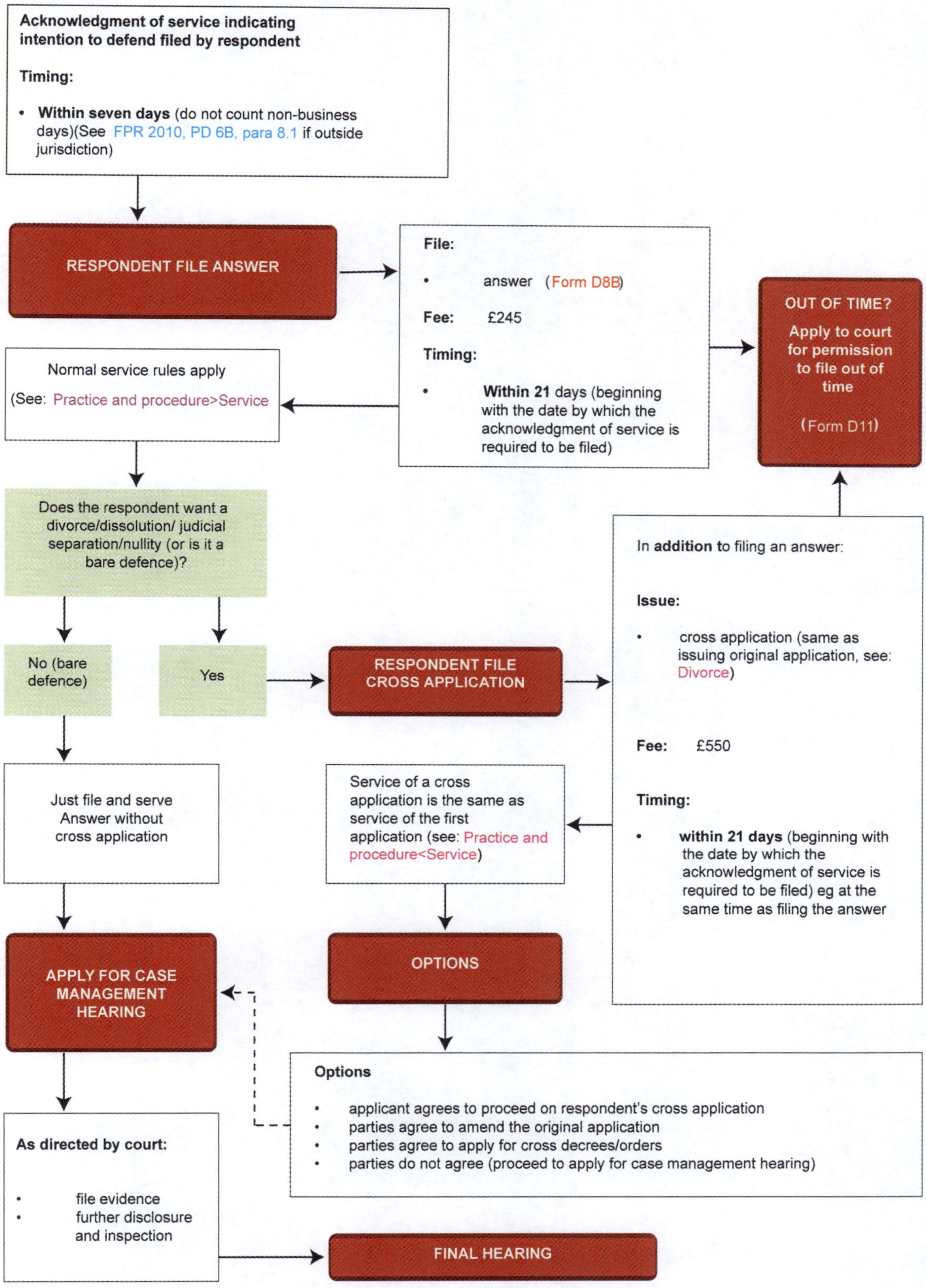

See also Procedural Guide (PG) B4 in Family Court Practice (The Red Book)

Undefended (judicial) separation

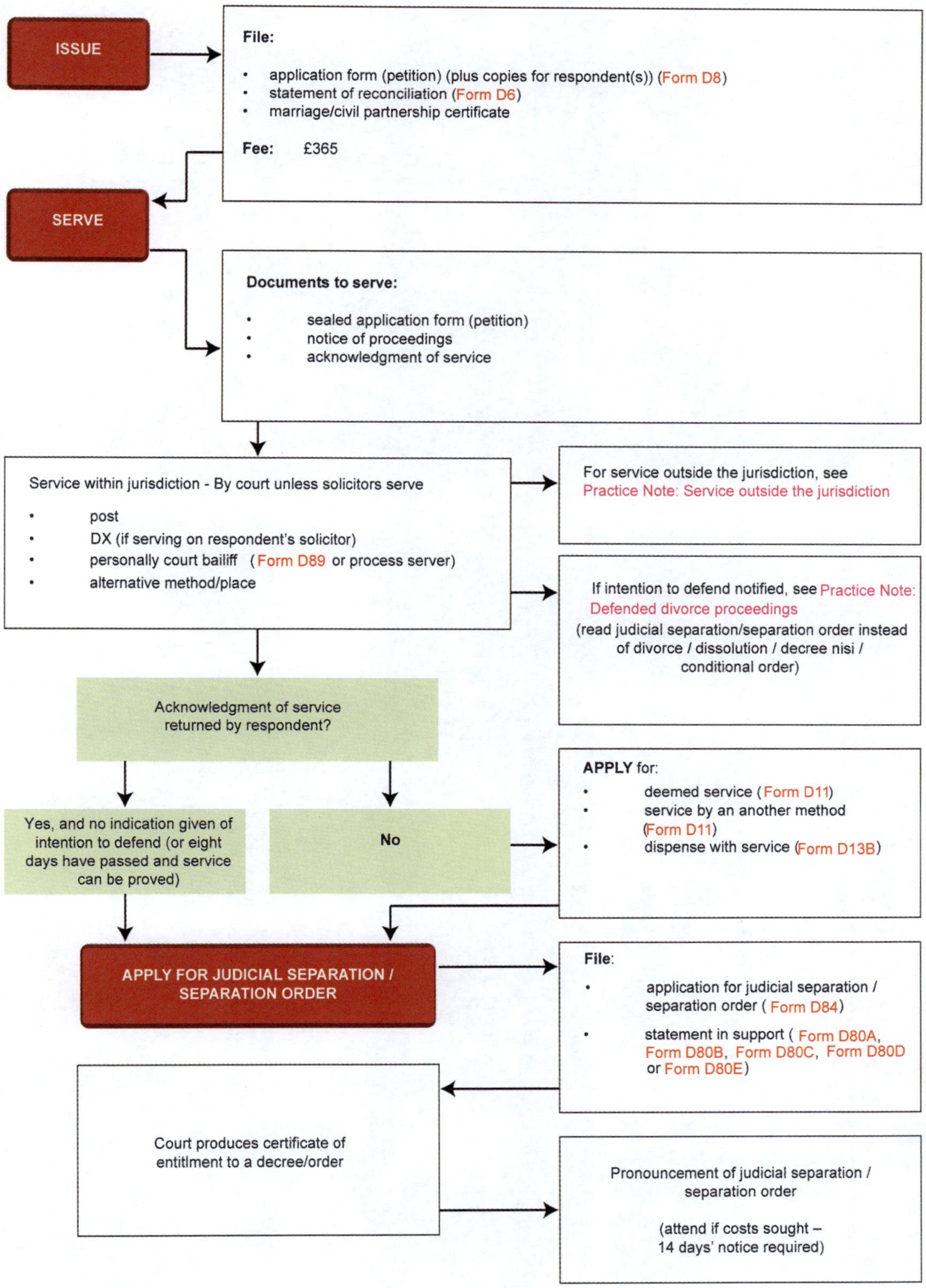

See also Procedural Guide (PG) B2 in Family Court Practice (The Red Book)

Undefended nullity

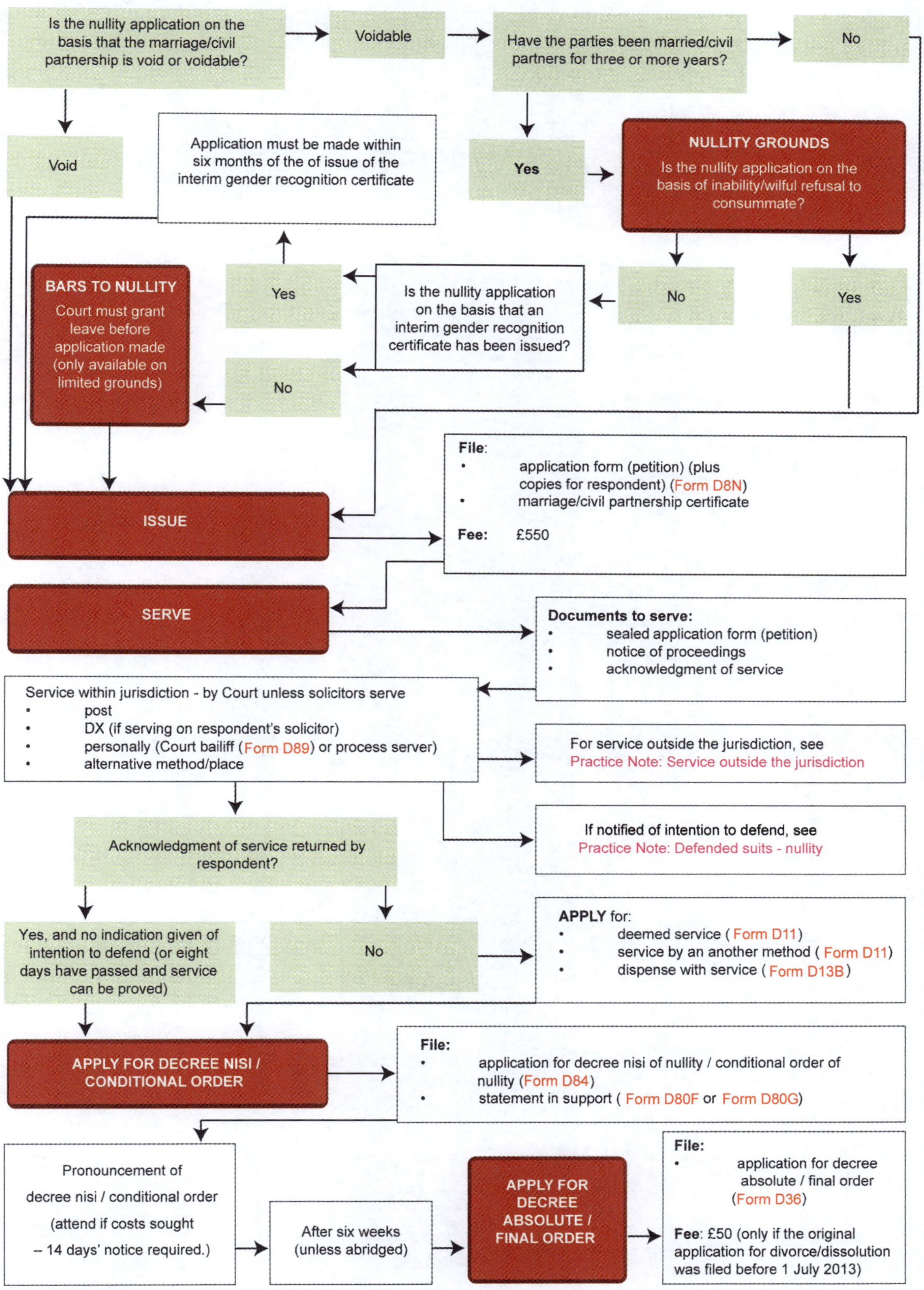

See also Procedural Guide (PG) B2 in Family Court Practice (The Red Book)

Amending an application for divorce/dissolution

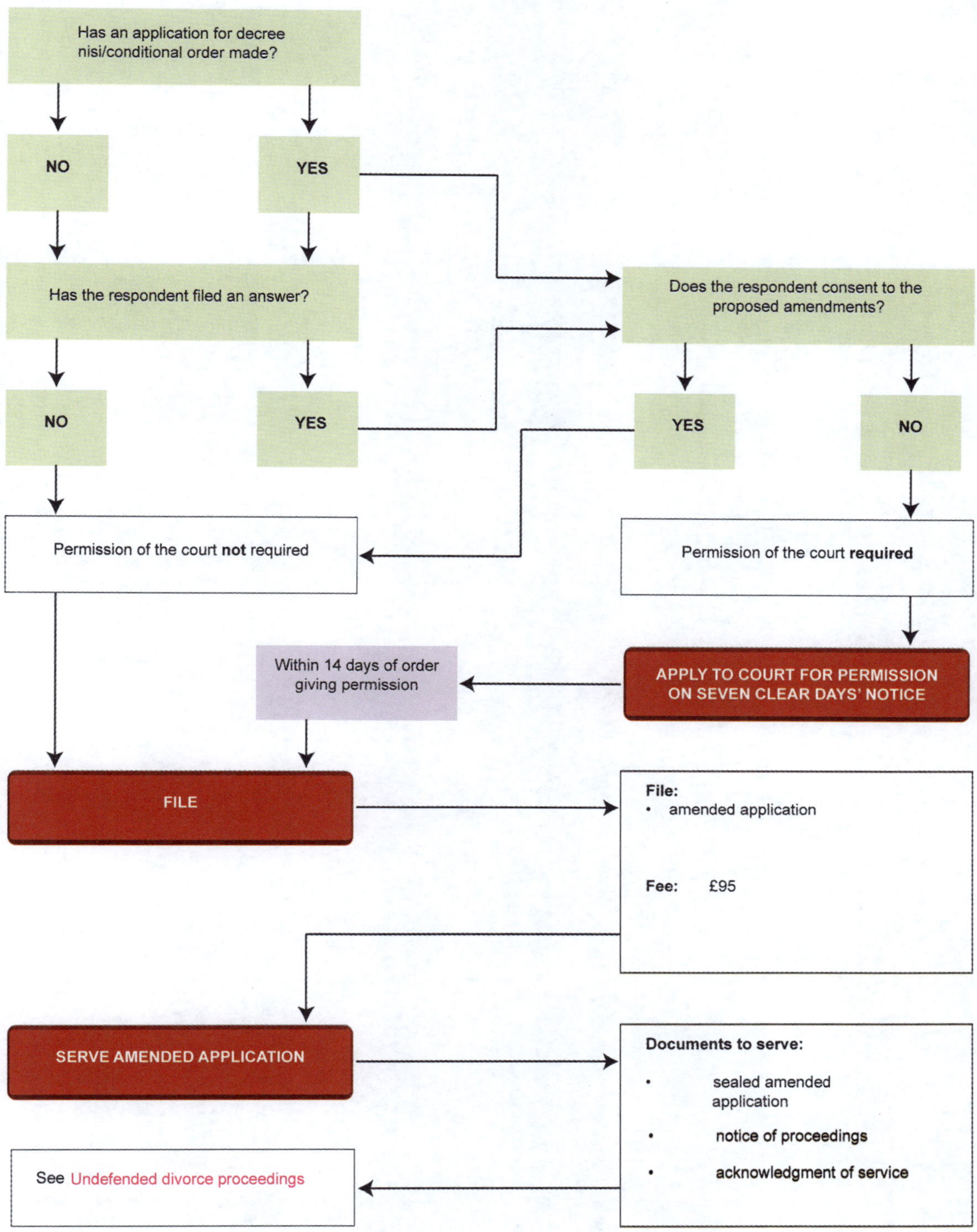

See also Procedural Guide (PG) B2 in Family Court Practice (The Red Book)

Declaration of marital/civil partnership status

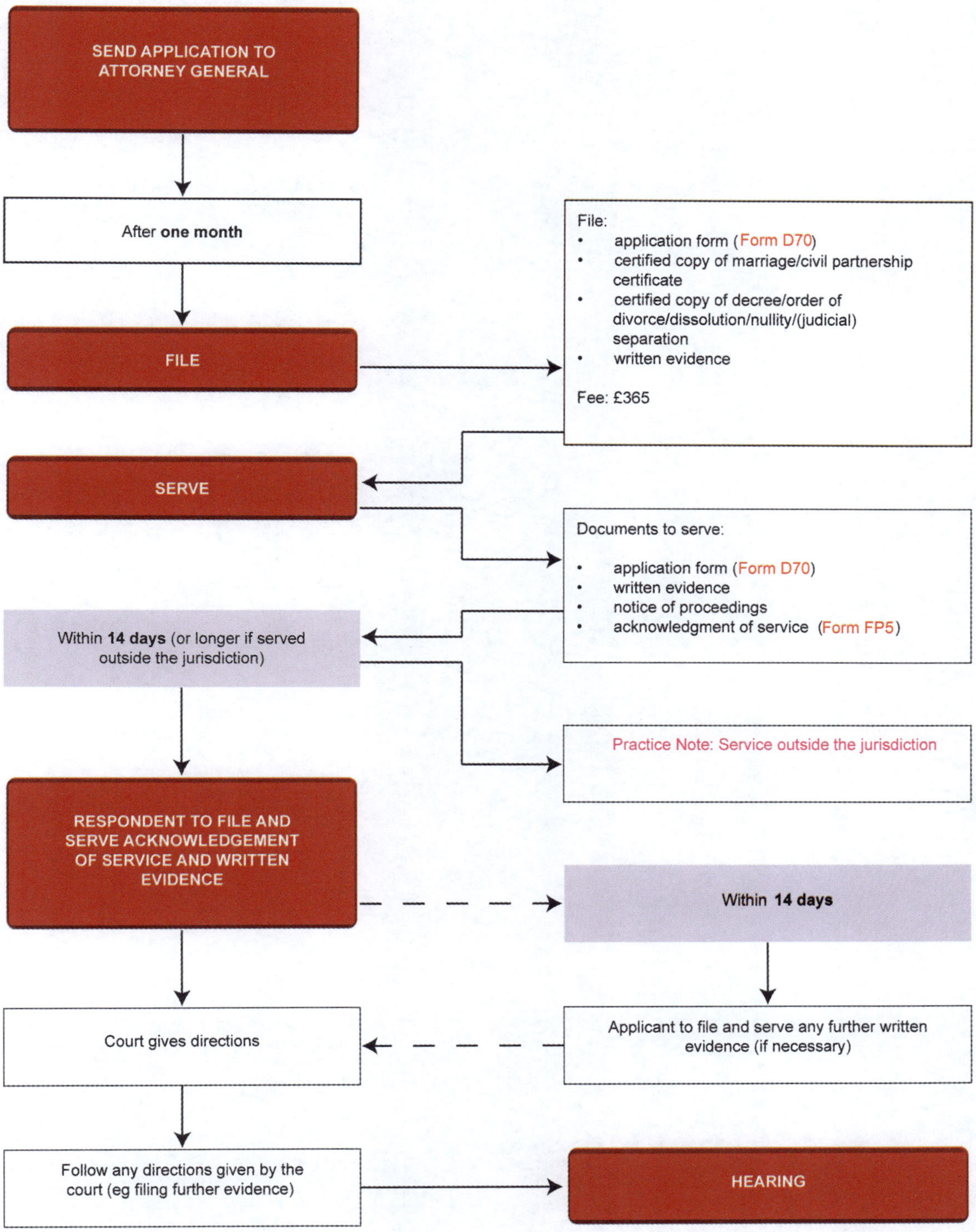

See also Procedural Guide (PG) B1 in Family Court Practice (The Red Book)

Staying grant of decree absolute under MCA 1973, s 10A

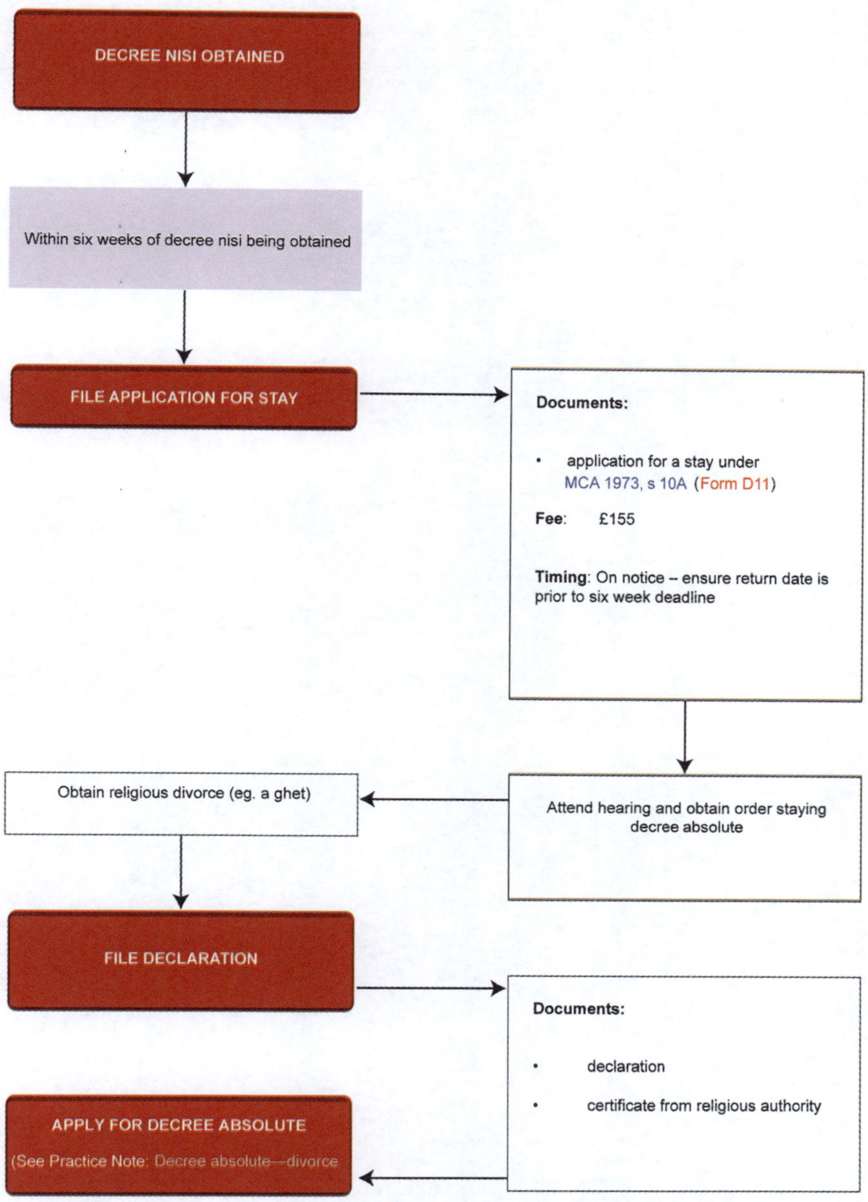

See also Procedural Guide (PG) B3 in Family Court Practice (The Red Book)

Service of an application for a matrimonial order/civil partnership order outside the jurisdiction

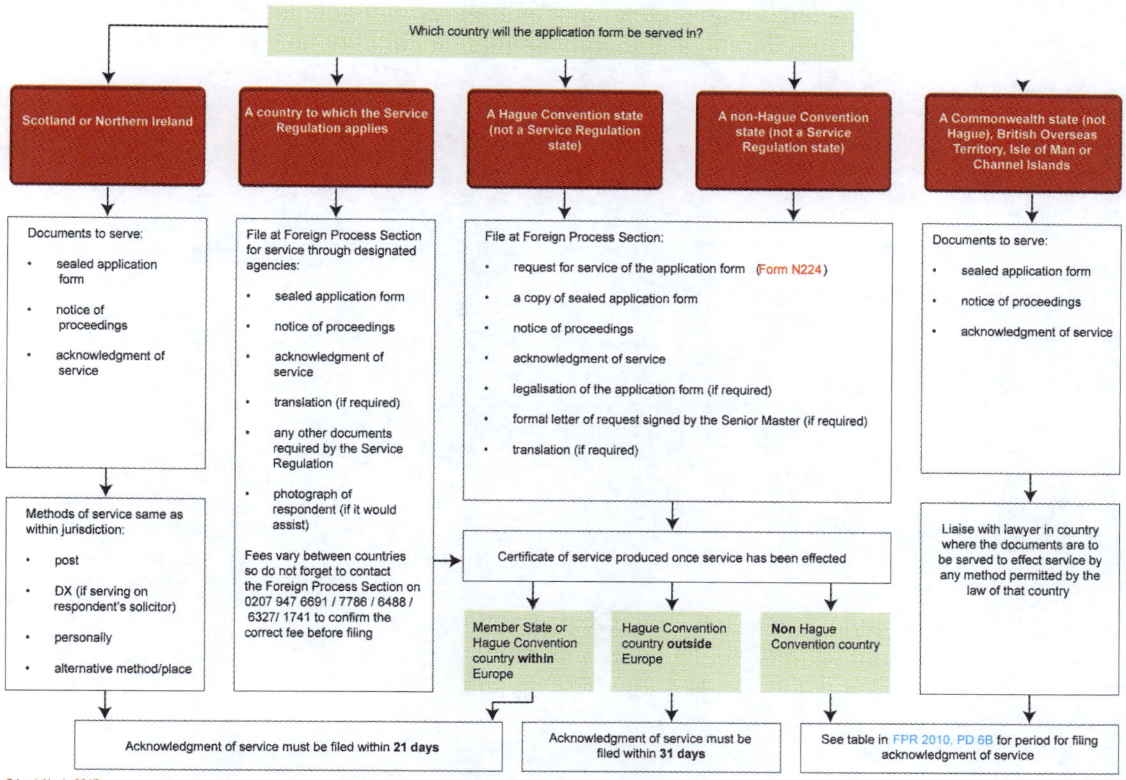

See also the Family Court Practice (The Red Book)

DOMESTIC ABUSE

Application for a non-molestation order under Part IV of the Family Law Act 1996

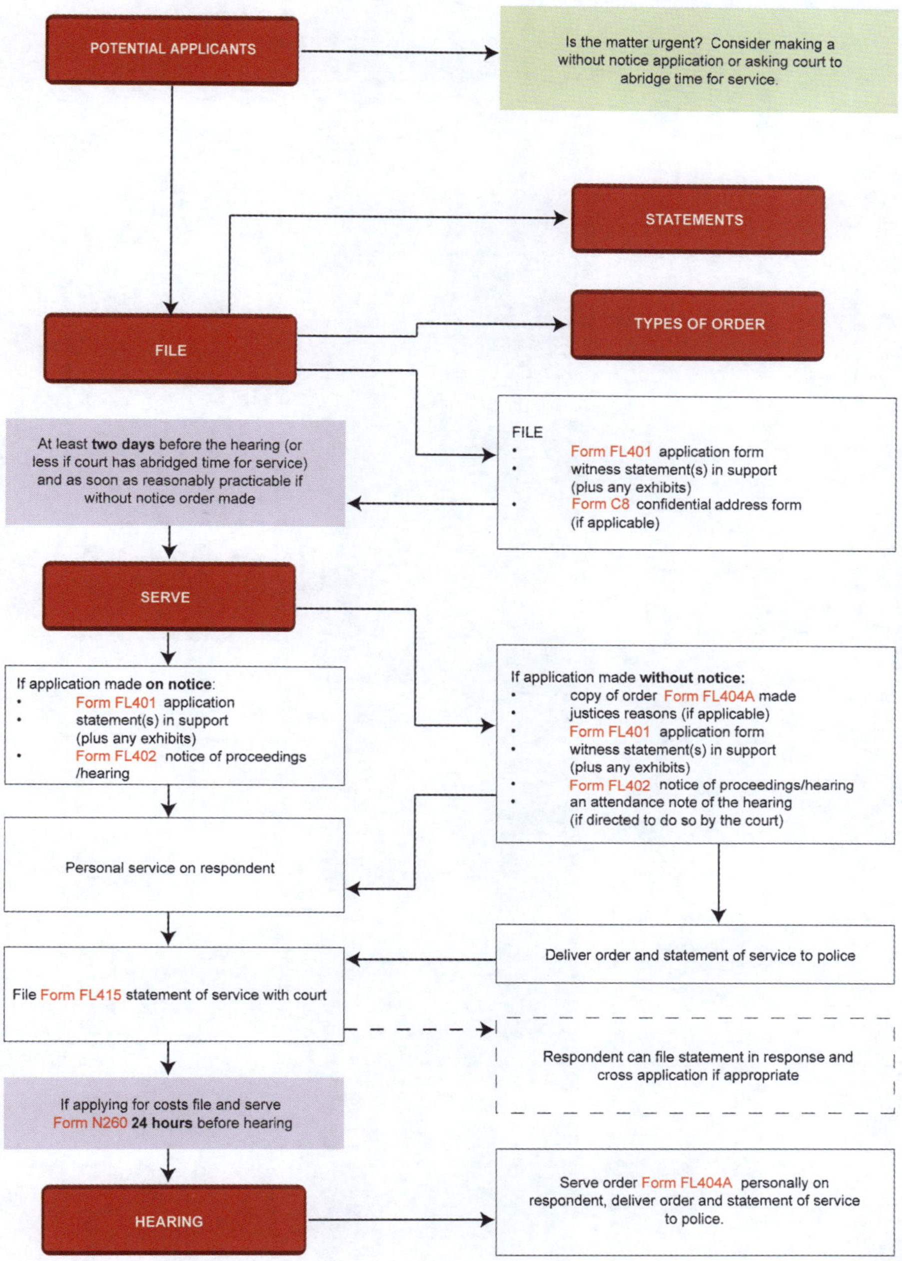

See also Procedural Guide (PG) A8 in Family Court Practice (The Red Book)

Application for an occupation order under Part IV of the Family Law Act 1996

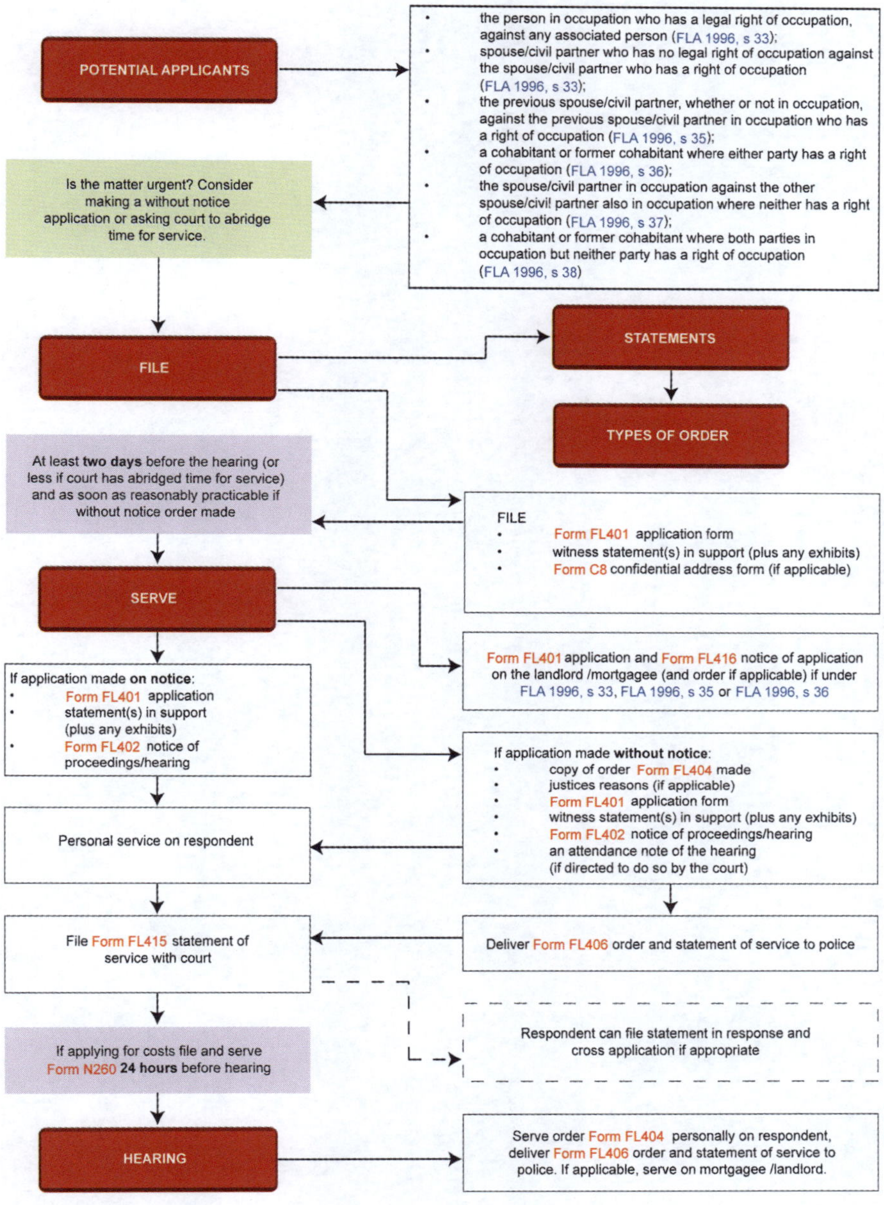

See also Procedural Guide (PG) A8 in Family Court Practice (The Red Book)

Application for a forced marriage protection order under Part 4A of the Family Law Act 1996

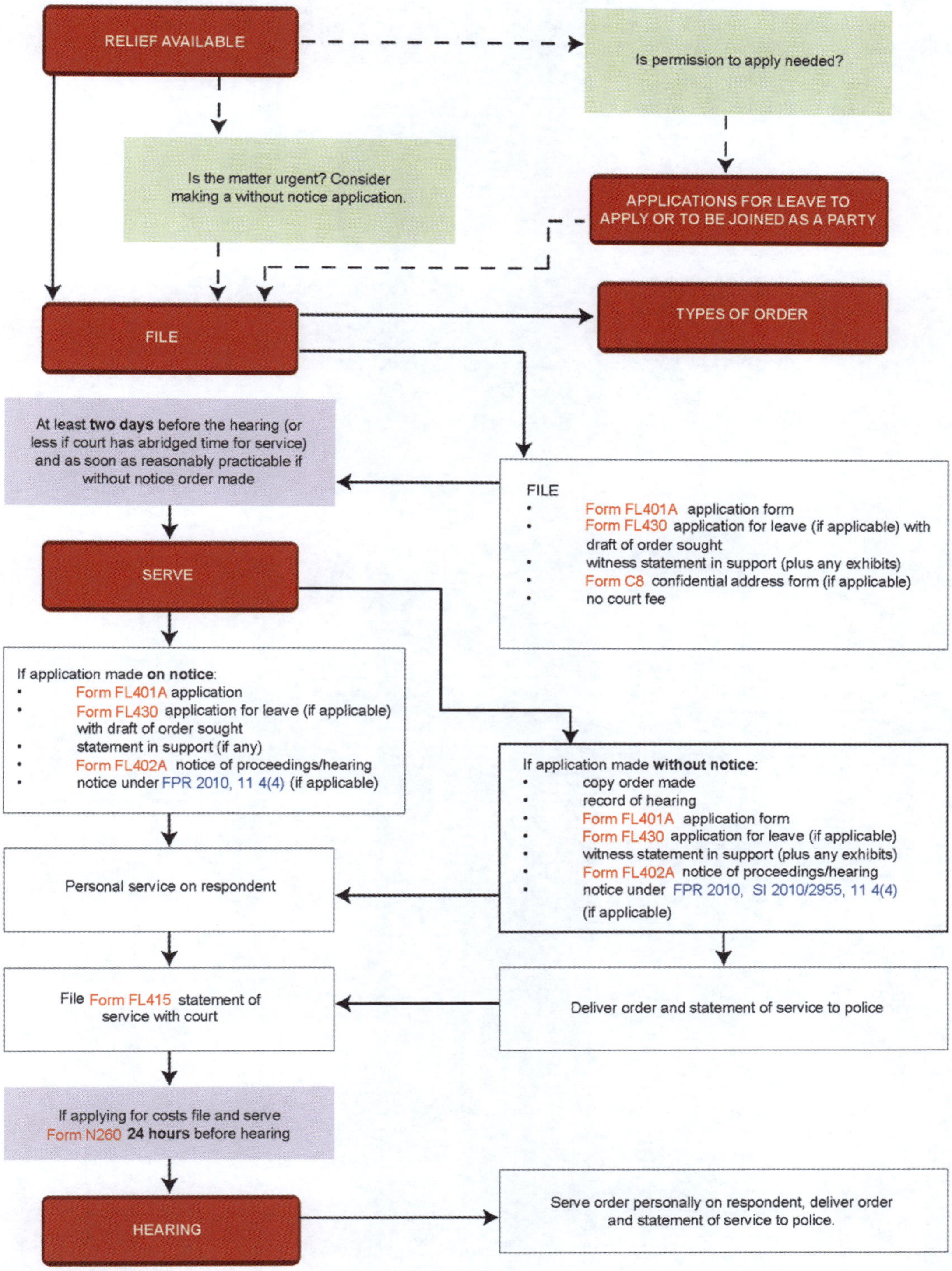

See also Procedural Guide (PG) A9 in Family Court Practice (The Red Book)

Claims under the Protection from Harassment Act 1997

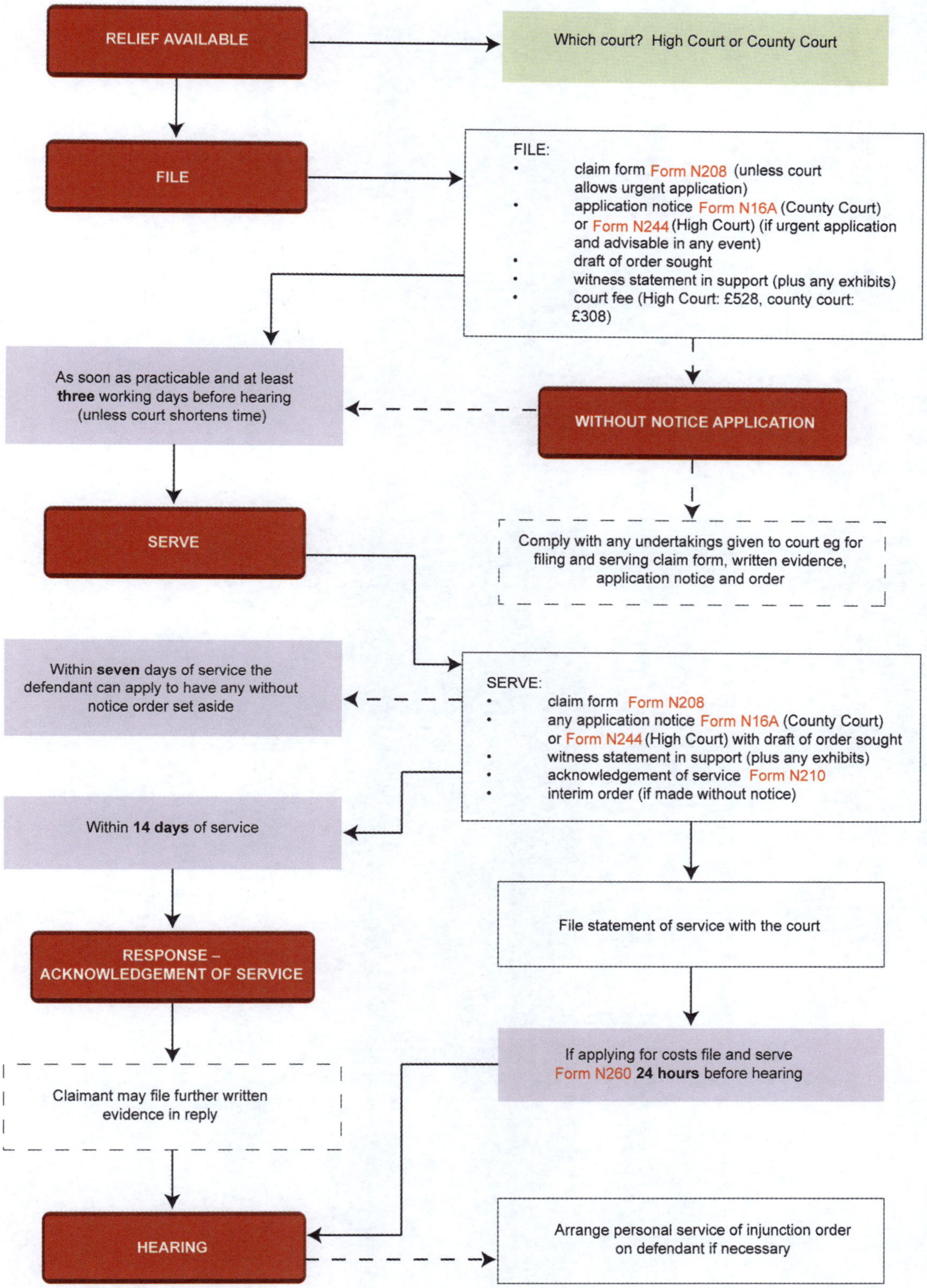

See also Procedural Guide (PG) A10 in Family Court Practice (The Red Book)

Application for variation, extension or discharge of a non-molestation or occupation order under Family Law Act 1996

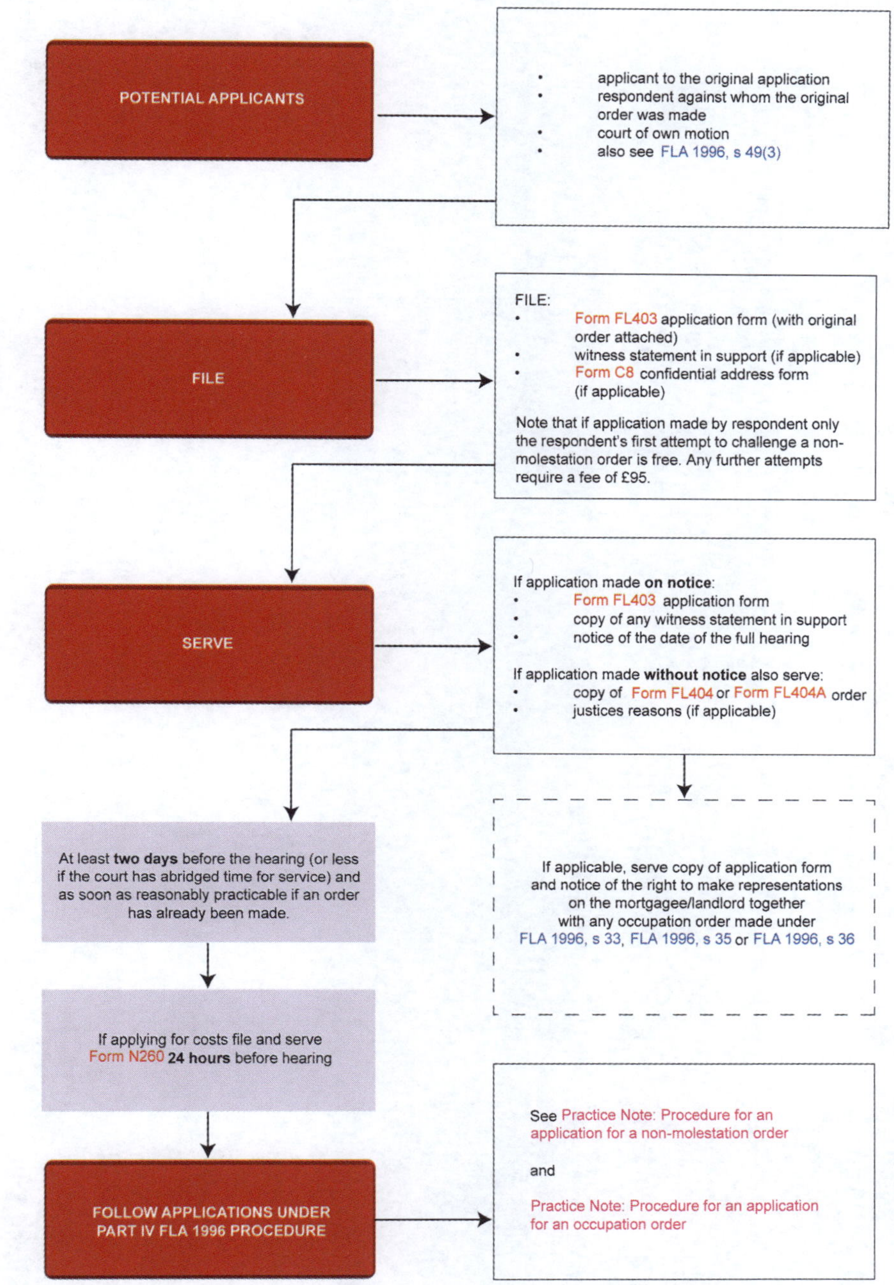

See also Procedural Guide (PG) A8 in Family Court Practice (The Red Book)

GENERAL

Service (not of an application for a matrimonial civil partnership order)

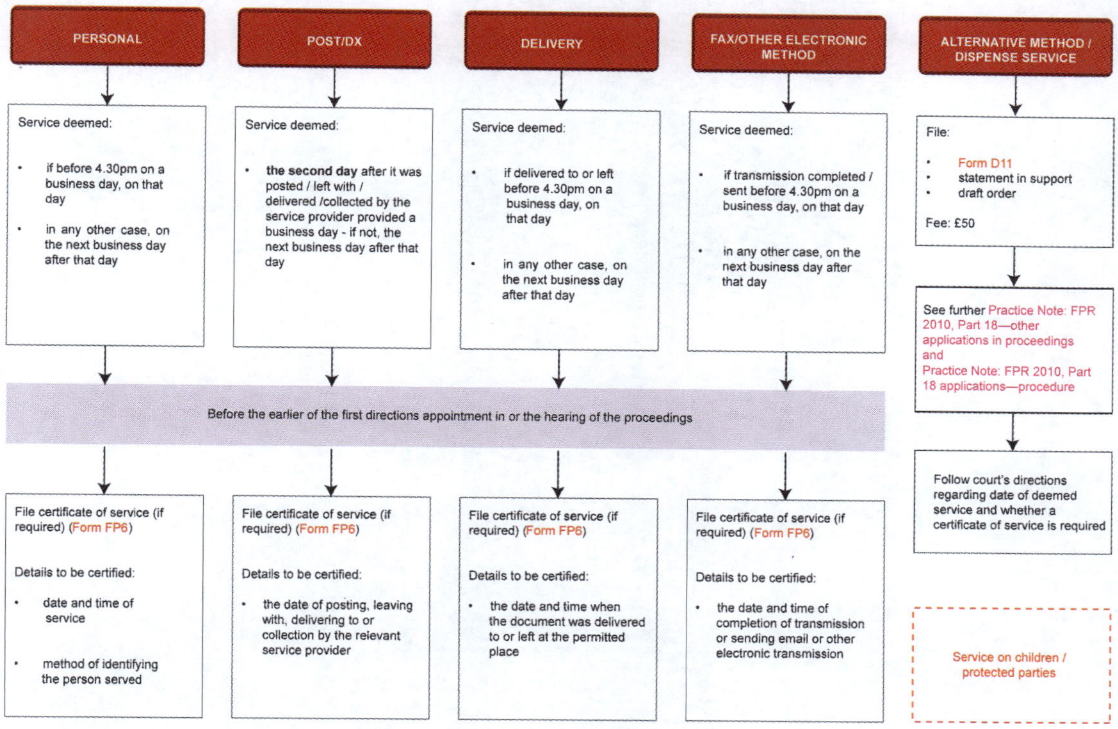

See also the Family Court Practice (The Red Book)

Service of a document (not an application for a matrimonial order civil partnership order) outside the jurisdiction

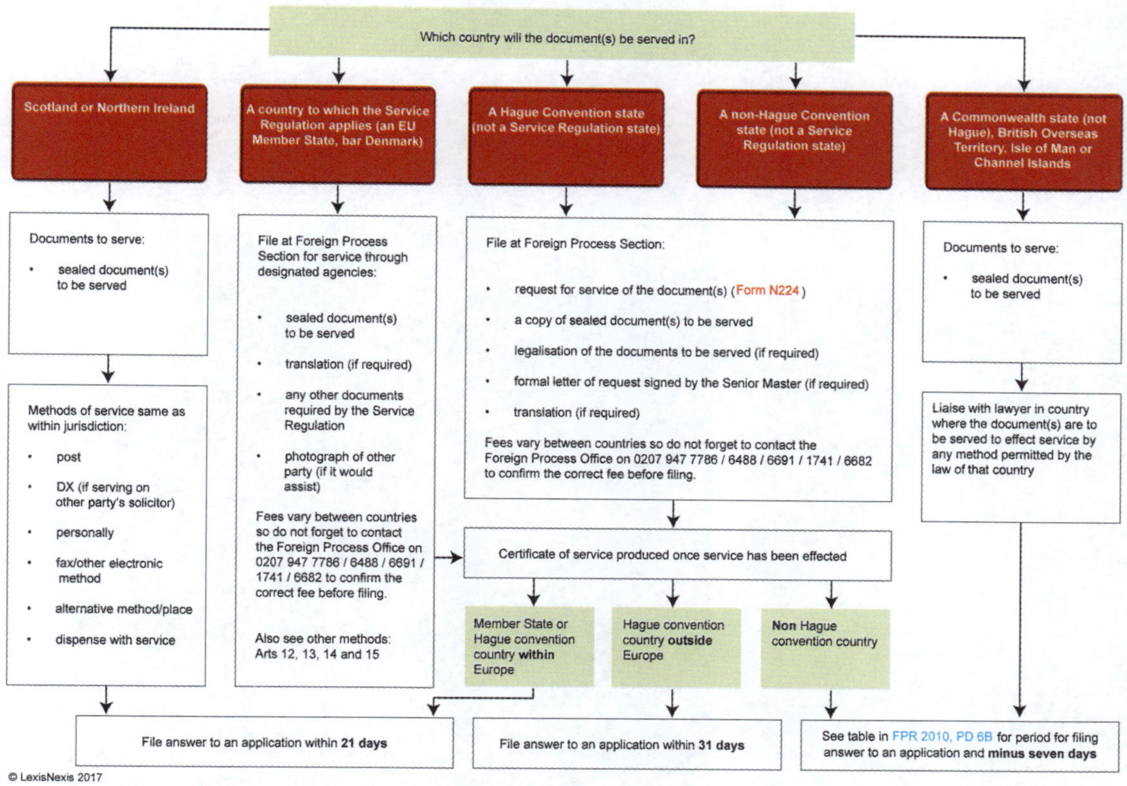

See also the Family Court Practice (The Red Book)

Applications under Part 18 of the Family Procedure Rules 2010

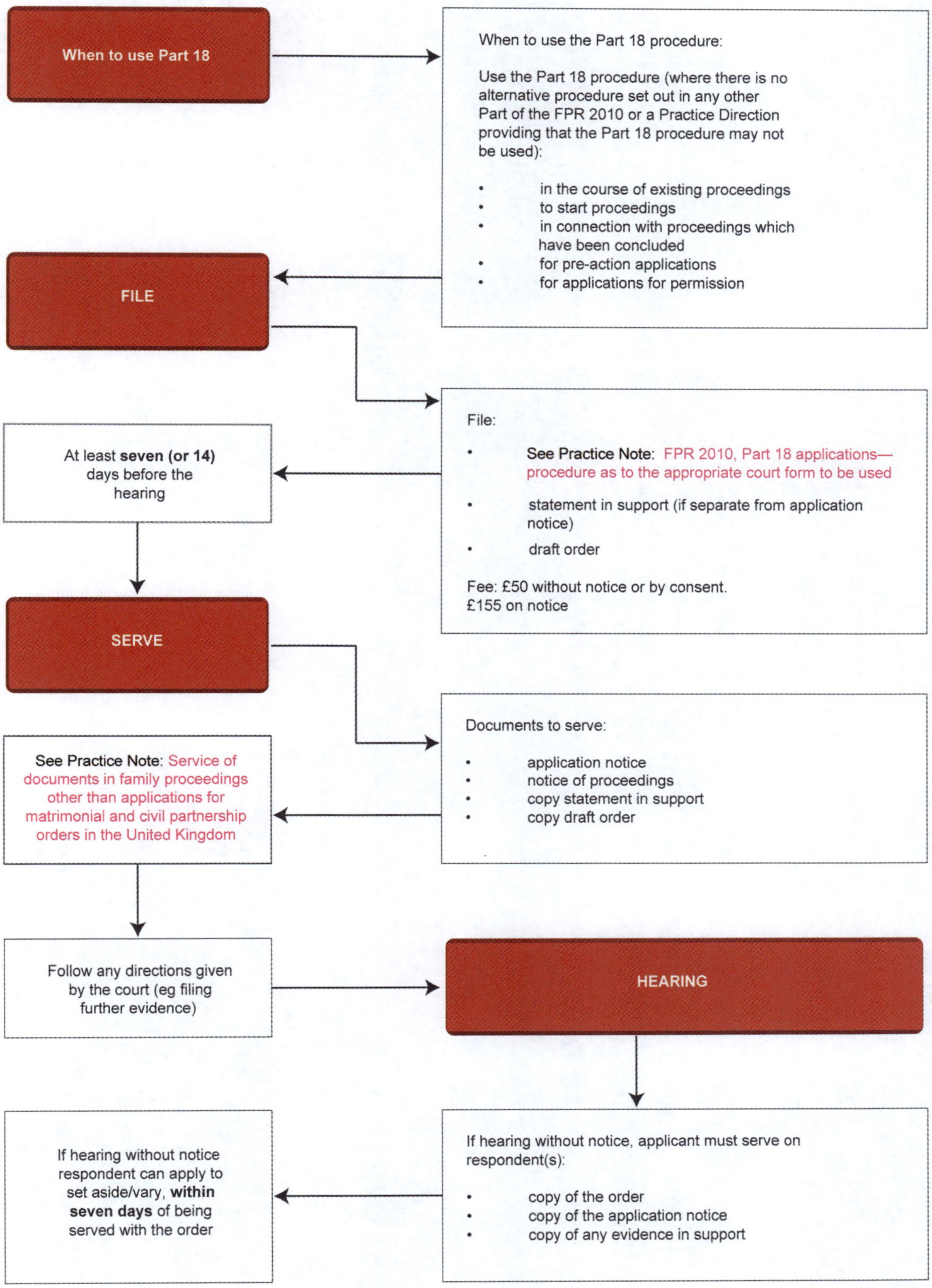

See also the Family Court Practice (The Red Book)

CHILDREN

Child arrangements orders (Part 1)—pre-proceedings to FHDRA

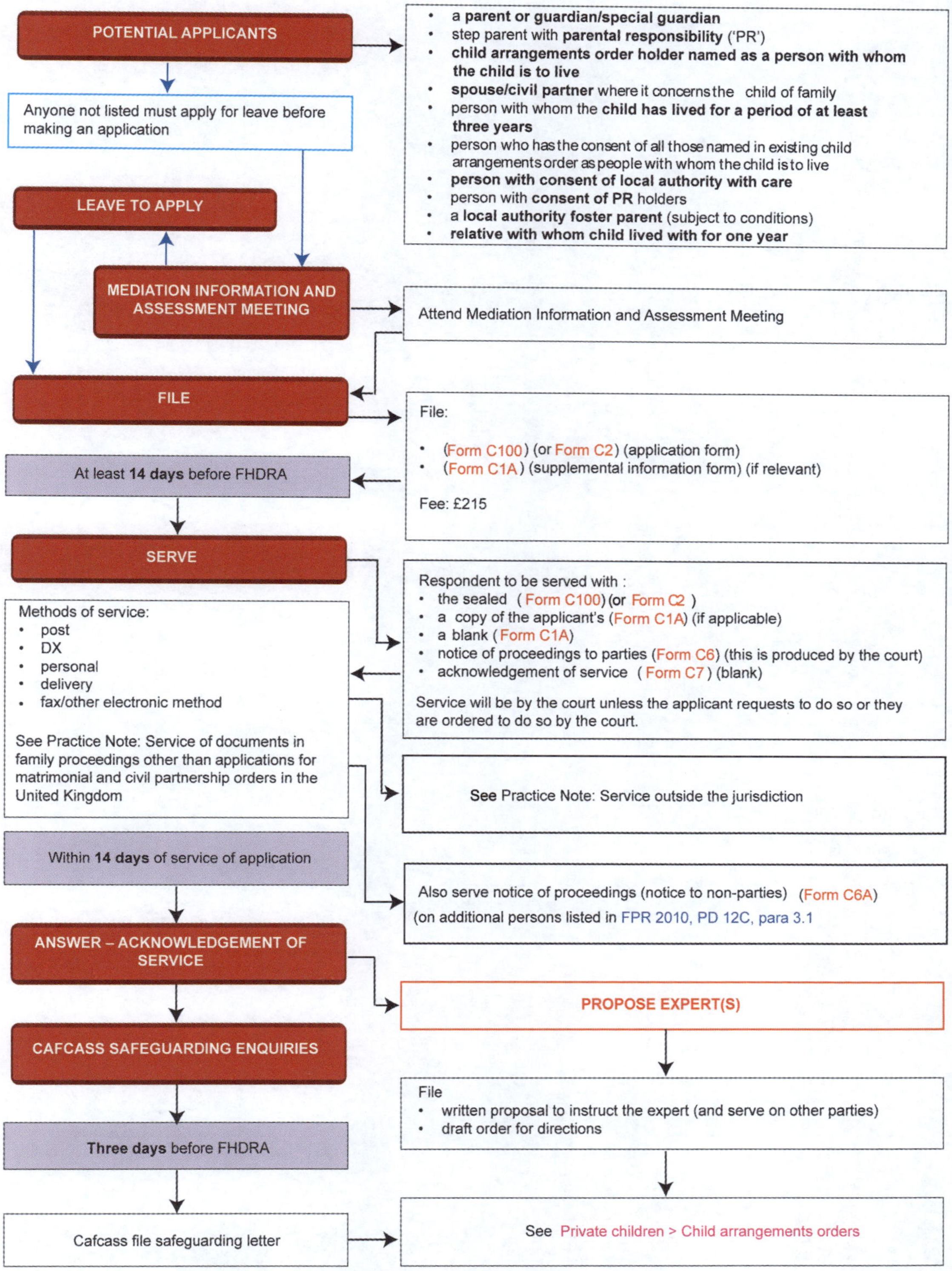

See also Procedural Guide (PG) D7 in Family Court Practice (The Red Book)

Child arrangements orders (Part 2)—FHDRA to fact finding

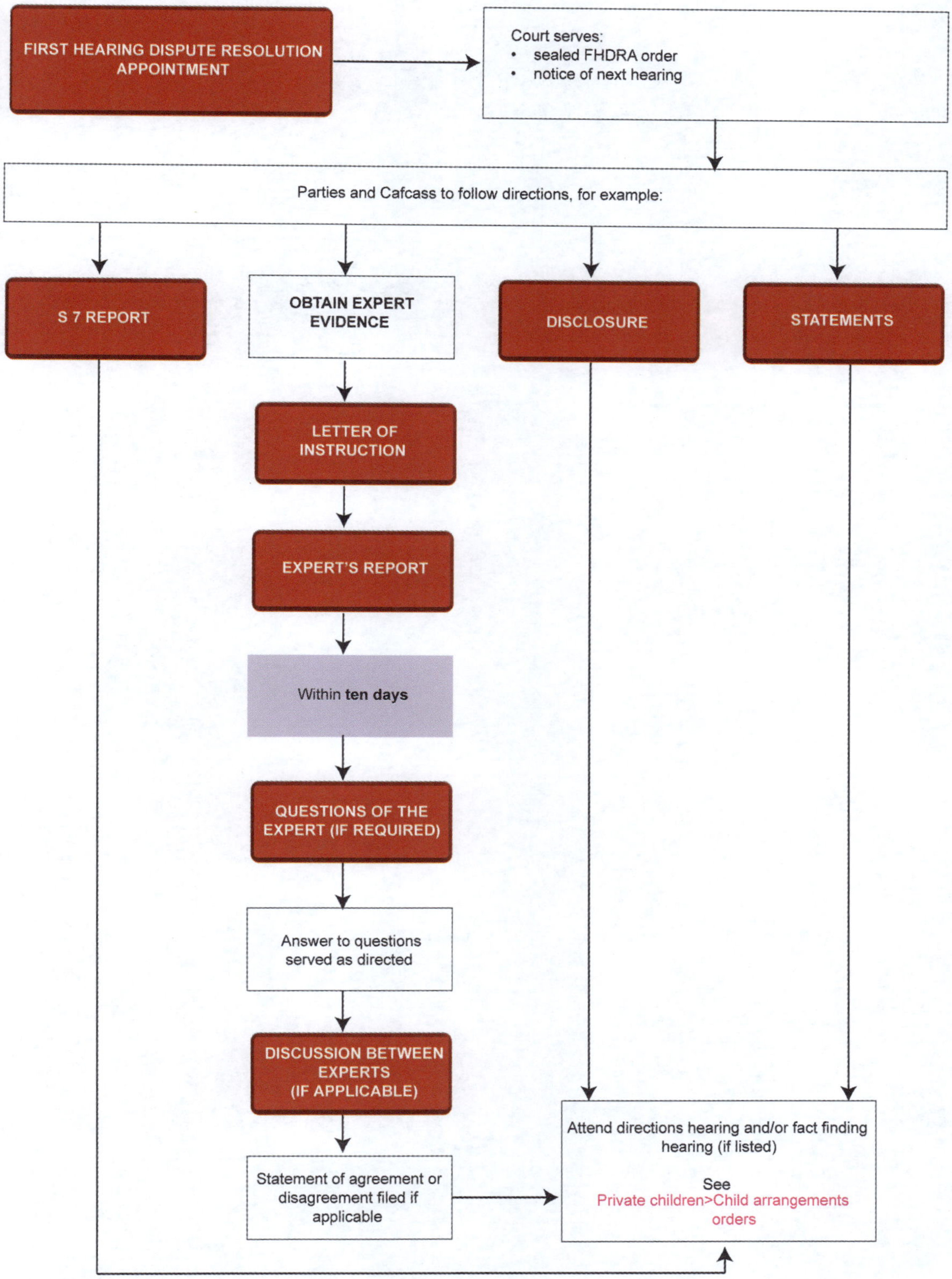

See also Procedural Guide (PG) D7 in Family Court Practice (The Red Book)

Child arrangements orders (Part 3)—fact finding to final hearing

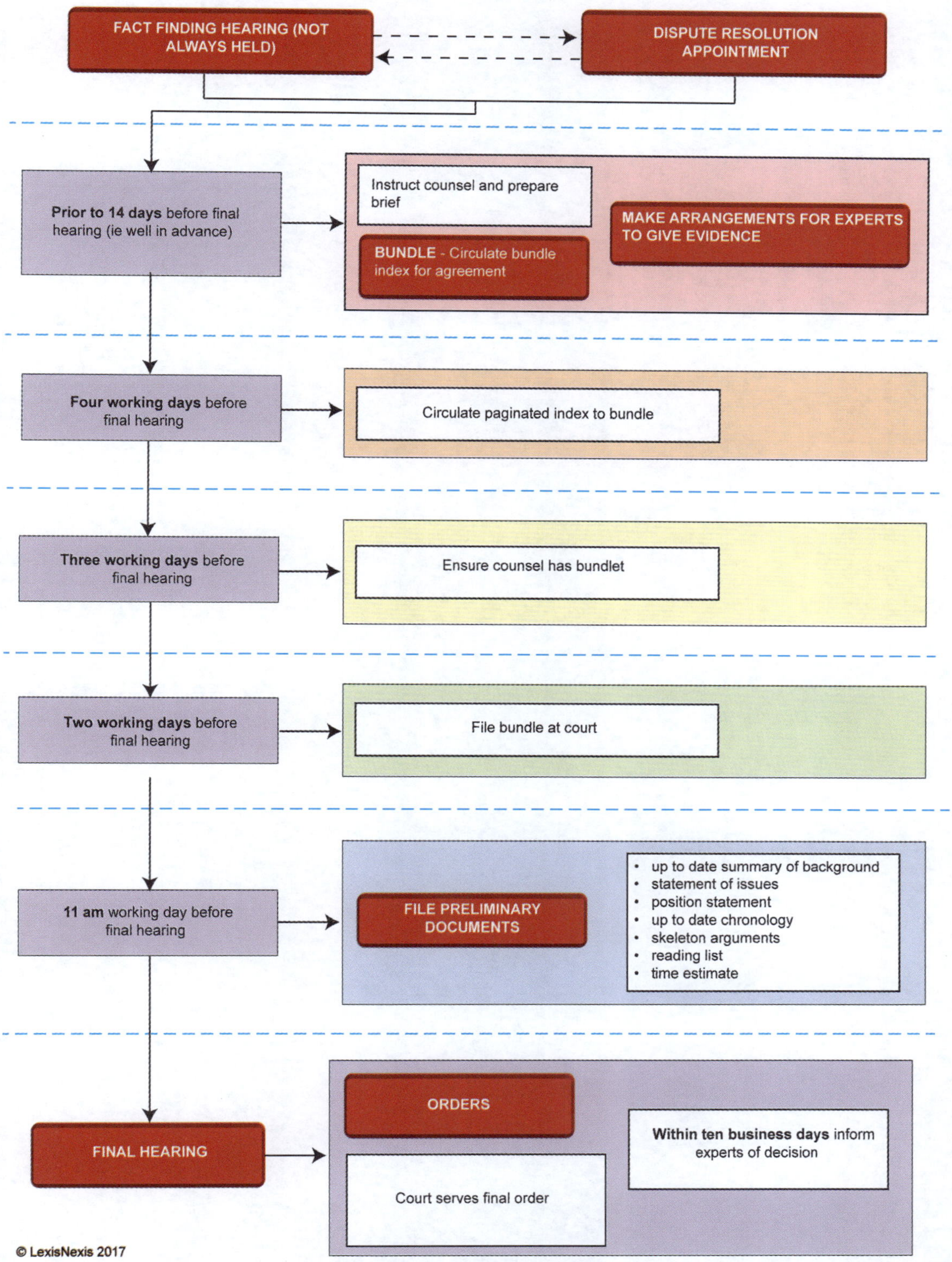

See also Procedural Guide (PG) D7 in Family Court Practice (The Red Book)

Parental responsibility orders (Part 1)—pre-proceedings to FHDRA

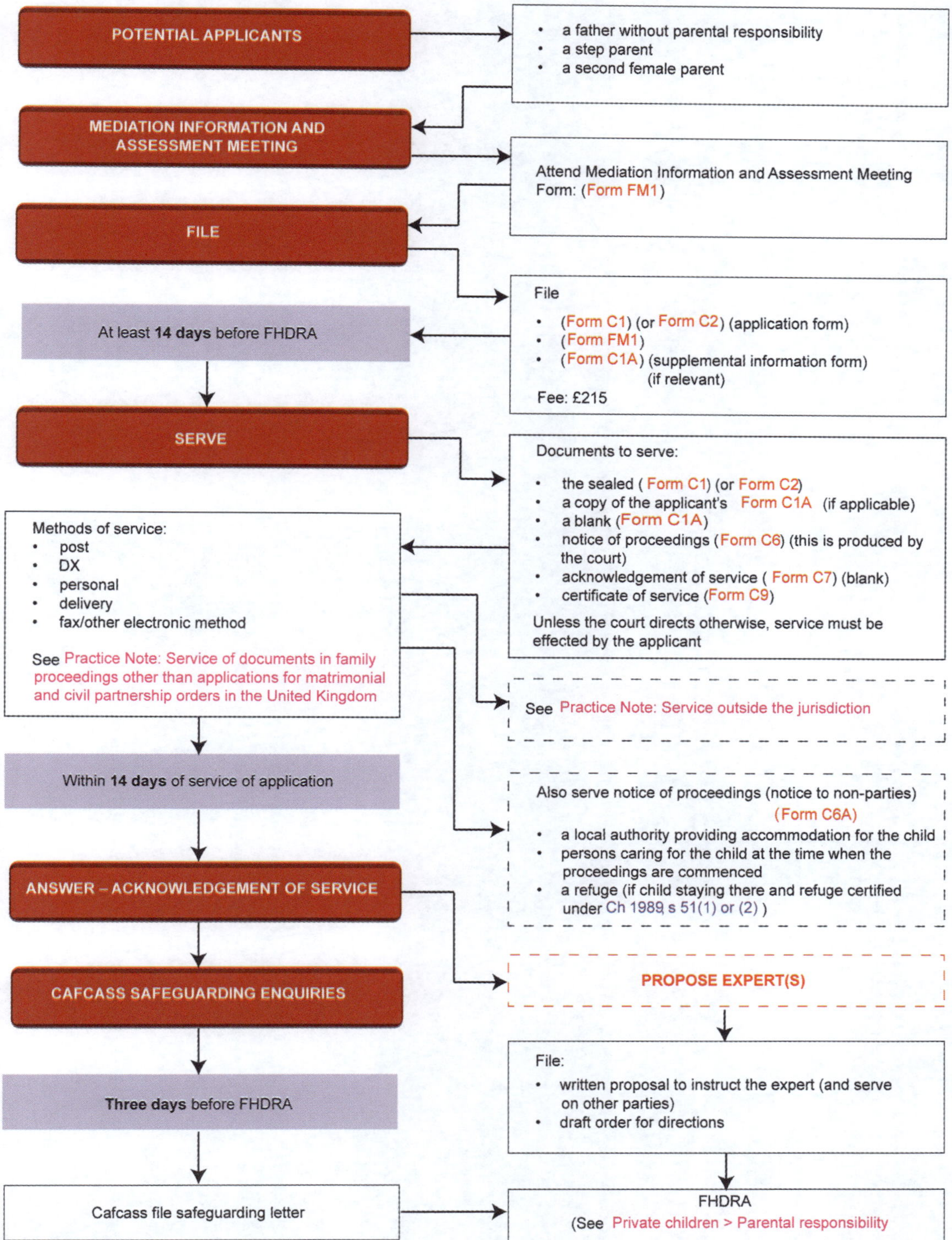

See also Procedural Guide (PG) D6 in Family Court Practice (The Red Book)

Parental responsibility orders (Part 2)—FHDRA to fact finding hearing

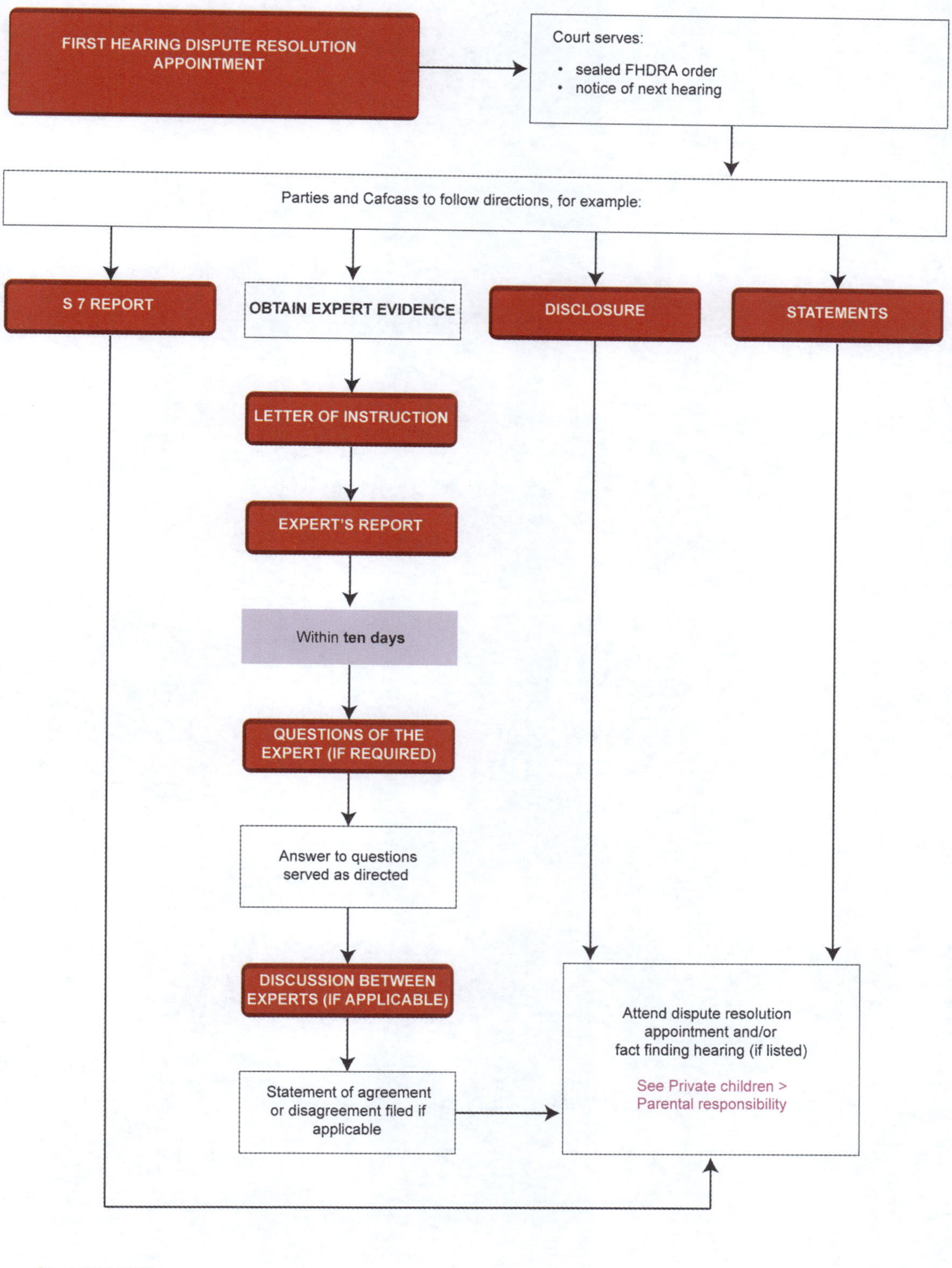

See also Procedural Guide (PG) D6 in Family Court Practice (The Red Book)

Parental responsibility orders (Part 3)—fact finding hearing to final hearing

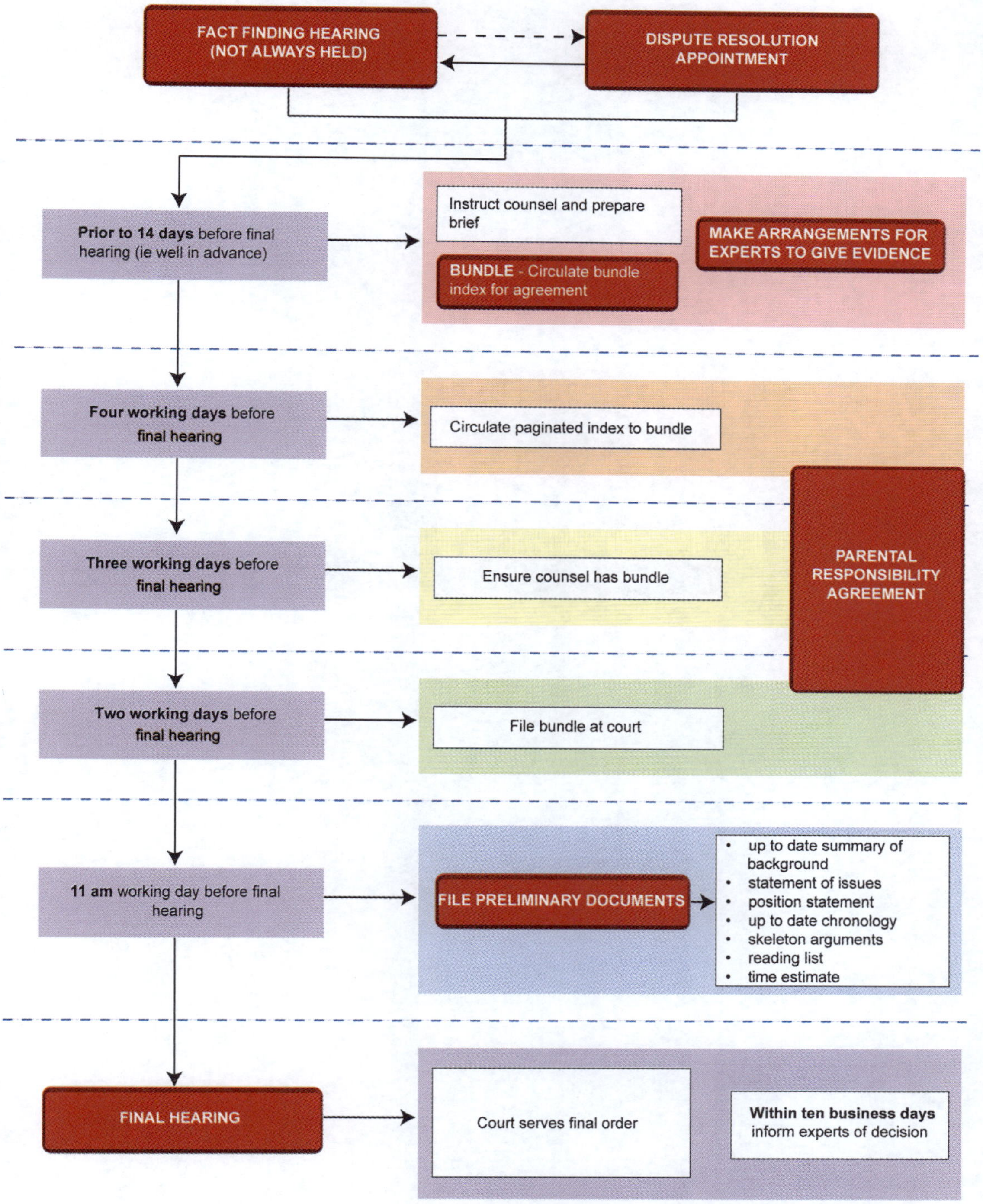

See also Procedural Guide (PG) D6 in Family Court Practice (The Red Book)

Prohibited steps and specific issue orders (Part 1)—pre-proceedings to FHDRA

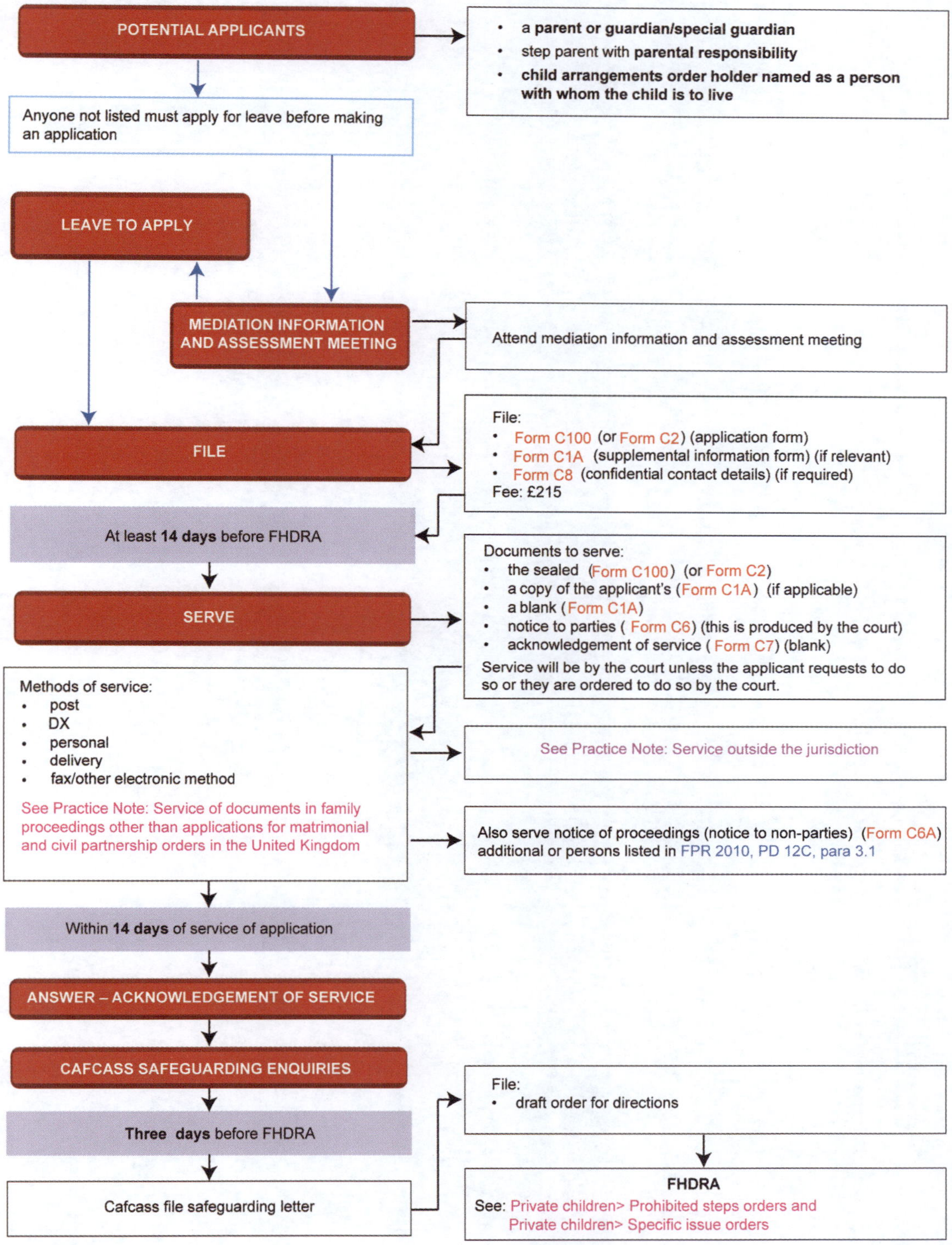

See also Procedural Guide (PG) D9 in Family Court Practice (The Red Book)

Prohibited steps and specific issue orders (Part 2)—FHDRA to fact finding hearing

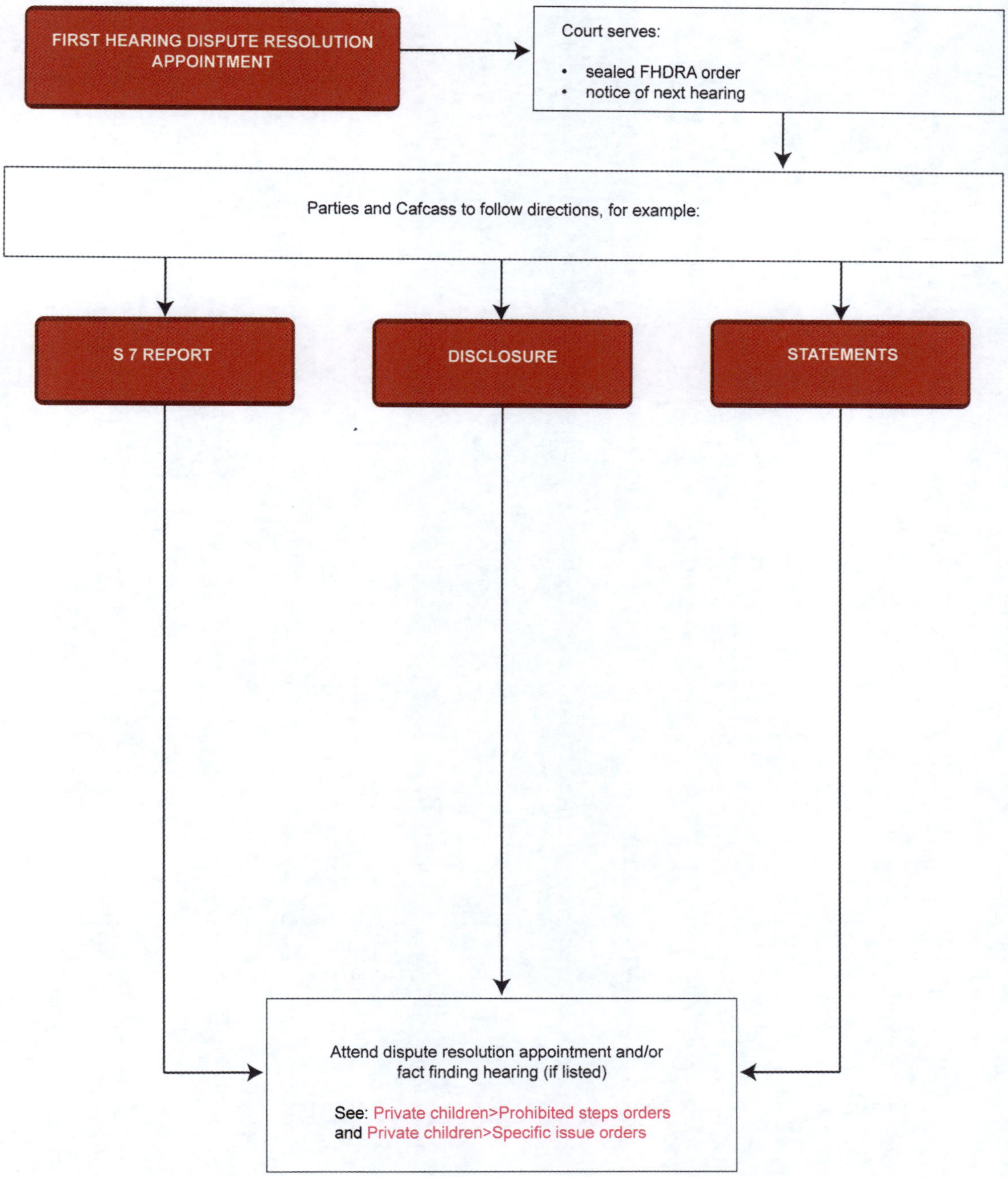

See also Procedural Guide (PG) D9 in Family Court Practice (The Red Book)

Prohibited steps and specific issue orders (Part 3)—fact finding hearing to final hearing

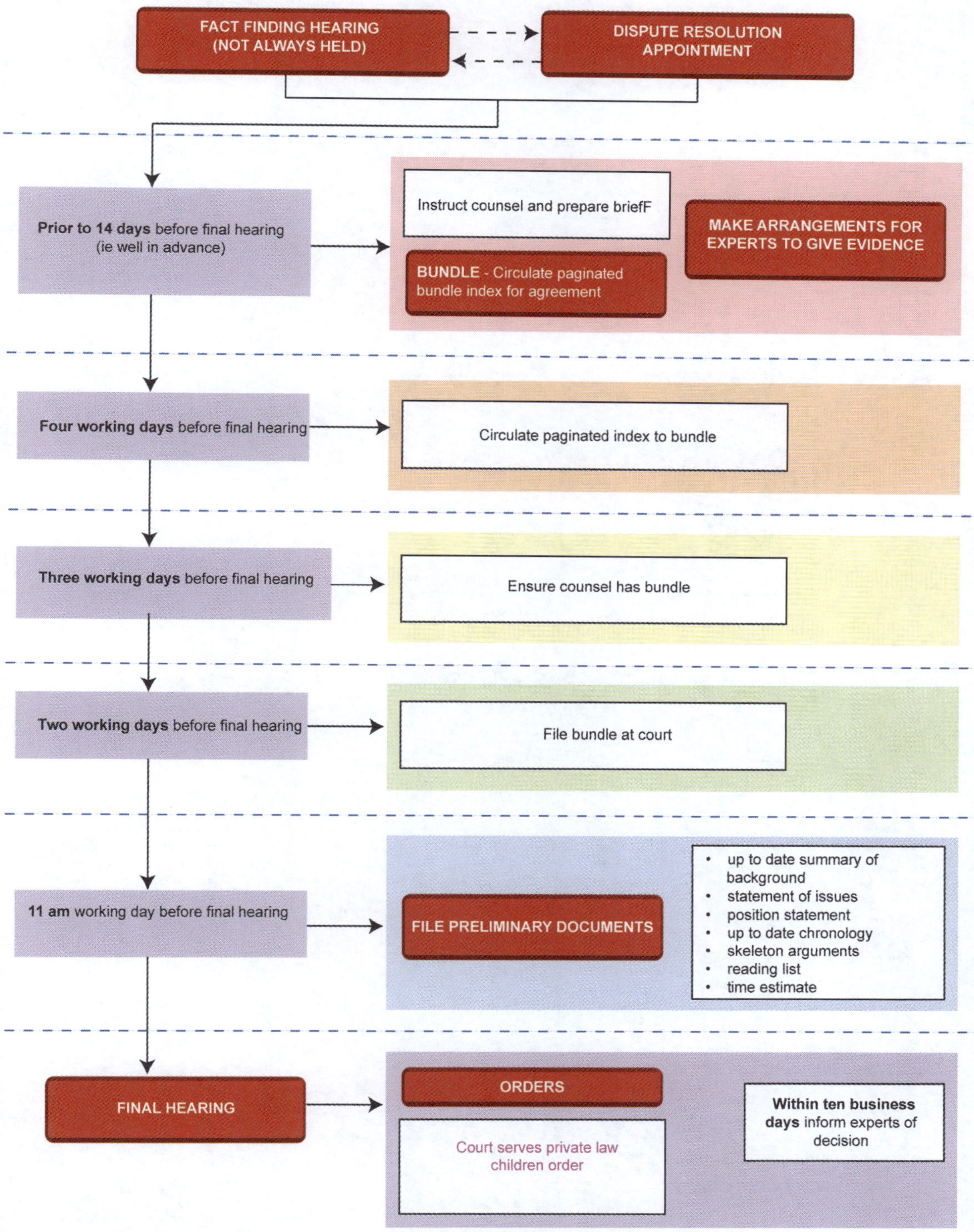

See also Procedural Guide (PG) D9 in Family Court Practice (The Red Book)

Discharge of a parental responsibility order or agreement

POTENTIAL APPLICANTS

- any person with parental responsibility for the child
- the child (but only with leave of the court)

APPLY FOR LEAVE (IF REQUIRED)

If the child is the applicant
File:
- (Form C2) (application for leave)
- statement
- draft (Form C1) (or Form C2)
- draft order
- (Form FM1)
- (Form C1A) (if relevant)
- (Form C8) (if relevant)

Fee: £215

FACTORS THE COURT WILL CONSIDER

- ChA 1989, s 1(1) – the welfare of the child is paramount
- ChA 1989, s 1(2) – the no delay principle
- ChA 1989, s 1(5)– the no order principle
- where there is no parental responsibility agreement or order in existence, what would be the court's response if such an application were made
- the fact that 'such an application…should not be allowed to become a weapon in the hands of the dissatisfied mother of the non-marital child: it should be used by the court as an appropriate step in the regulation of the child's life where the circumstances really do warrant it and not otherwise' (Re P (Terminating Parental Responsibility) [1995] 1 FLR 1048, A v D [2014] 1 FLR 1305)
- the fact that the court cannot terminate a parental responsibility order linked to a child arrangements order under ChA 1989, 12(1) while the child arrangements order concerned remains in force so far as providing for the child to live with that parent

FOLLOW PART 12 PROCEDURE

See Private children > Parental responsibility

See also Procedural Guide (PG) D6 in Family Court Practice (The Red Book)

Enforcement orders and financial compensation orders (child arrangements orders)

POTENTIAL APPLICANTS

- the person with whom the child lives
- the person in whose favour the order is made
- a person subject to a ChA 1989, s 11(7)condition or activity condition
- the child (subject to additional provisions)

APPLY TO ATTACH WARNING NOTICE (IF NECESSARY)

File:
- (Form C78)
- copy of contact order
- (Form C8) (if relevant)

Fee: £50

Ensure warning notice given to respondent or they are otherwise informed of the terms of it.

FILE

File:
- (Form C79)
- copy of child arrangements order
- receipts or documentary evidence
- (Form C8) (if relevant)

Fee: £215

At least **14 days** before FHDRA

SERVE

Documents to serve:
- the sealed (Form C79)
- notice to parties (Form C6) (this is produced by the court)
- acknowledgement of service (Form C7) (blank)

Methods of service:
- post
- DX
- personal
- delivery
- fax/other electronic method

See Practice Note: Service of documents in family proceedings other than applications for matrimonial and civil partnership orders in the United Kingdom

See Practice Note: Service outside the jurisdiction although note that an application for an enforcement order cannot be made against a person unless they are habitually resident in England and Wales.

Also serve **notice of proceedings** (Form C6A) on additional persons listed in FPR 2010, PD 12C, para 3.1

Within **14 days** of service of application

ANSWER

FOLLOW PART 12 PROCEDURE

See: Private children>Child arrangements orders

WHAT THE COURT WILL CONSIDER BEFORE MAKING AN ORDER

ORDER

Serve enforcement order **personally** on respondent

See also Procedural Guide (PG) D8 in Family Court Practice (The Red Book)

FINANCIAL PROVISION

Application for a financial order (not an interim order) under MCA 1973 or CPA 2004—pre-proceedings to first appointment

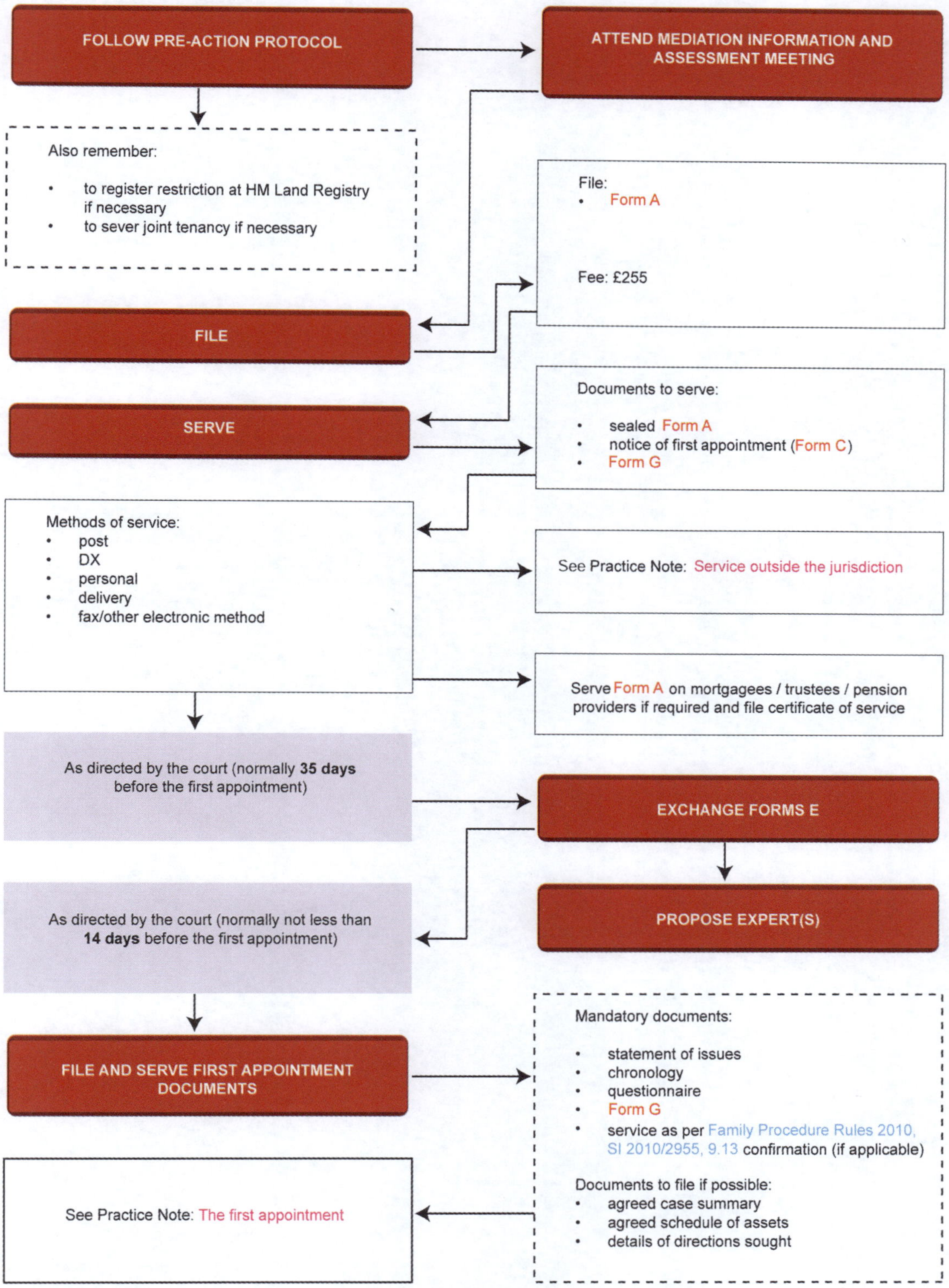

See also Procedural Guide (PG) B5 in Family Court Practice (The Red Book)

Applications for a financial order (not an interim order) under MCA 1973 or CPA 2004—first appointment to FDR

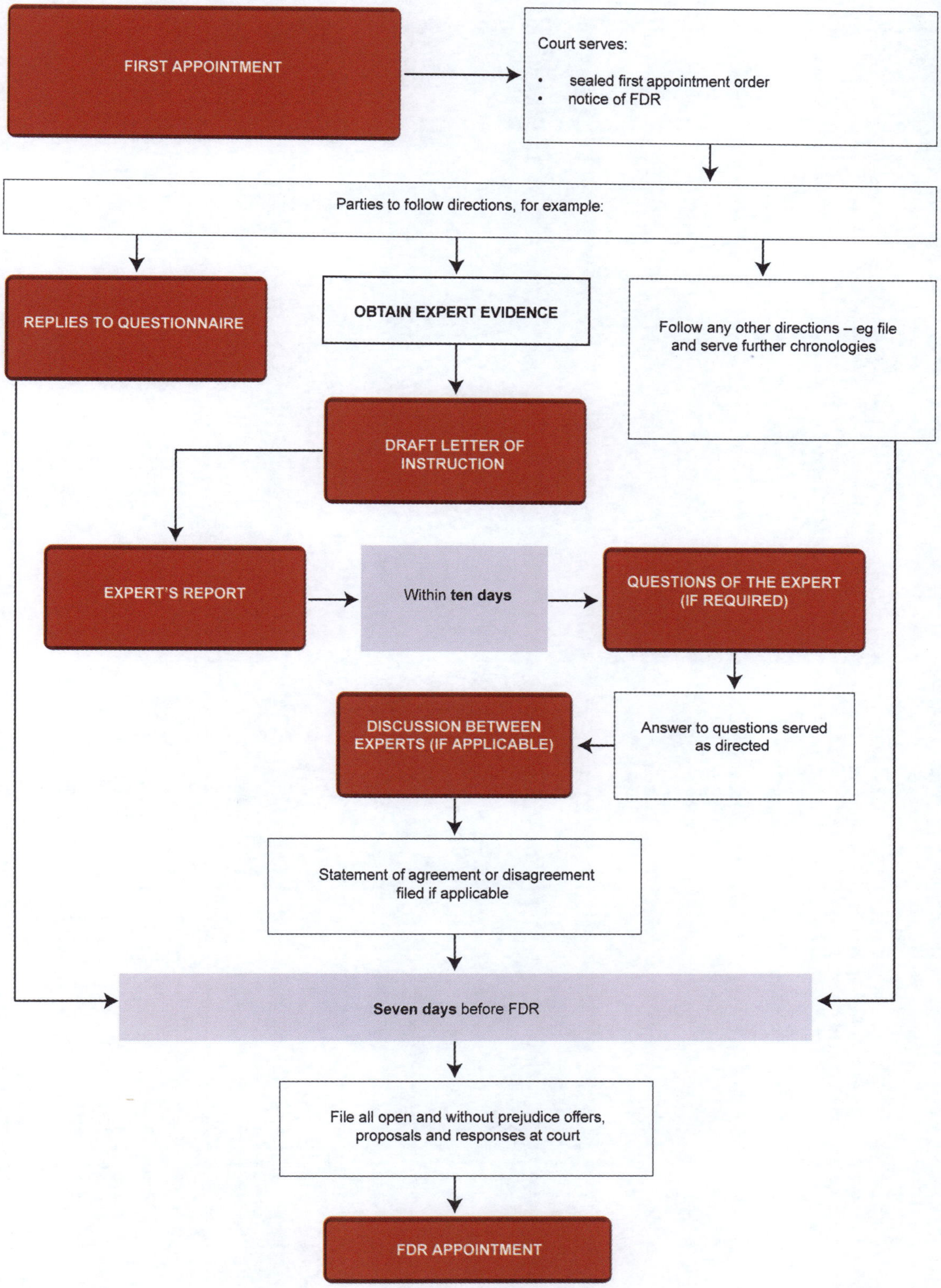

See also Procedural Guide (PG) B5 in Family Court Practice (The Red Book)

Application for a financial order (not an interim order) under MCA 1973 or CPA 2004—FDR to final hearing

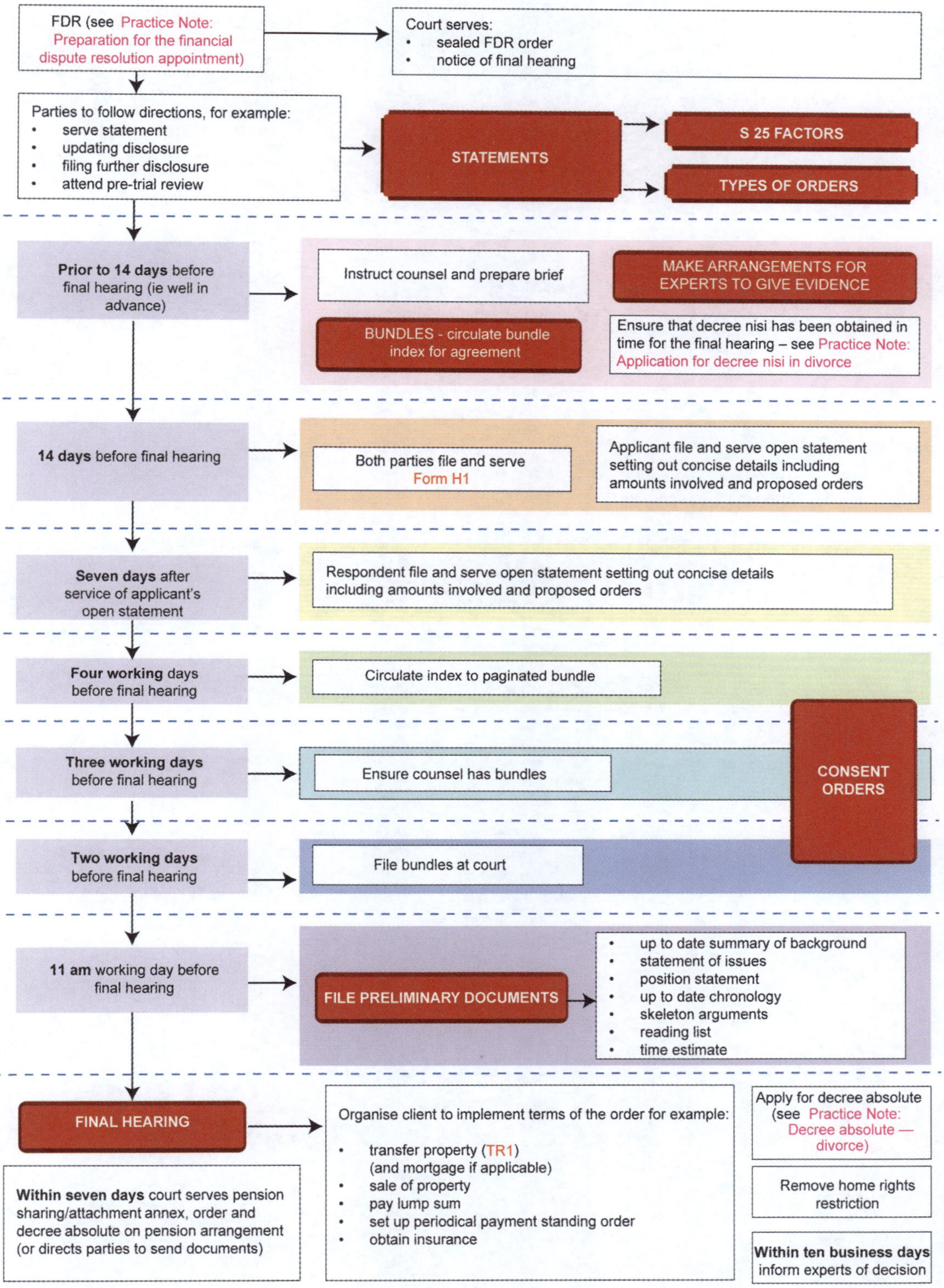

See also Procedural Guide (PG) B5 in Family Court Practice (The Red Book)

Interim financial orders

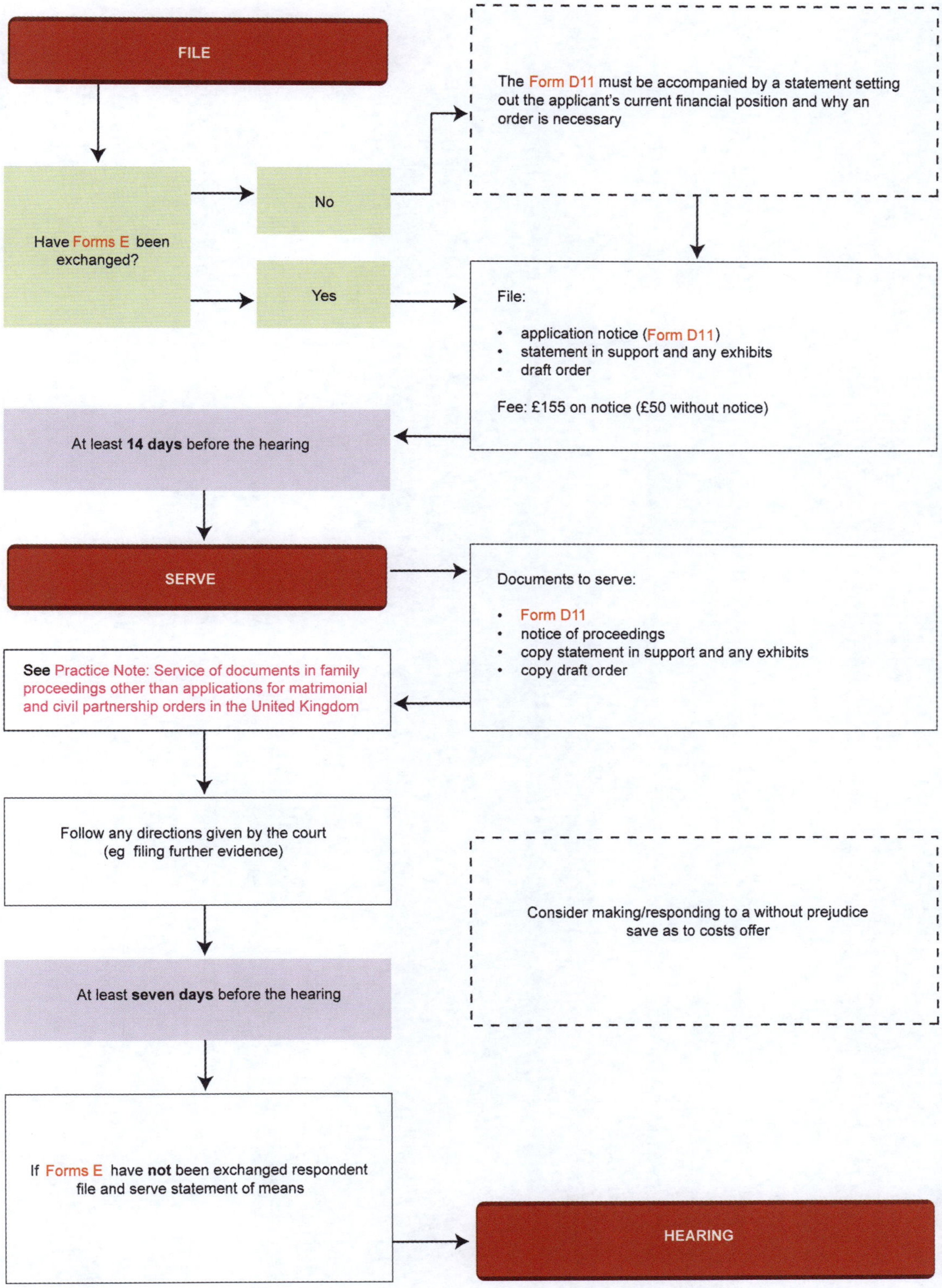

See also Procedural Guide (PG) B5 in Family Court Practice (The Red Book)

Variation of a financial order

TYPES OF ORDERS THAT CAN BE VARIED →

- maintenance pending suit / interim order for maintenance
- periodical payments
- secured periodical payments
- lump sum **by instalments**
- deferred order for a lump sum which include provision by way of pension (or pension compensation) attachment
- settlement of property or for a variation of settlement on or after the grant of a decree of **judicial separation or civil partnership separation order**
- sale of property
- pension (compensation) sharing order made **before the decree absolute / final order**

FACTORS THE COURT WILL CONSIDER →

- all the circumstances of the case
- first consideration to be given to the welfare of any child (under 18)
- any change in any of the matters to which the court was required to have regard when making the order to which the application relates
- whether to capitalise periodical payments and whether periodical payments can be terminated without undue hardship
- if the party against whom the order was made has died, the changed circumstances resulting from that person's death

FOLLOW SHORTENED PART 9 PROCEDURE →

See Practice Note: Accelerated (shortened) financial remedy procedure:

See also Procedural Guide (PG) B5 in Family Court Practice (The Red Book)

Application after an overseas divorce

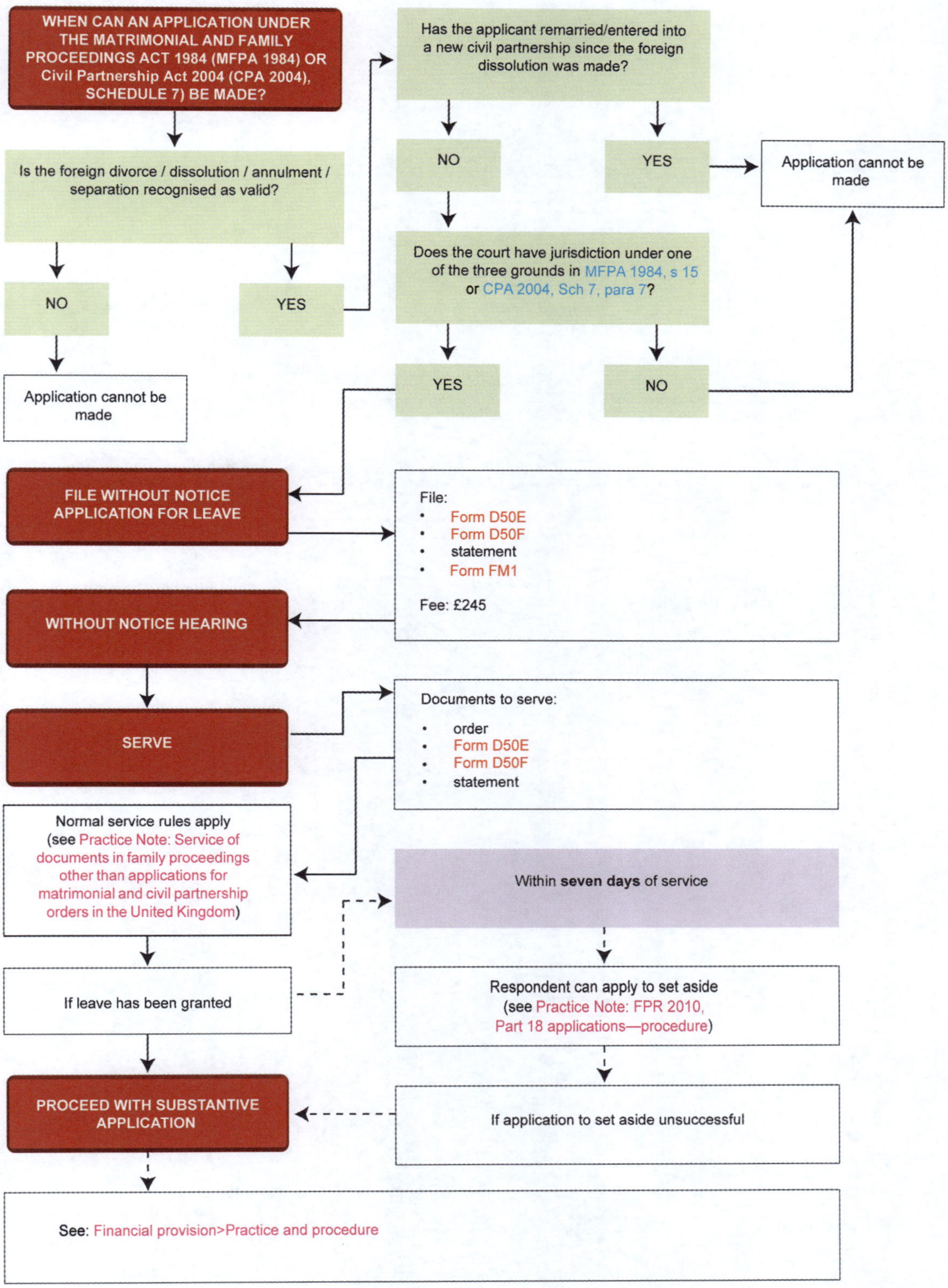

See also Procedural Guide (PG) B7 in Family Court Practice (The Red Book)

Application for an injunction

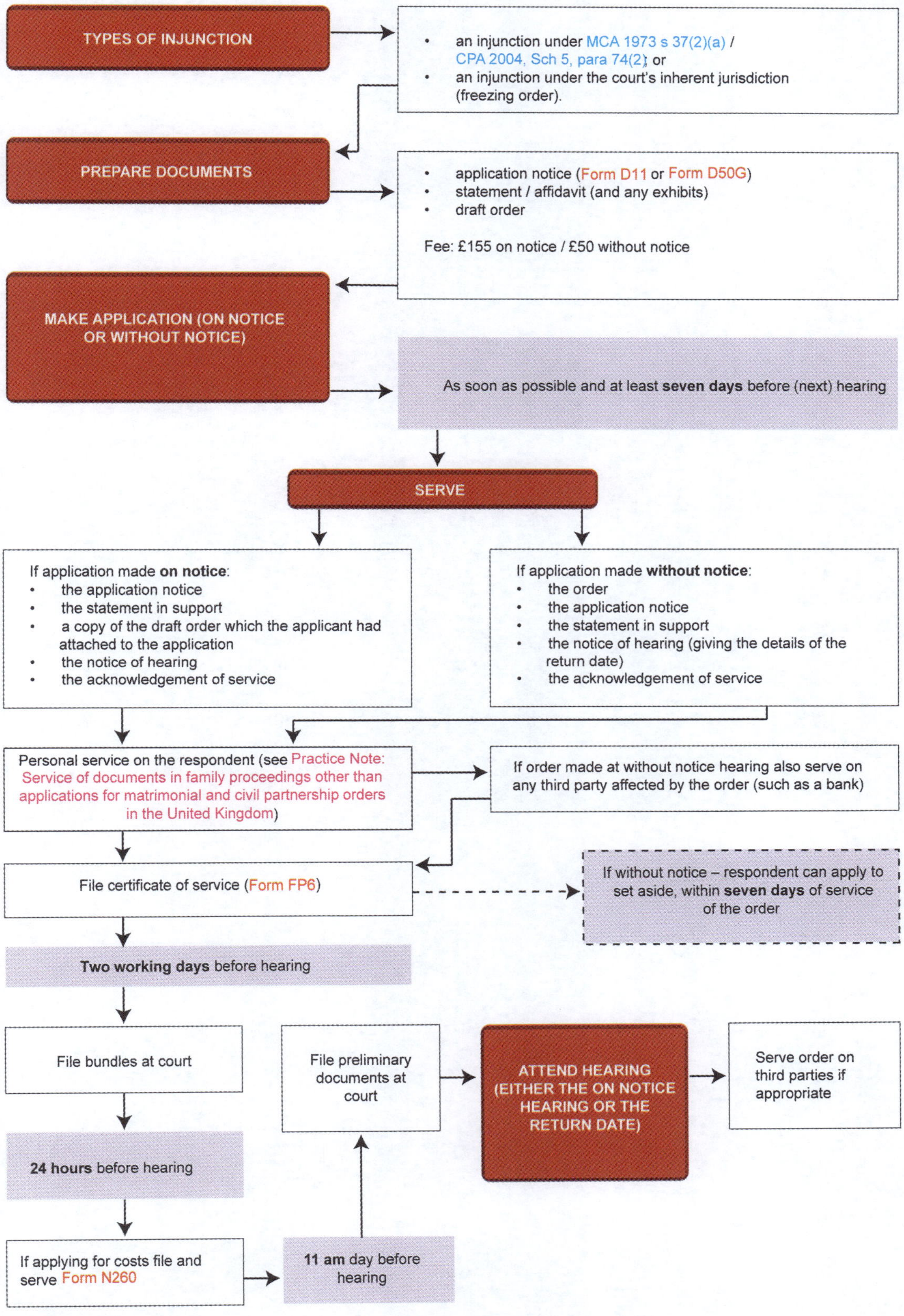

See also Procedural Guide (PG) B6 in Family Court Practice (The Red Book)

Application for a search order (Anton Piller)

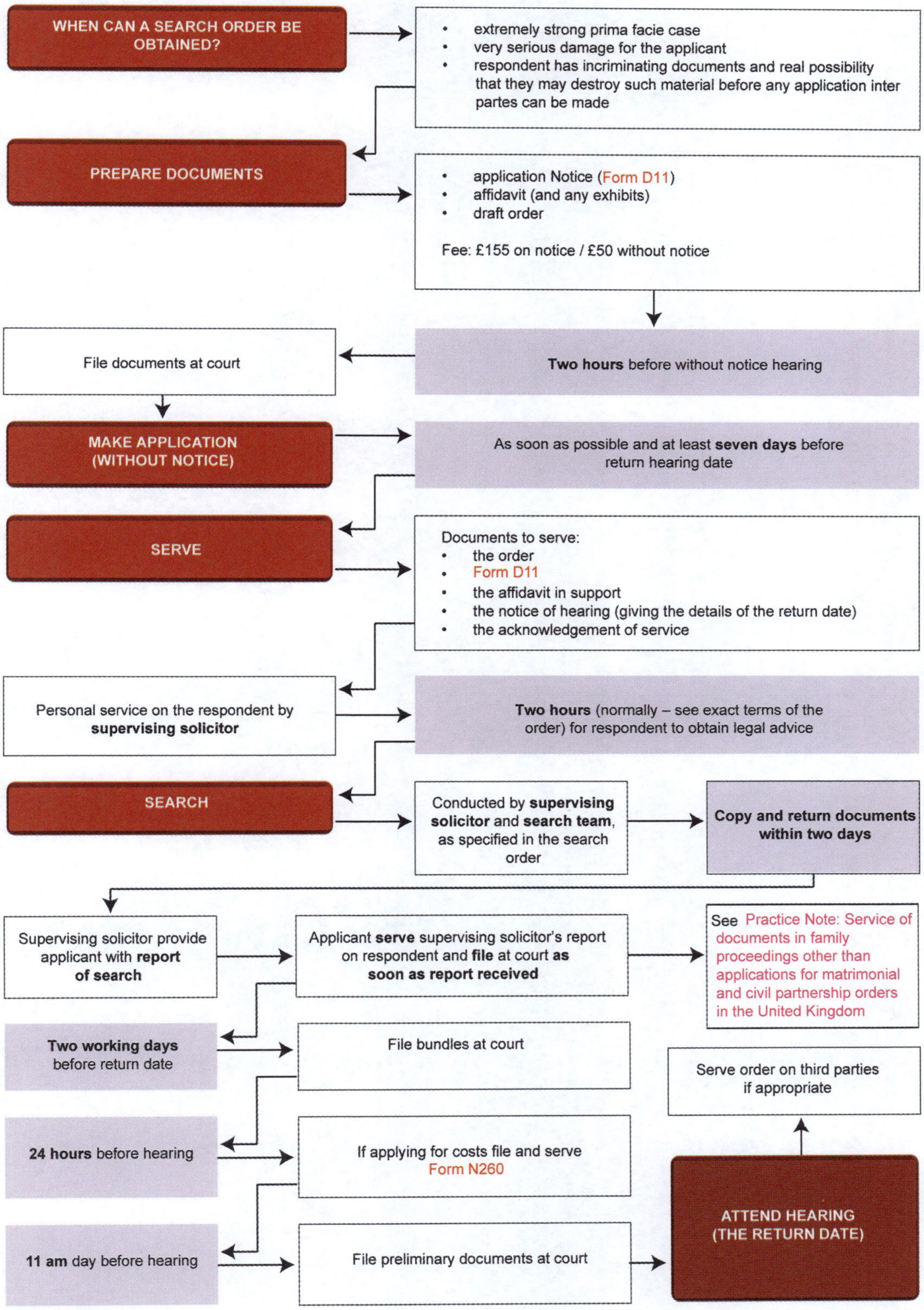

See also Procedural Guide (PG) B6 in Family Court Practice (The Red Book)

Contested applications under Trusts of Land and Appointment of Trustees Act 1996, s 14, under CPR 1998, Pt 7

POTENTIAL APPLICANTS → **FOLLOW PRE-ACTION CONDUCT PRACTICE DIRECTION**

ISSUE

File:
- Form N1 with particulars of claim (in the form or separately)

Fee: In the High Court £480
In the County Court £355

SERVE

Documents to serve:

- claim form
- particulars of claim (if separate to the claim form)
- form for defending the claim (Form N9D)
- form for admitting the claim (Form N9C)
- form for acknowledging service (Form N9)

Timing:

- claim form: before **12.00 midnight on the calendar day four months** after the date of issue of the claim form
- particulars of claim: can be served separately but within **14 days after service of the claim form** (but no later than the latest time for serving the claim form)

Methods of service

- post or DX
- delivery
- personally
- fax
- other electronic method (eg email)

For service outside the jurisdiction see CPR 1998, SI 1998/3132, Part 6, Section IV and PD 6B

DEFENDANT FILE ACKNOWLEDGMENT OF SERVICE

File:
- acknowledgment of service (Form N9)

Timing:
- within **14 days** after service of the claim form (or particulars of claim if served separately

(See CPR 1998), SI 1998/3132, r 6.35 and CPR 1998 Part 6, Section IV and PD 6B where the defendant is outside the jurisdiction)

Defendant may file an admission – see CPR 1998, SI 1998/3132, Part 14

DEFENDANT FILE AND SERVE A DEFENCE

Document:
- defence (Form N9D)

Timing:
- if no acknowledgment of service - within **14 days** after service of the particulars of claim
- if acknowledgment of service filed - **28 days** after service of the particulars of claim

If the claim form was served out of the jurisdiction, see CPR 1998, SI 1998/3132, r 6.35 or 6.37

No acknowledgment of service or defence received?

- certificate of service
- default judgment

DIRECTIONS QUESTIONNAIRE, DIRECTIONS, BUDGET, DISCLOSURE REPORT AND REPLY

Documents:
- directions questionnaire (Form N180 or Form N181)
- draft directions
- precedent H (Budget) (if multi-track)
- disclosure report (Form N263) (if multi-track)
- reply to defence

Timing:
- **directions questionnaire**: by the date specified in it (not less than **28 days** after the date it is deemed served (14 days in small-track cases) (the reply must be filed and served at the same time)
- **draft directions**: same time as directions questionnaire (in any event no later than **seven days** before CMC)
- **precedent H**: same date as directions questionnaire (**seven days** or no later than 21)
- **disclosure report** (Form N263): not less than **14 days** before the CMC

DIRECTIONS AND CASE MANAGEMENT CONFERENCE (CMC)

- disclosure
- witness statements
- expert evidence

→ **PRE-TRIAL CHECKLIST** → Fee payable - **£1,090** (multi-track) → If applying for costs file and serve Form N260 24 hours before hearing → **TRIAL**

See also Procedural Guide (PG) A4 in Family Court Practice (The Red Book)

Contested applications under Trusts of Land and Appointment of Trustees Act 1996, s 14, under CPR 1998, Pt 8

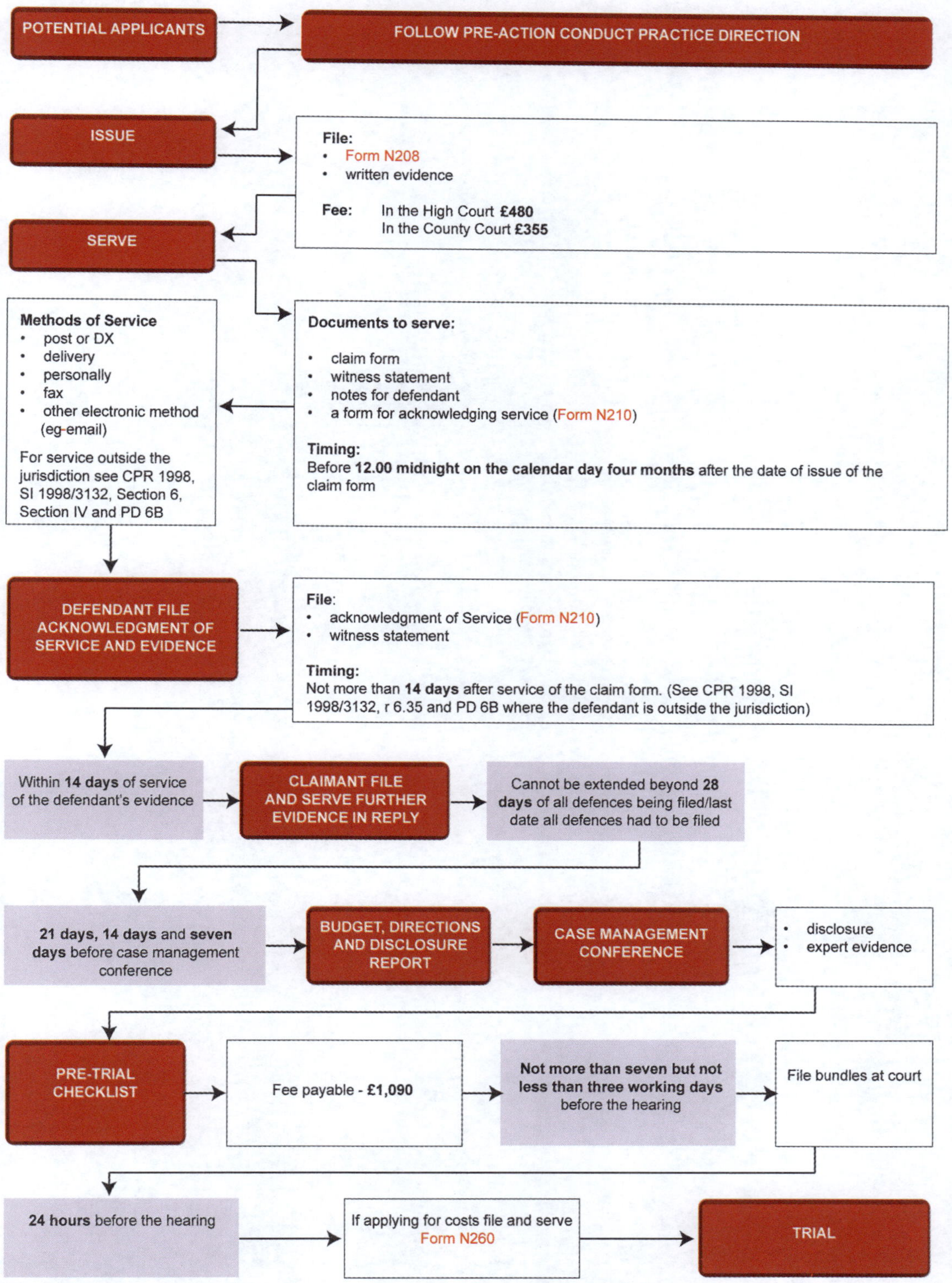

See also the Family Court Practice (The Red Book)

Applications under Schedule 1 to the Children Act 1989 (shortened procedure)—before first hearing

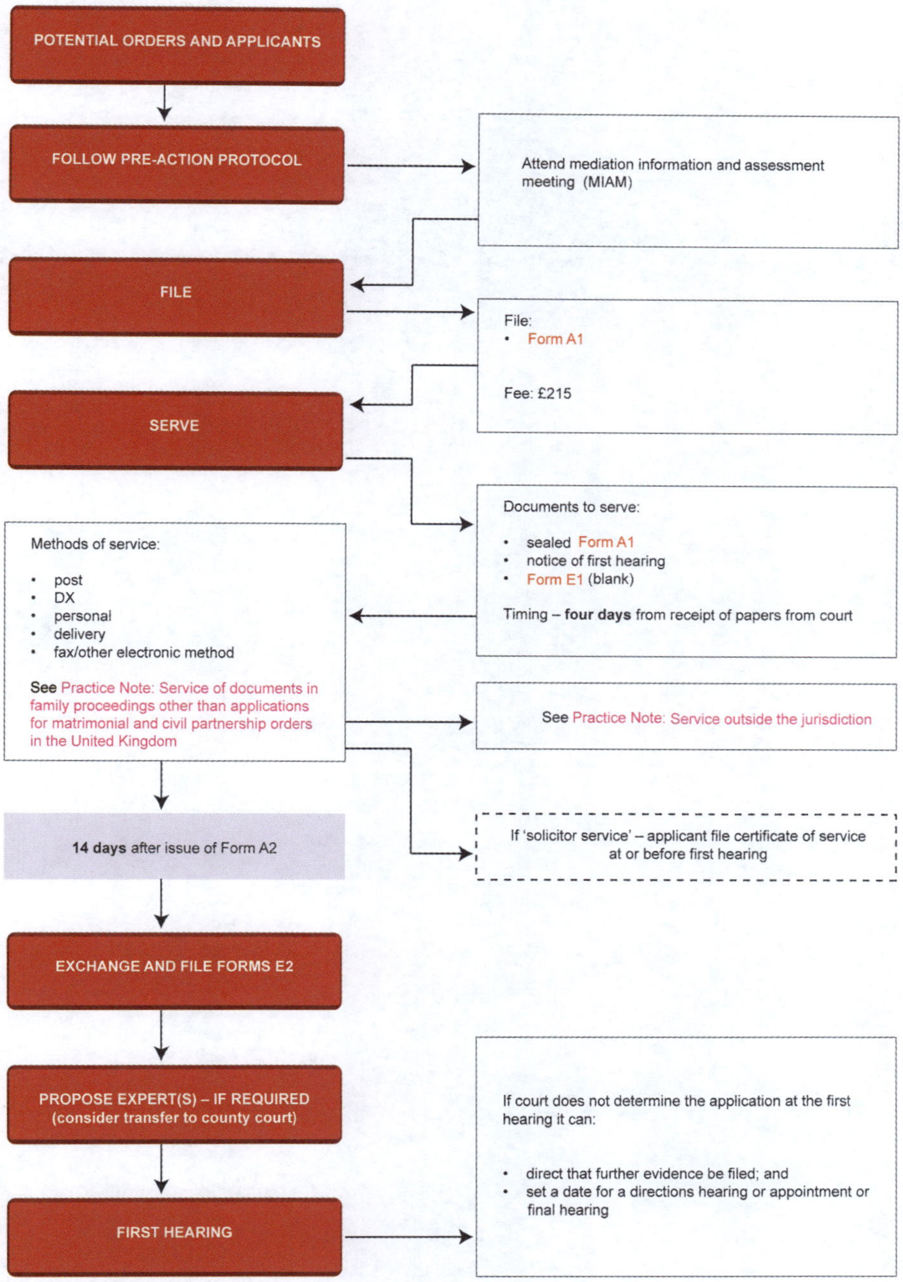

See also Procedural Guide (PG) A2 in Family Court Practice (The Red Book)

Applications under Schedule 1 to the Children Act 1989 (shortened procedure)—after first hearing

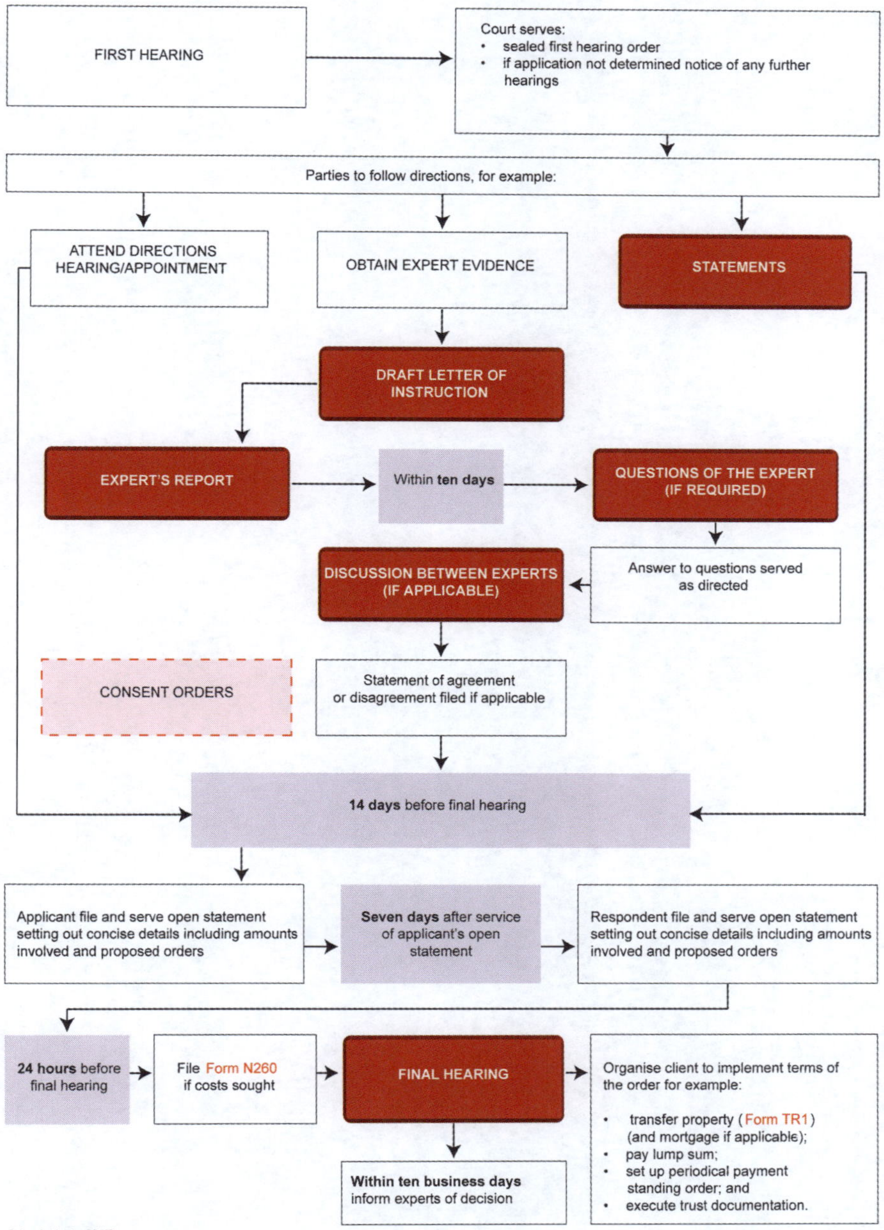

See also Procedural Guide (PG) A2 in Family Court Practice (The Red Book)

Variation of a Schedule 1 order

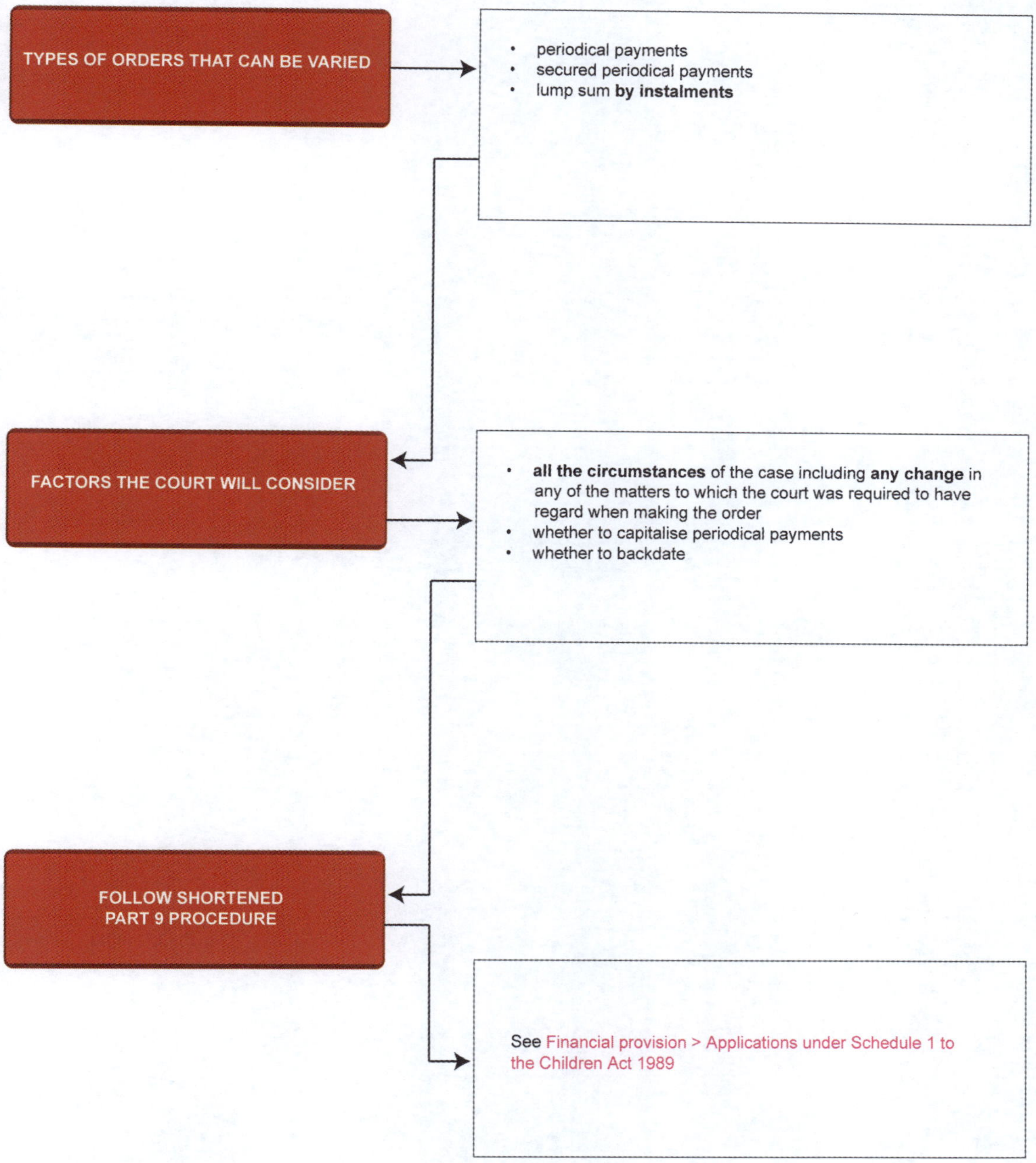

See also Procedural Guide (PG) A2 in Family Court Practice (The Red Book)

Application under MCA 1973, s 10(2)/CPA 2004, s 48(2)

An order under MCA 1973, s 10(2) or CPA 2004, s 48(2) allows the court to consider the respondent's financial position before allowing the decree nisi/conditional order to be made absolute/final. It is only available if the divorce or dissolution is based on:

- five years' separation; or
- two years' separation with consent.

FACTORS THE COURT WILL CONSIDER

- all the circumstances of the case
- age
- health
- conduct
- earning capacity
- financial resources
- financial obligations
- the financial position of the respondent as, having regard to the divorce/dissolution, it is likely to be after the death of the petitioner should the petitioner die first.

After application for matrimonial/civil partnership order (petition) filed but **before** decree absolute/final order

FOLLOW PART 9 PROCEDURE

See: Financial provision > Practice and procedure

See also Procedural Guide (PG) B5 in Family Court Practice (The Red Book)

Pensions on divorce/dissolution/nullity/(judicial) separation (Part 1)—to first appointment

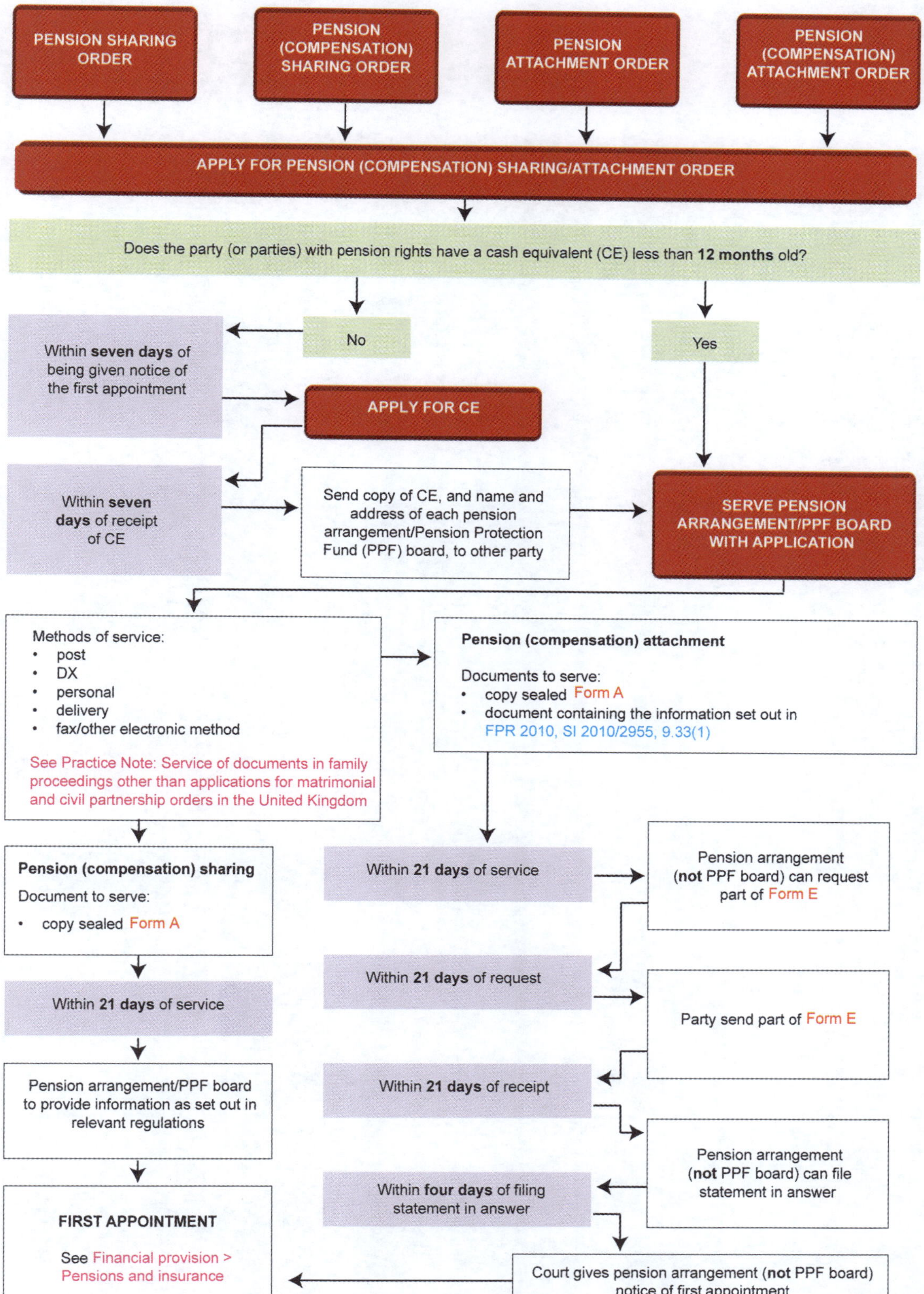

See also Procedural Guide (PG) B5 in Family Court Practice (The Red Book)

Pensions on divorce/dissolution/nullity/(judicial) separation (Part 2)—first appointment to implementation

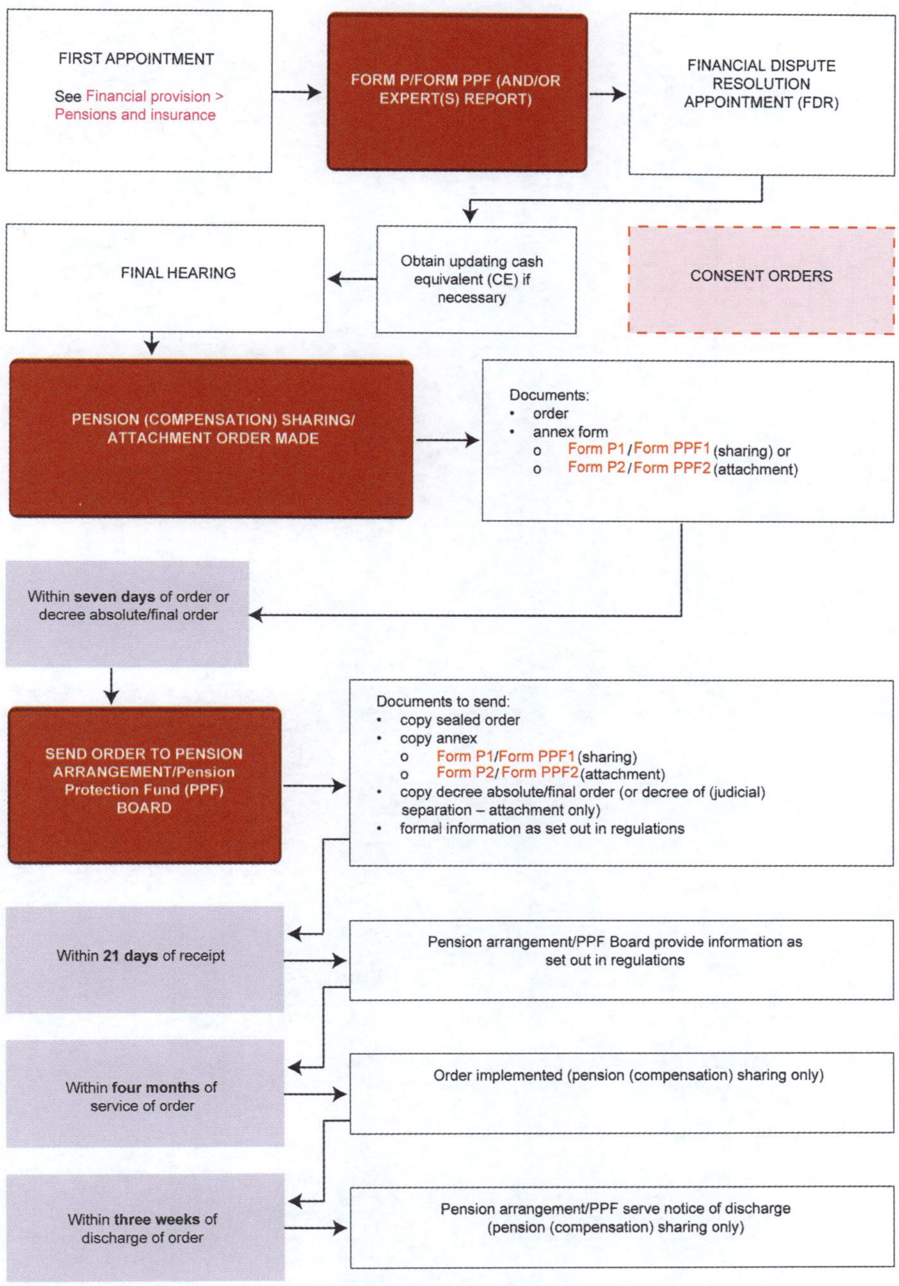

See also Procedural Guide (PG) B5 in Family Court Practice (The Red Book)

APPEALS

Application for judicial review

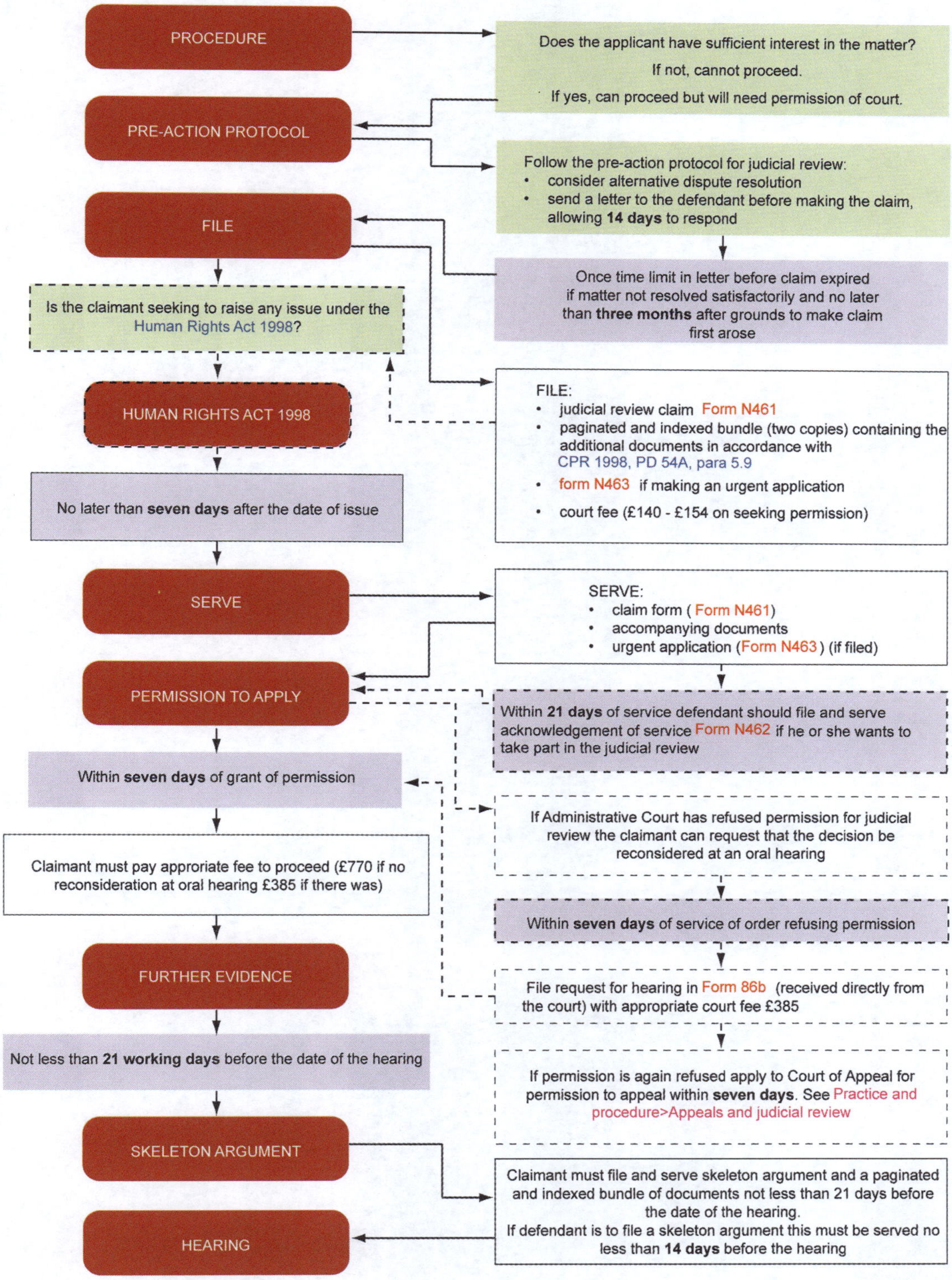

See also Procedural Guide (PG) E1 in Family Court Practice (The Red Book)

Family Court—appeal from lay justice or district judge level to circuit judge, or from district judge (High Court level) to judge of the High Court (Part 1)

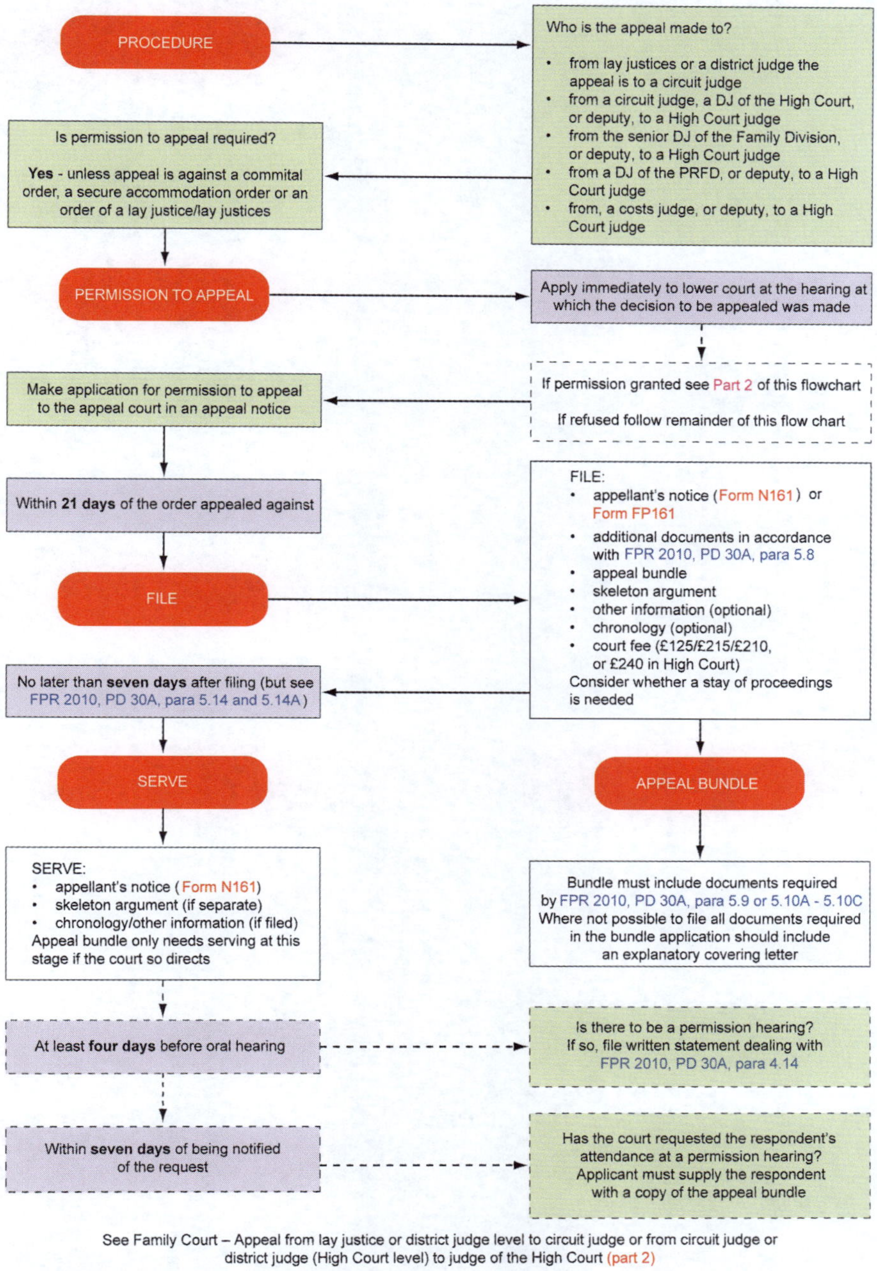

See also Procedural Guide (PG) E2 in Family Court Practice (The Red Book)

Family Court—appeal from lay justice or district judge level to circuit judge, or from district judge (High Court level) to judge of the High Court (Part 2)

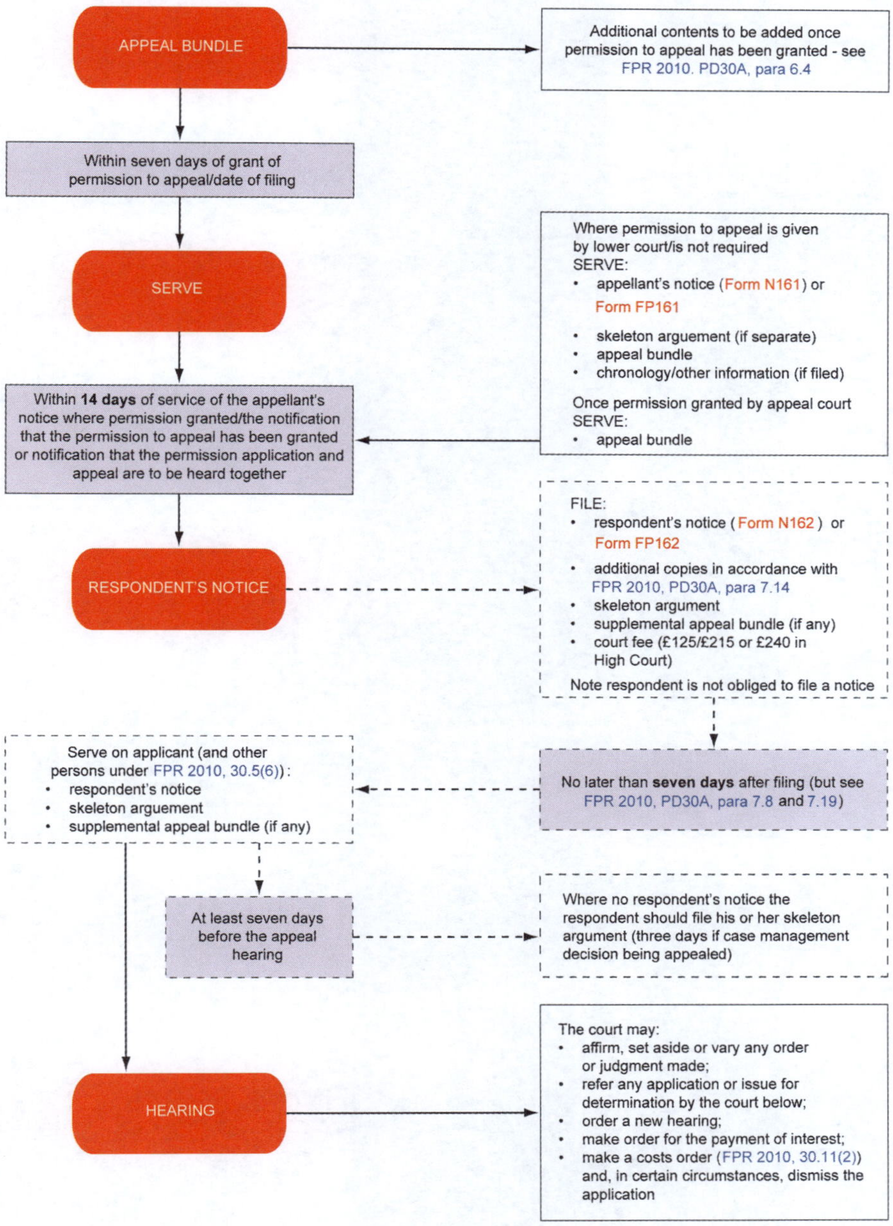

See also Procedural Guide (PG) E2 in Family Court Practice (The Red Book)

Family Court—appeal from judge of circuit judge level or a judge of High Court level to the Court of Appeal (Part 1)

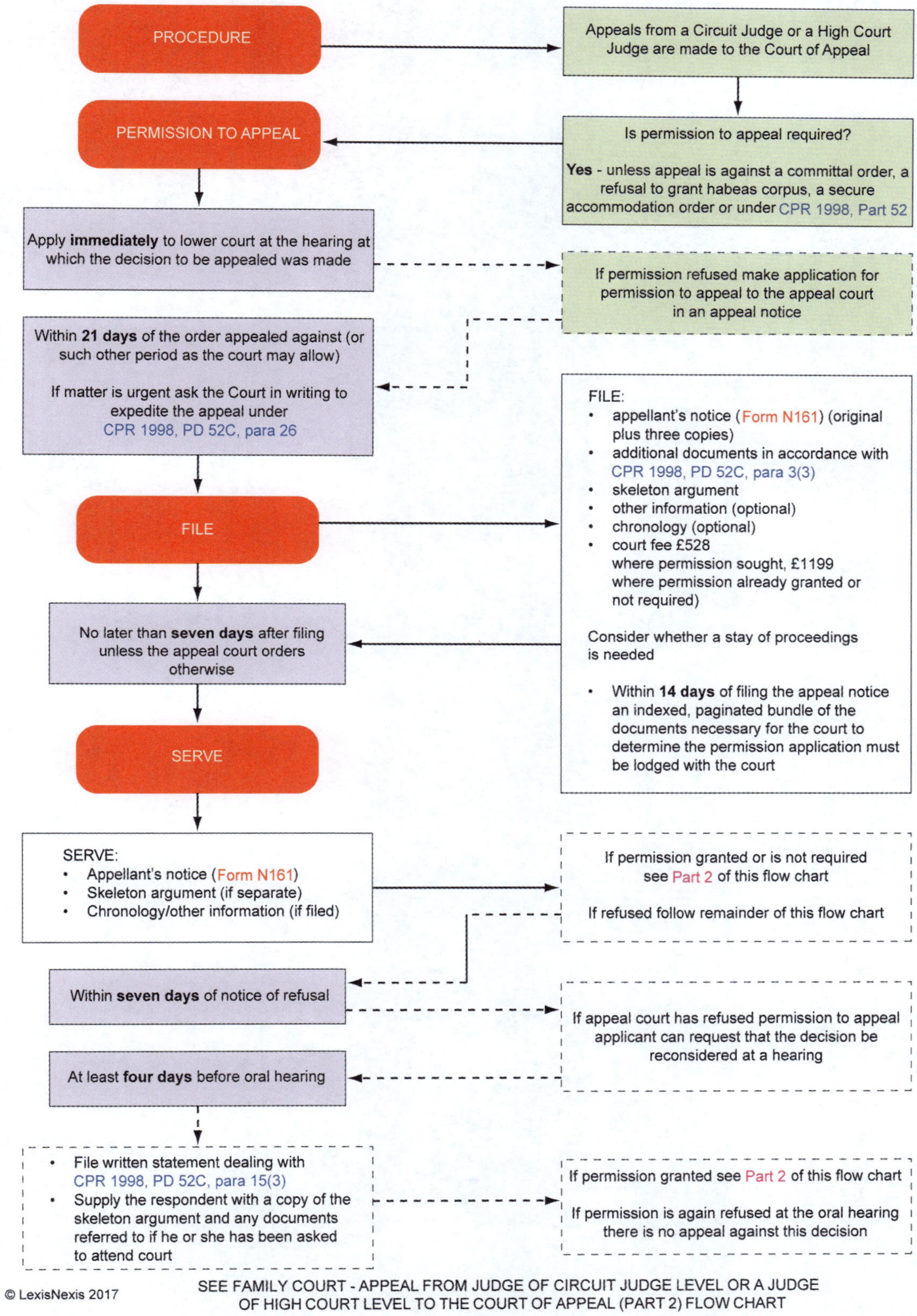

See also Procedural Guide (PG) E5 in Family Court Practice (The Red Book)

Family Court—appeal from judge of circuit judge level or a judge of High Court level to the Court of Appeal (Part 2)

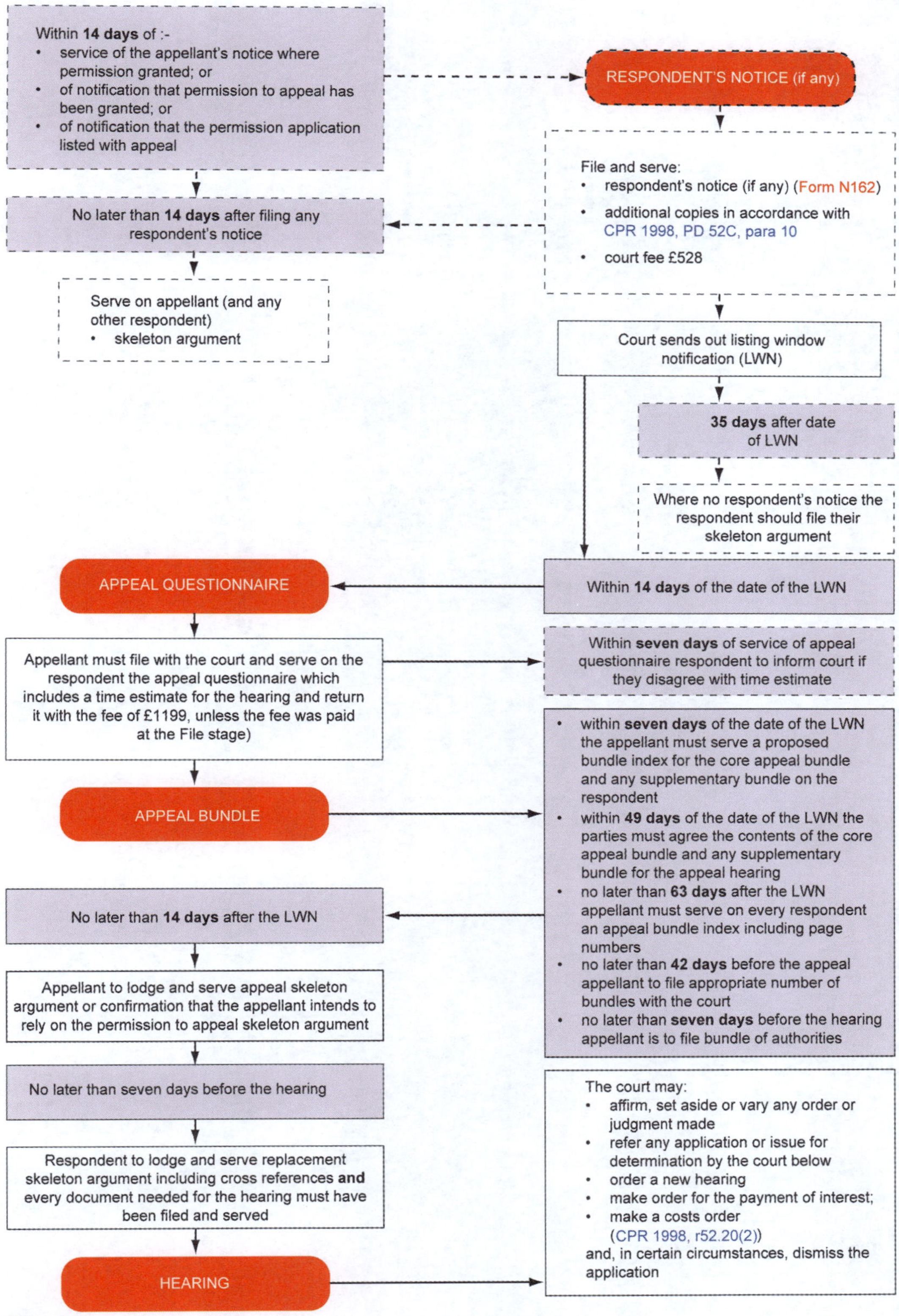

See also Procedural Guide (PG) E5 in Family Court Practice (The Red Book)

Applications to set aside a financial remedy order

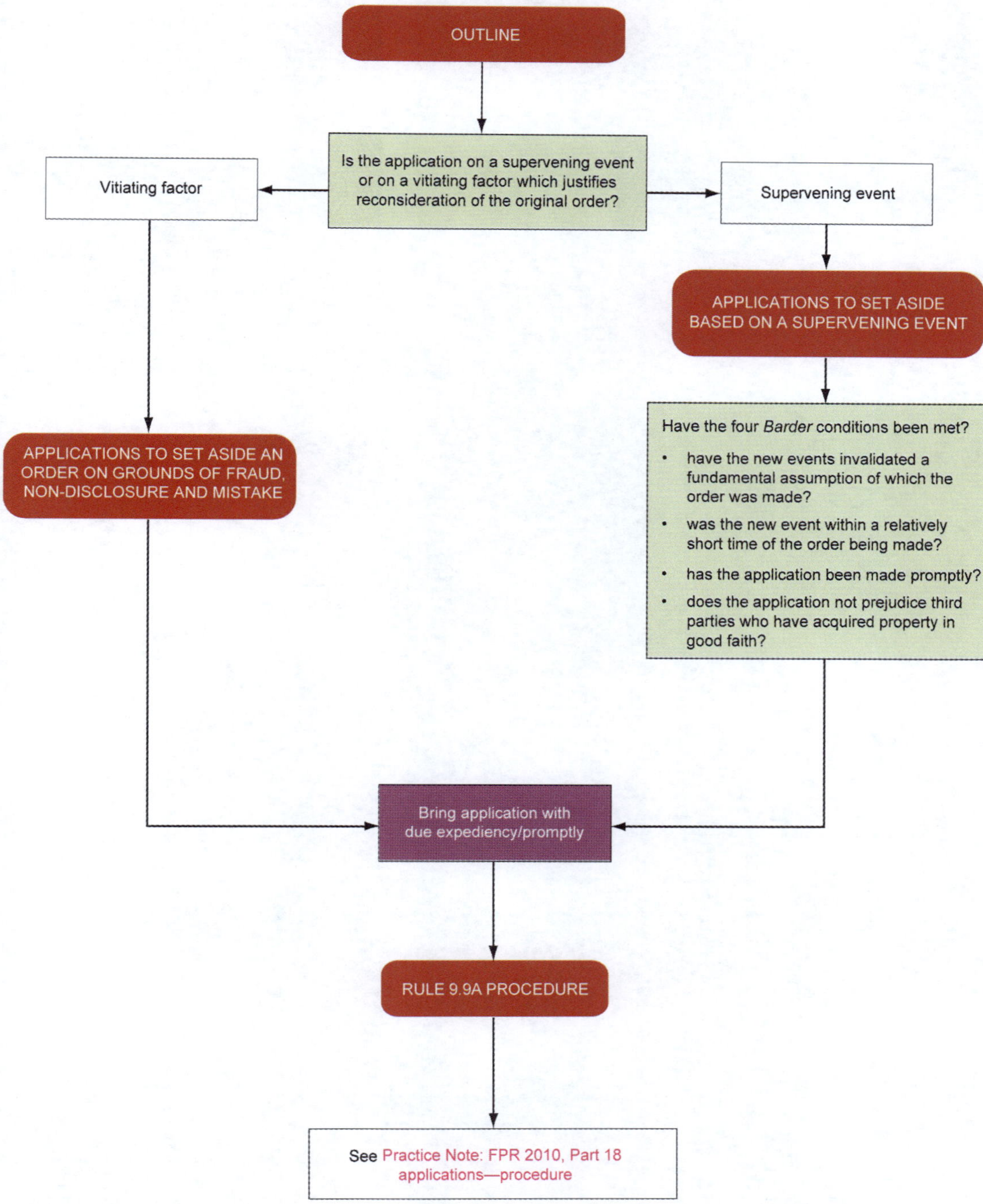

See also Procedural Guide (PG) E7(2) in Family Court Practice (The Red Book)

Family Court—appeal from judge of the High Court or from the Court of Appeal to the Supreme Court

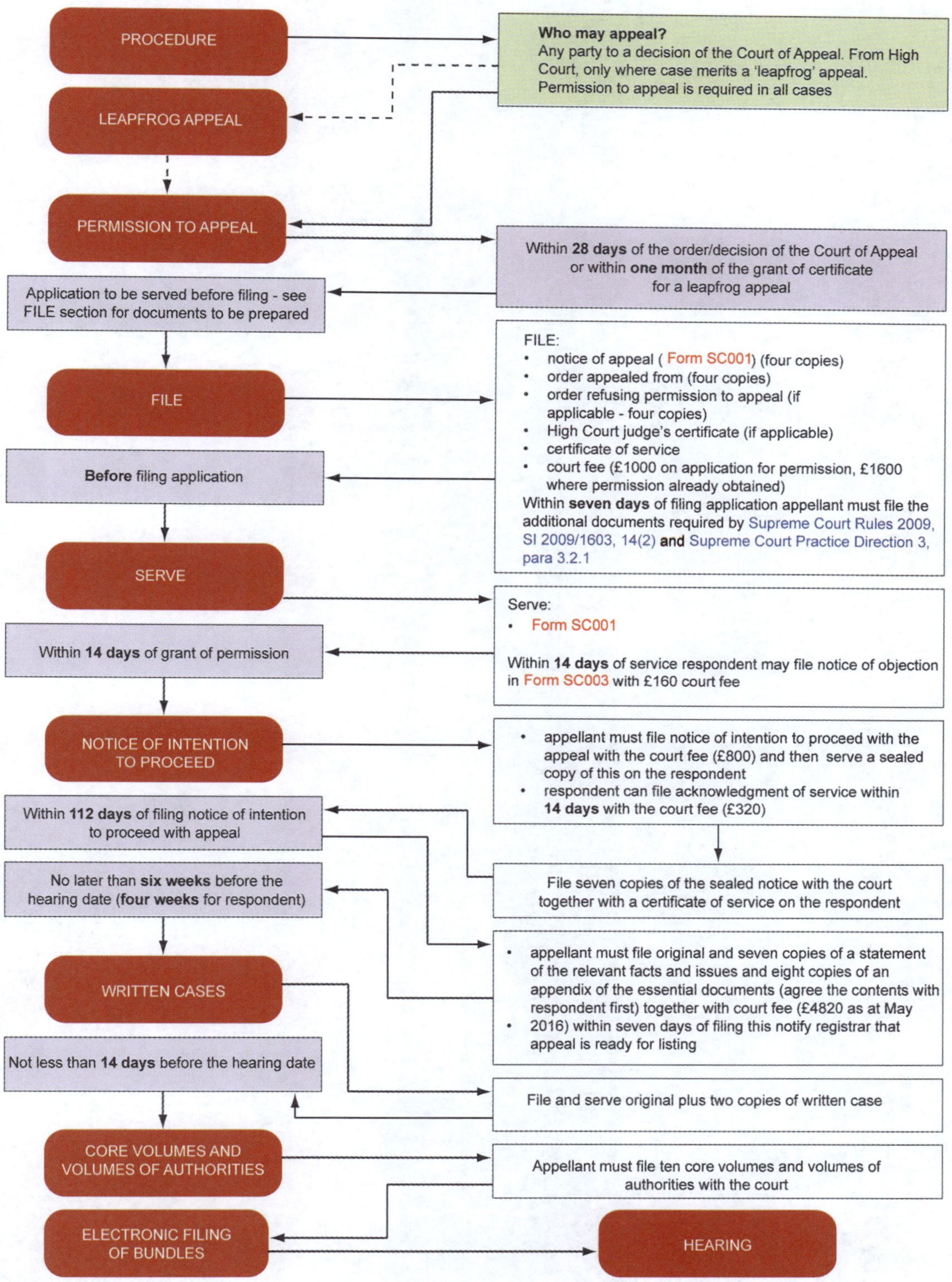

See also Procedural Guide (PG) E4 in Family Court Practice (The Red Book)

Family Court—appeal from magistrates to the Family Court under Child Support Act 1991

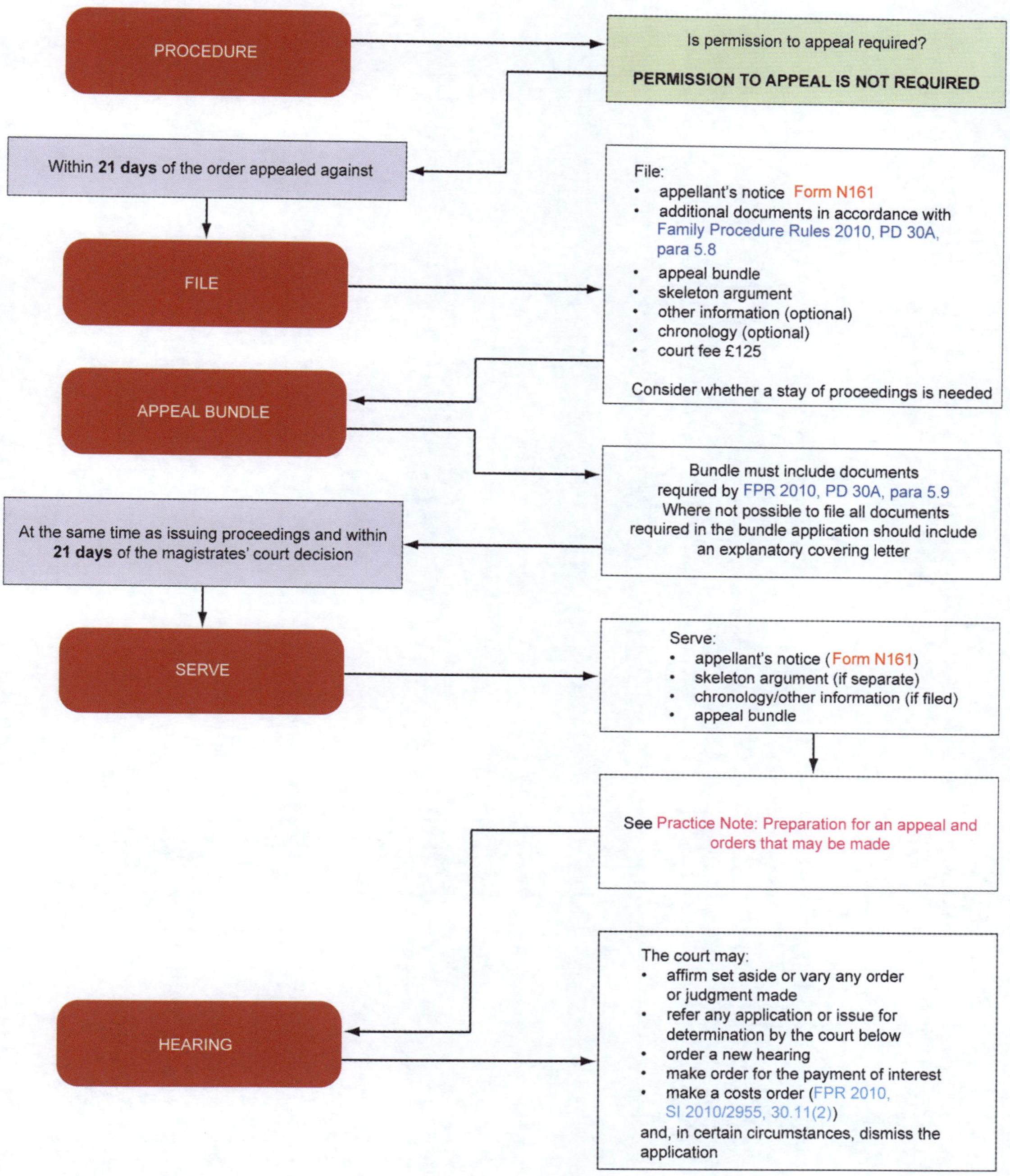

See also Procedural Guide (PG) E3 in Family Court Practice (The Red Book)

ENFORCEMENT

Enforcement options (Part 1)—non-monetary issues

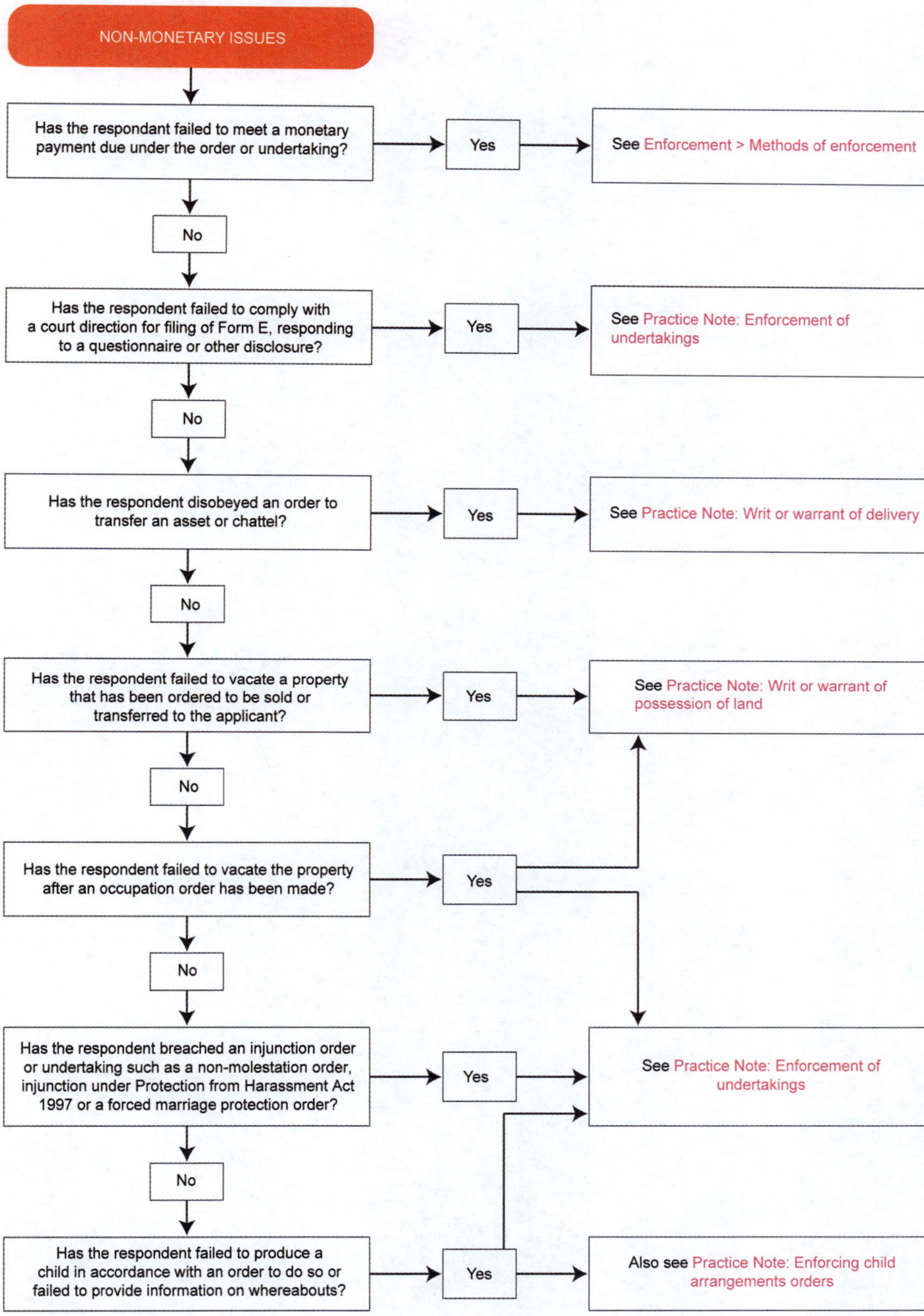

See also the Family Court Practice (The Red Book)

Enforcement options (Part 2)—monetary issues

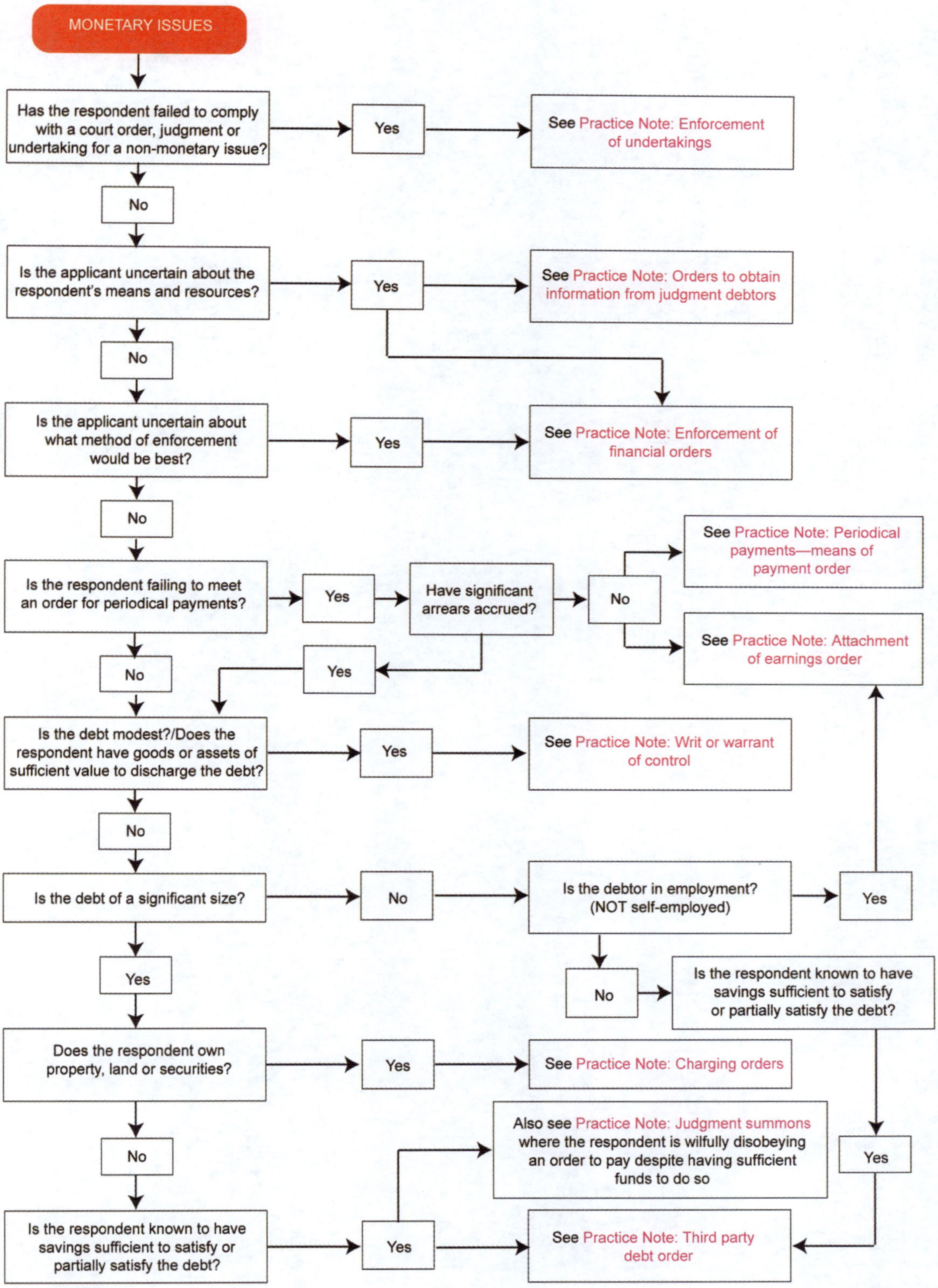

See also the Family Court Practice (The Red Book)

Obtaining information from the debtor

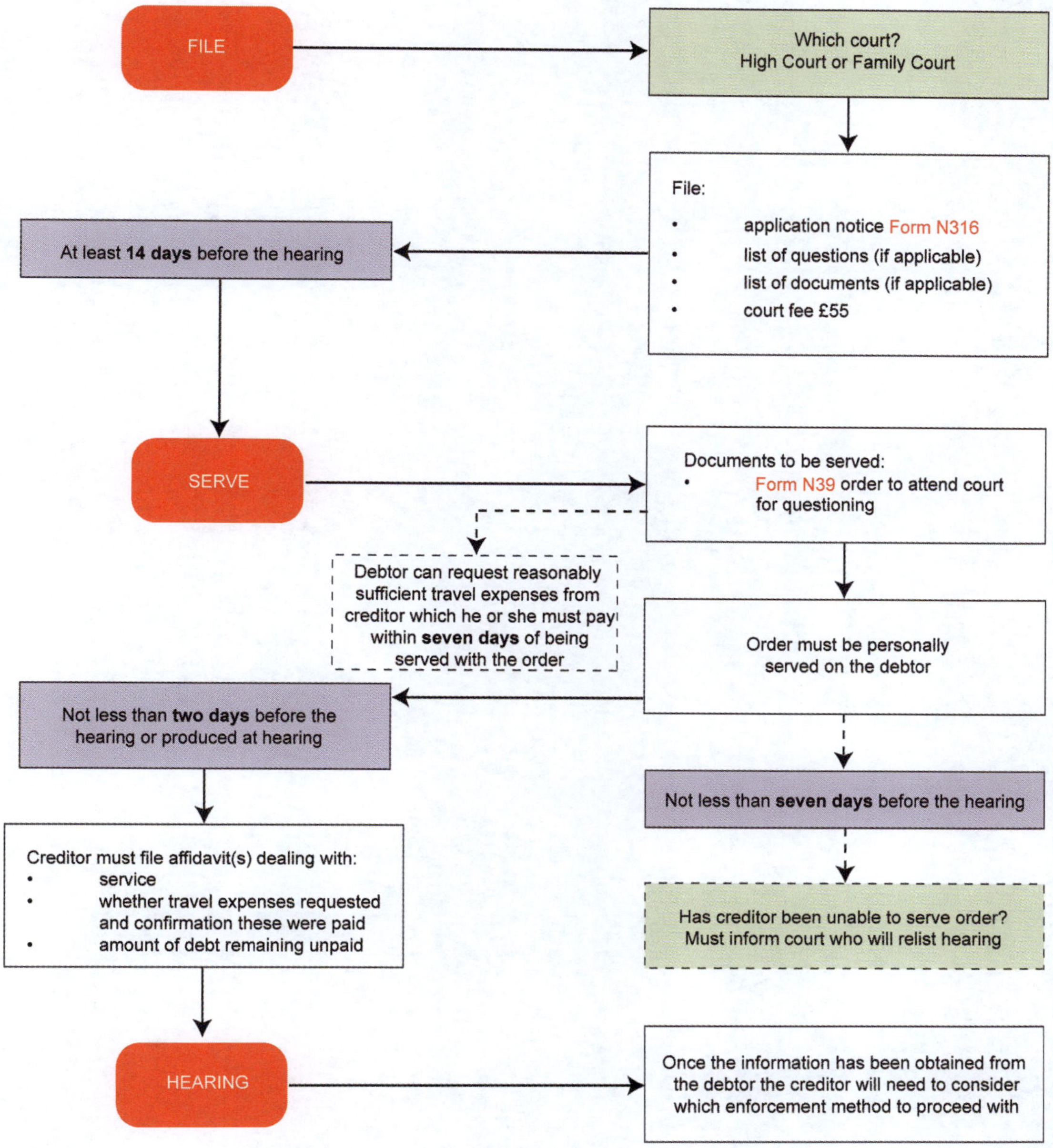

See also Procedural Guide (PG) C12 in Family Court Practice (The Red Book)

Order for such method of enforcement as the court may consider appropriate

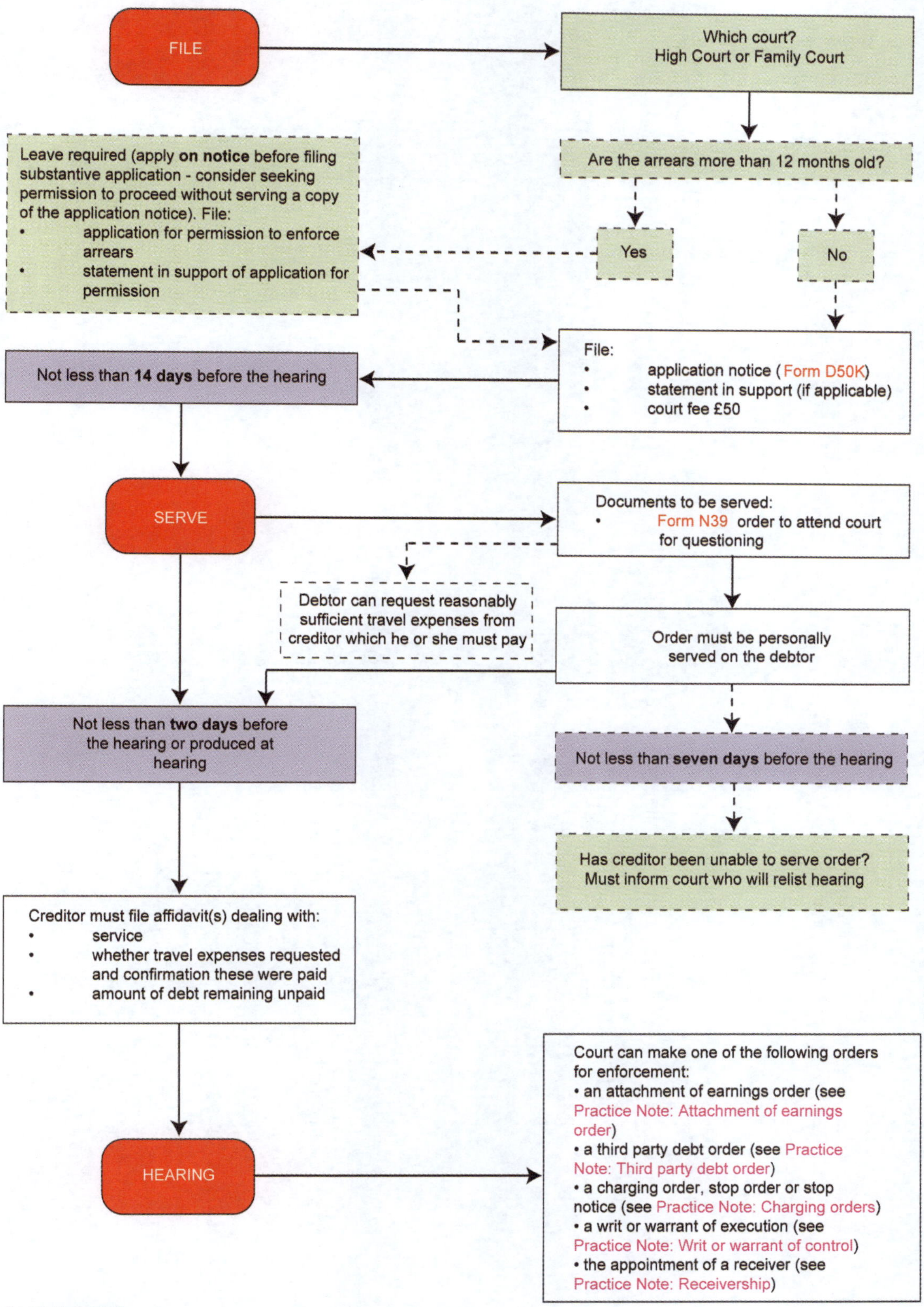

See also Procedural Guide (PG) C11 in Family Court Practice (The Red Book)

Committal for breach of an order or undertaking in the Family Court and High Court—matrimonial and civil partnership financial proceedings

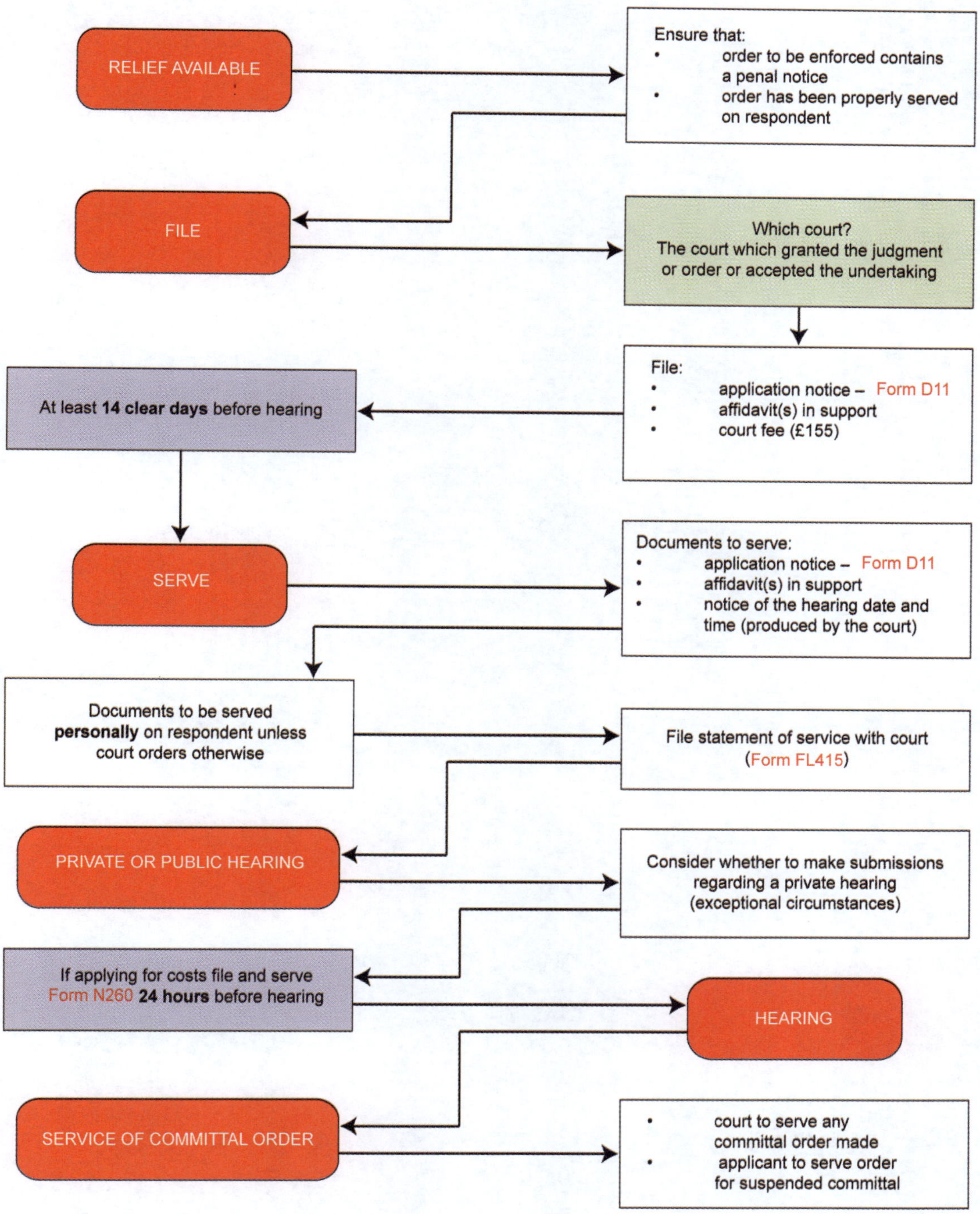

See also the Family Court Practice (The Red Book)

Committal and arrest for disobedience of an injunctive order or breach of an undertaking in the High Court, Family Court or County Court

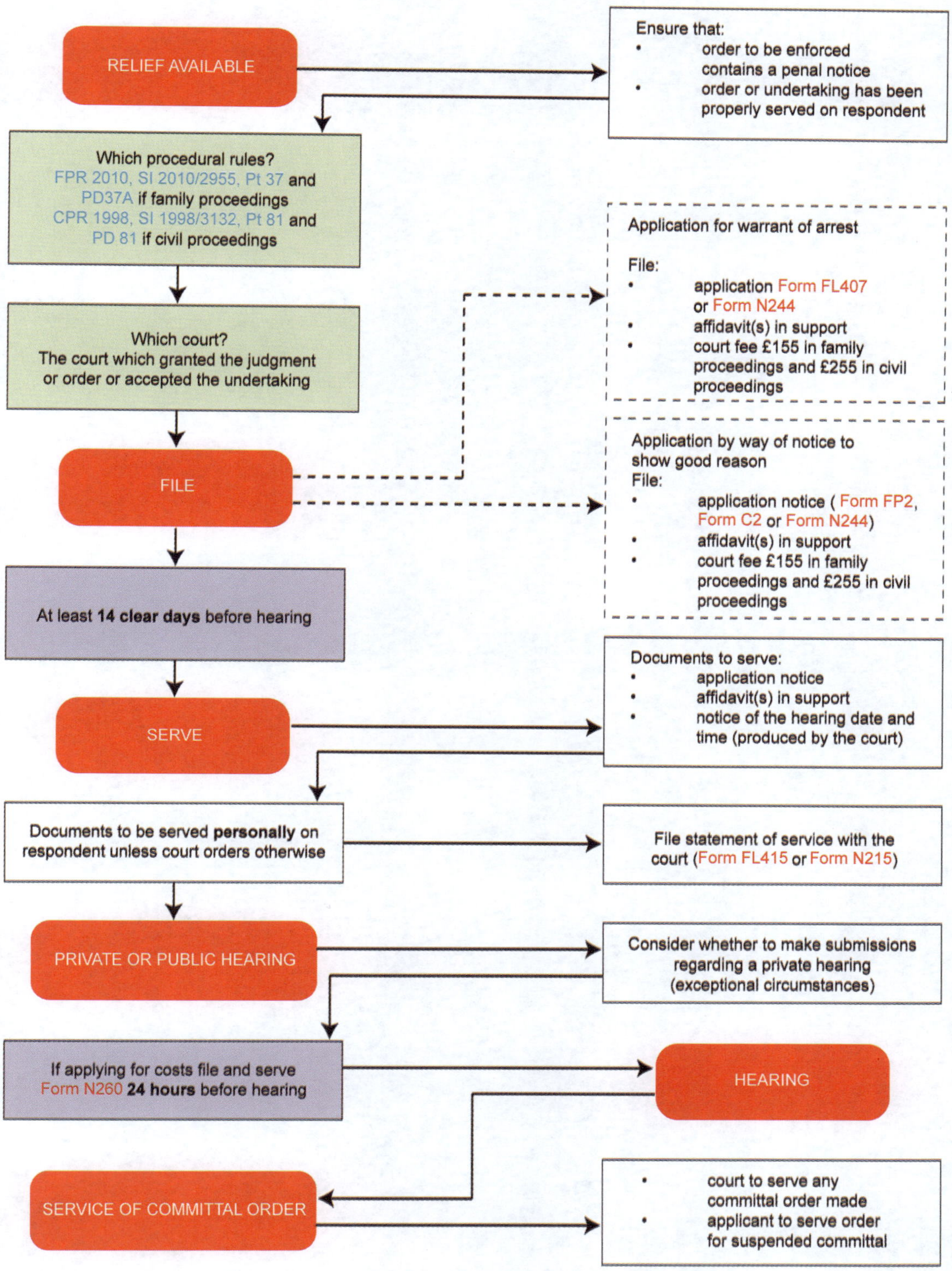

See also Procedural Guide (PG) C14 in Family Court Practice (The Red Book)

Attachment of earnings order

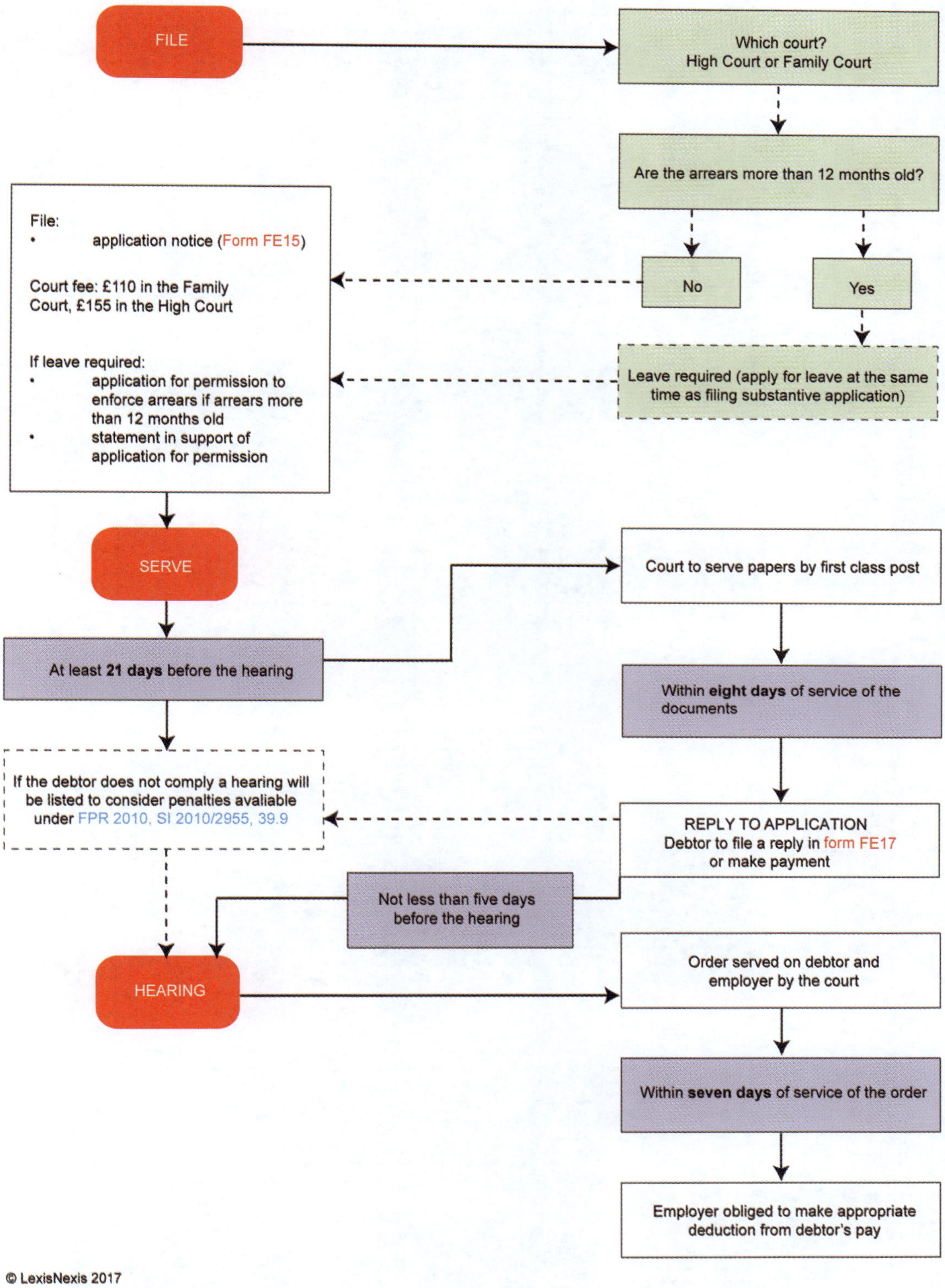

See also Procedural Guide (PG) C4 in Family Court Practice (The Red Book)

Charging order

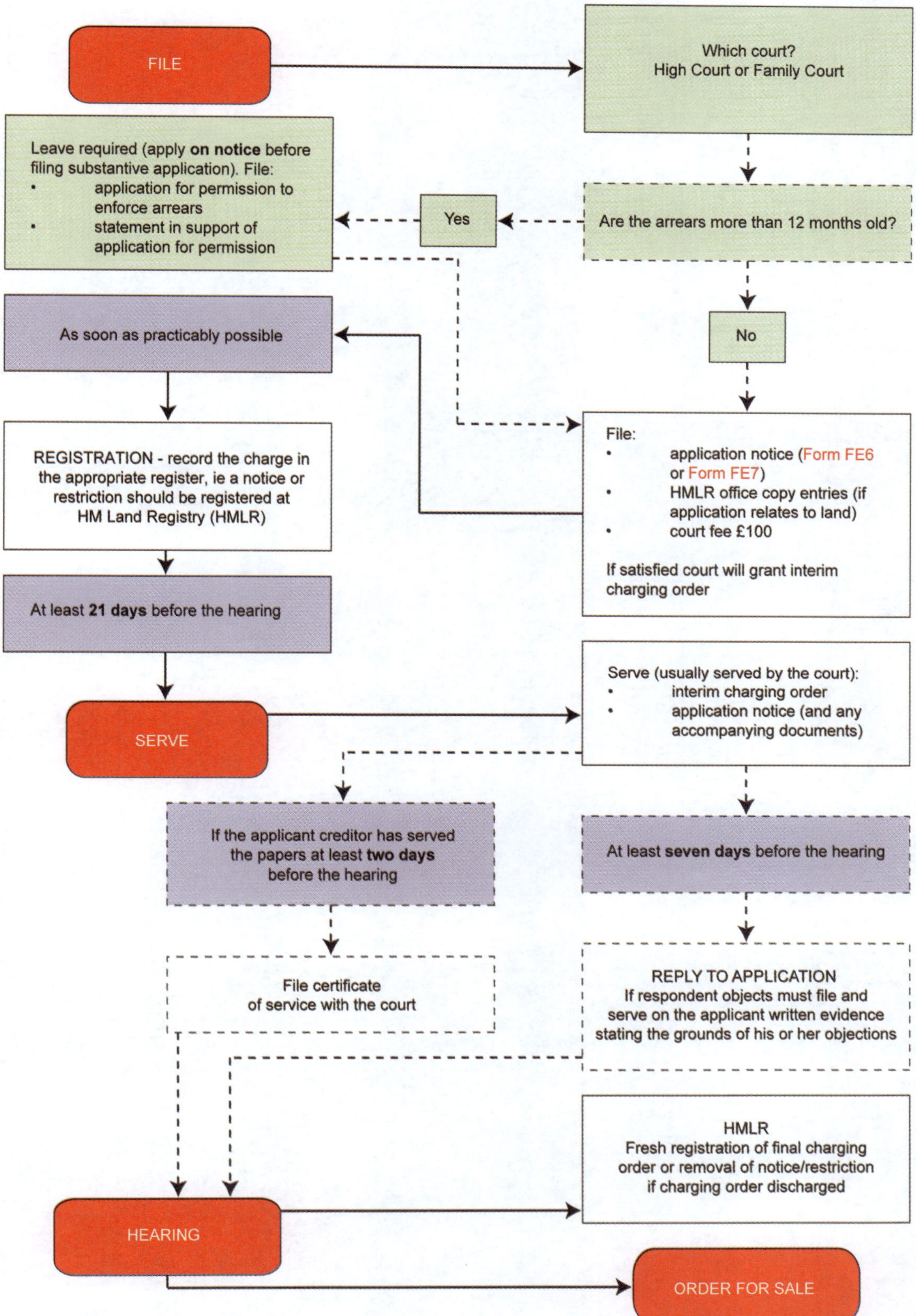

See also Procedural Guide (PG) C5 in Family Court Practice (The Red Book)

Writ or warrant of delivery

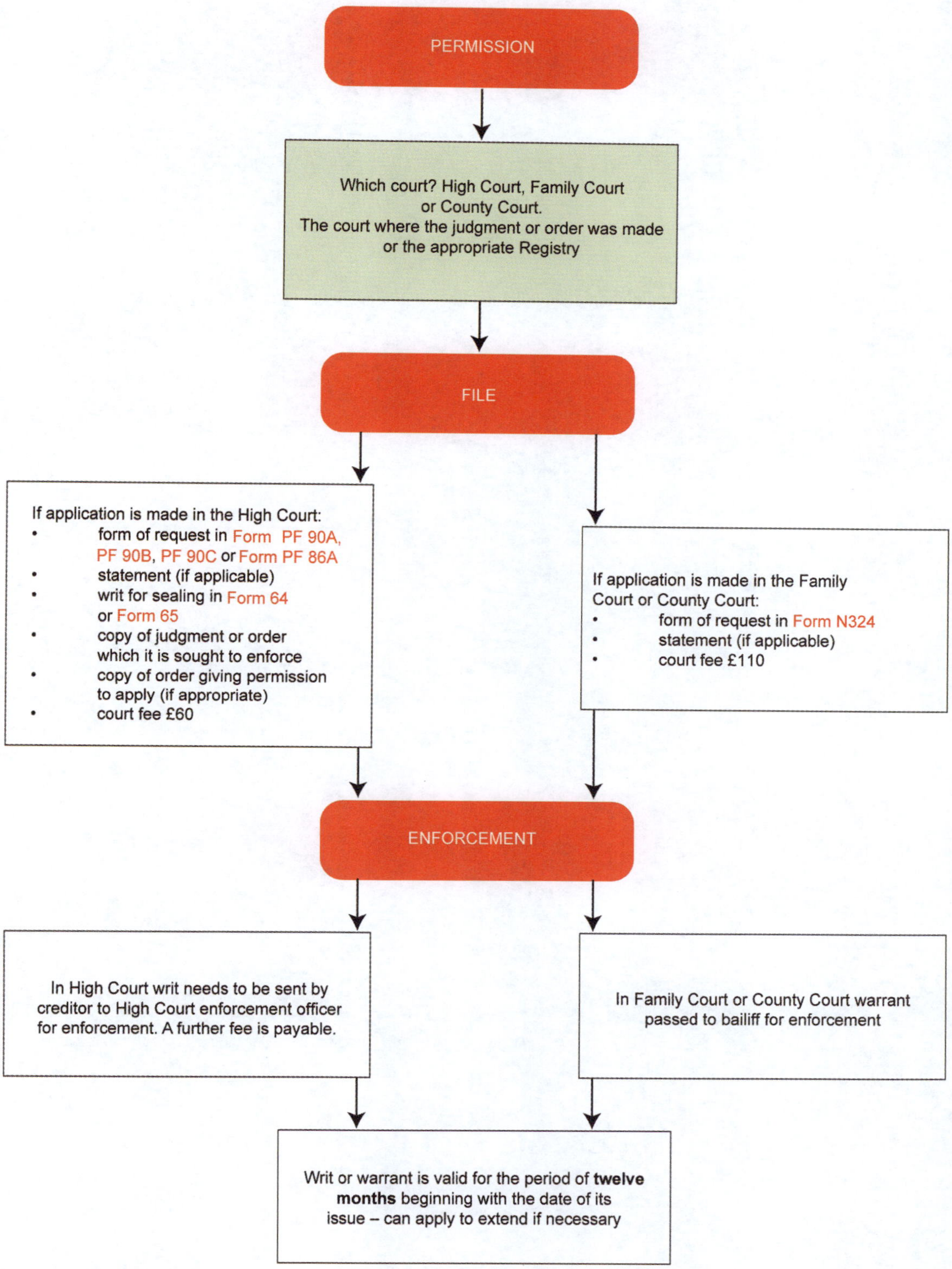

See also Procedural Guide (PG) C6 in Family Court Practice (The Red Book)

Execution against goods—writ or warrant of control

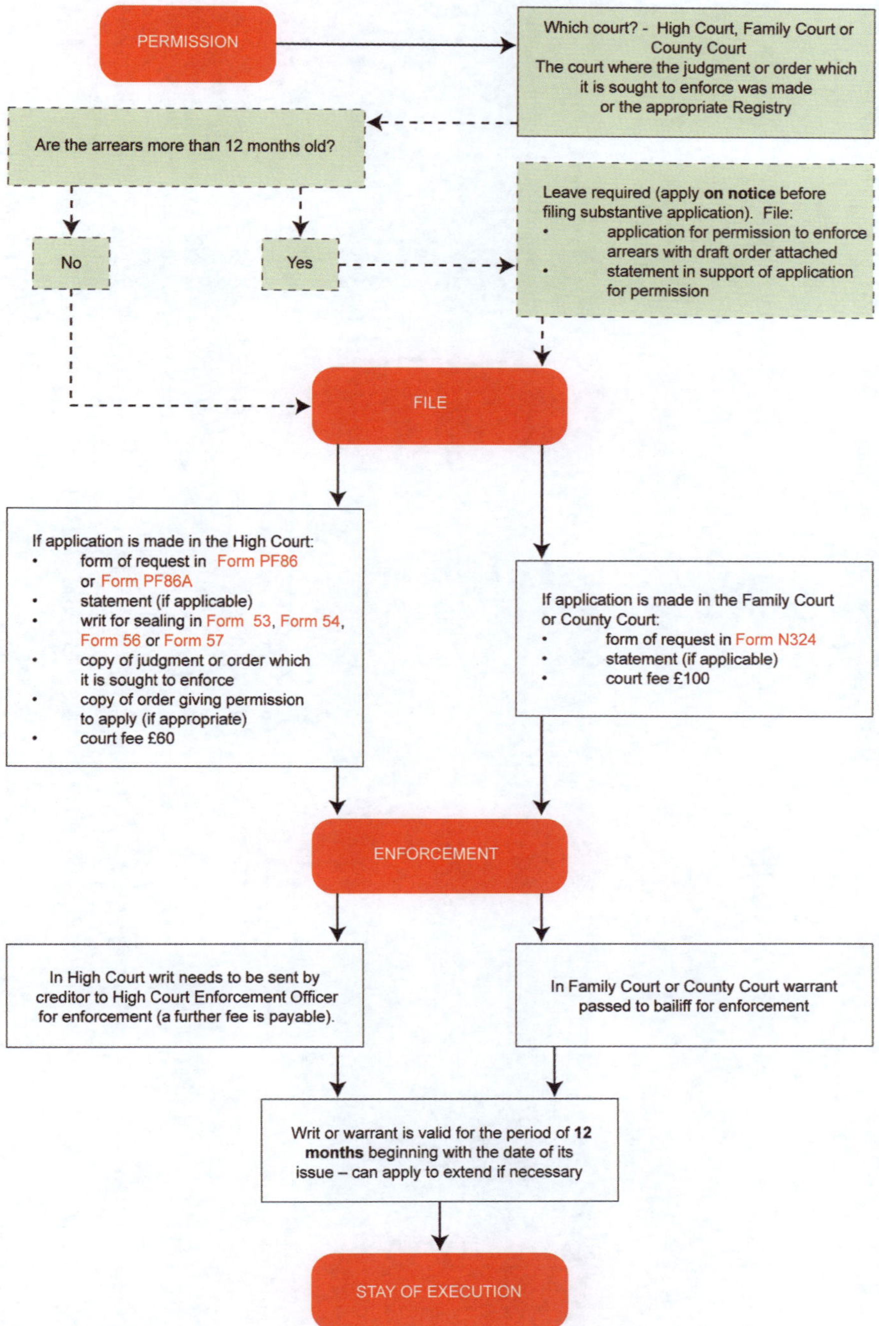

See also Procedural Guide (PG) C7 in Family Court Practice (The Red Book)

Application for a third party debt order

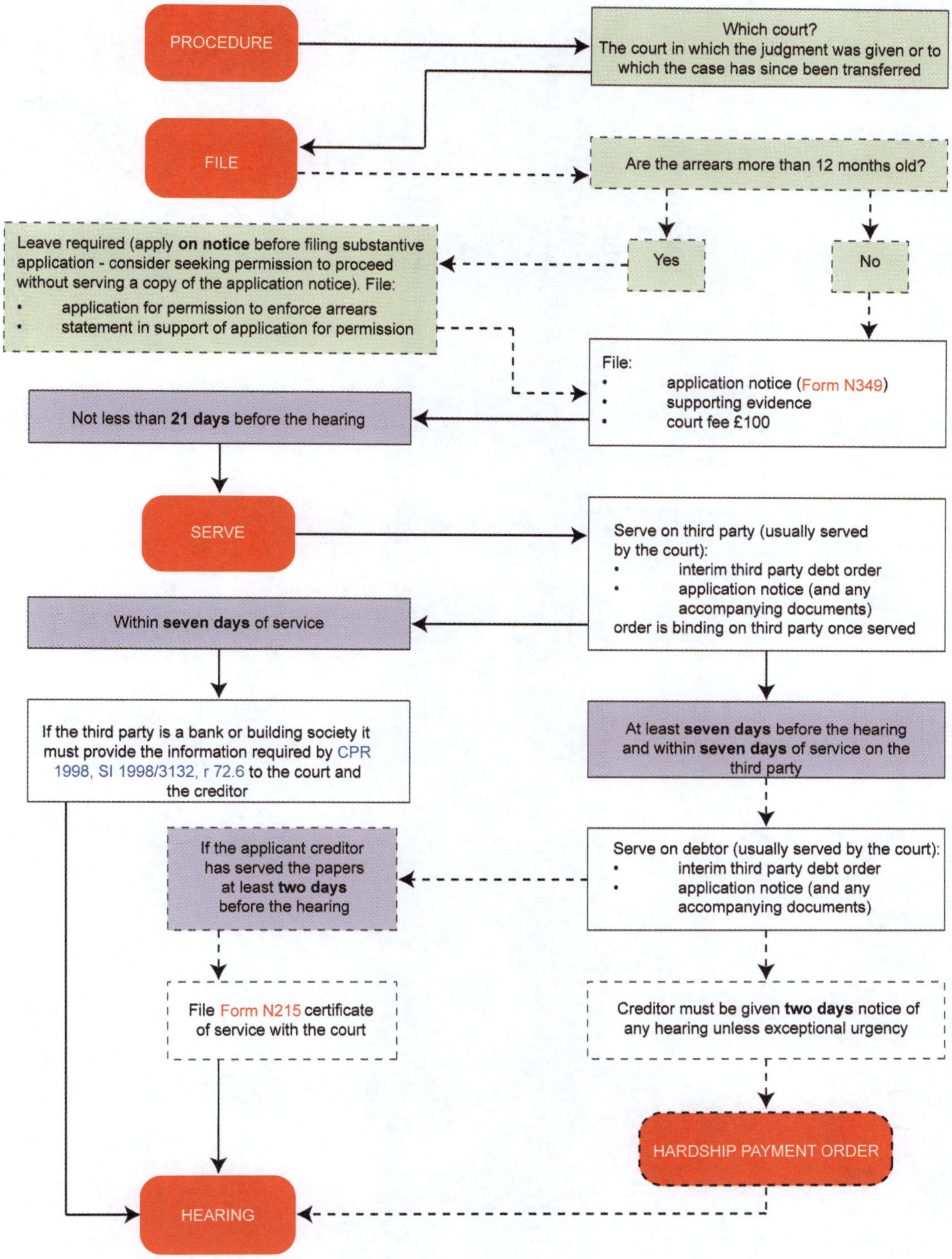

See also Procedural Guide (PG) C8 in Family Court Practice (The Red Book)

Committal by way of judgment summons

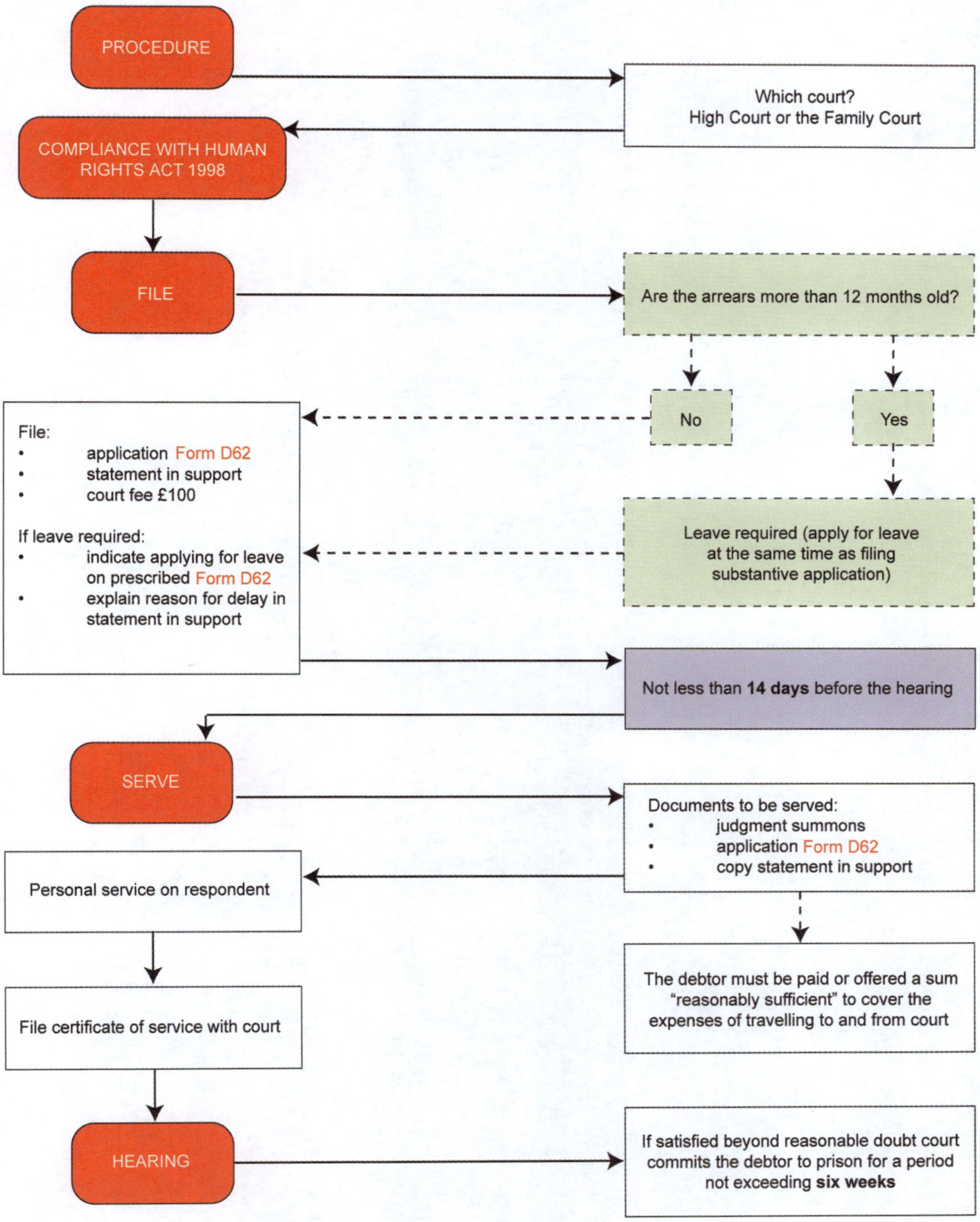

See also Procedural Guide (PG) C9 in Family Court Practice (The Red Book)

Means of payment order

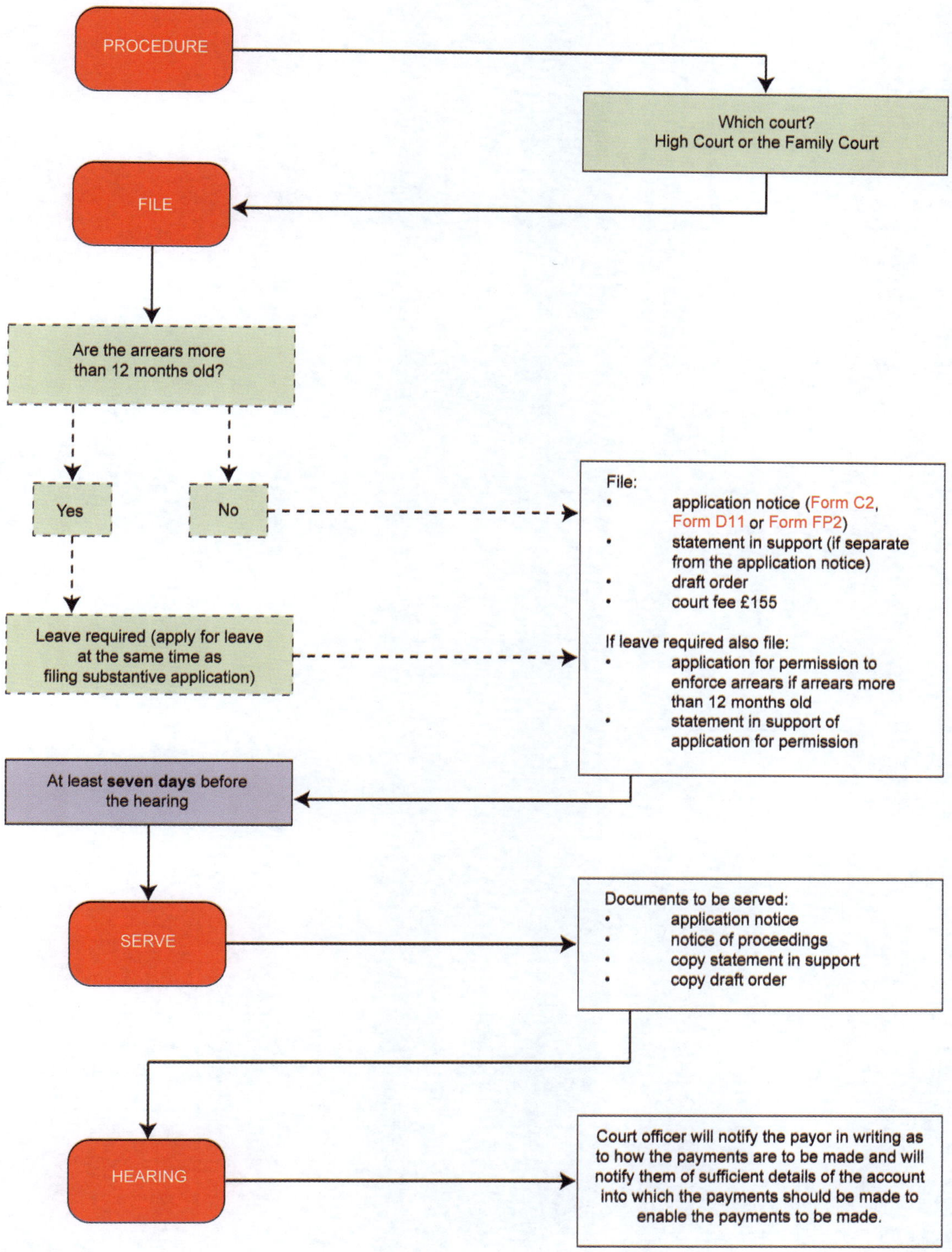

See also Procedural Guide (PG) C10 in Family Court Practice (The Red Book)

Writ or warrant of possession of land

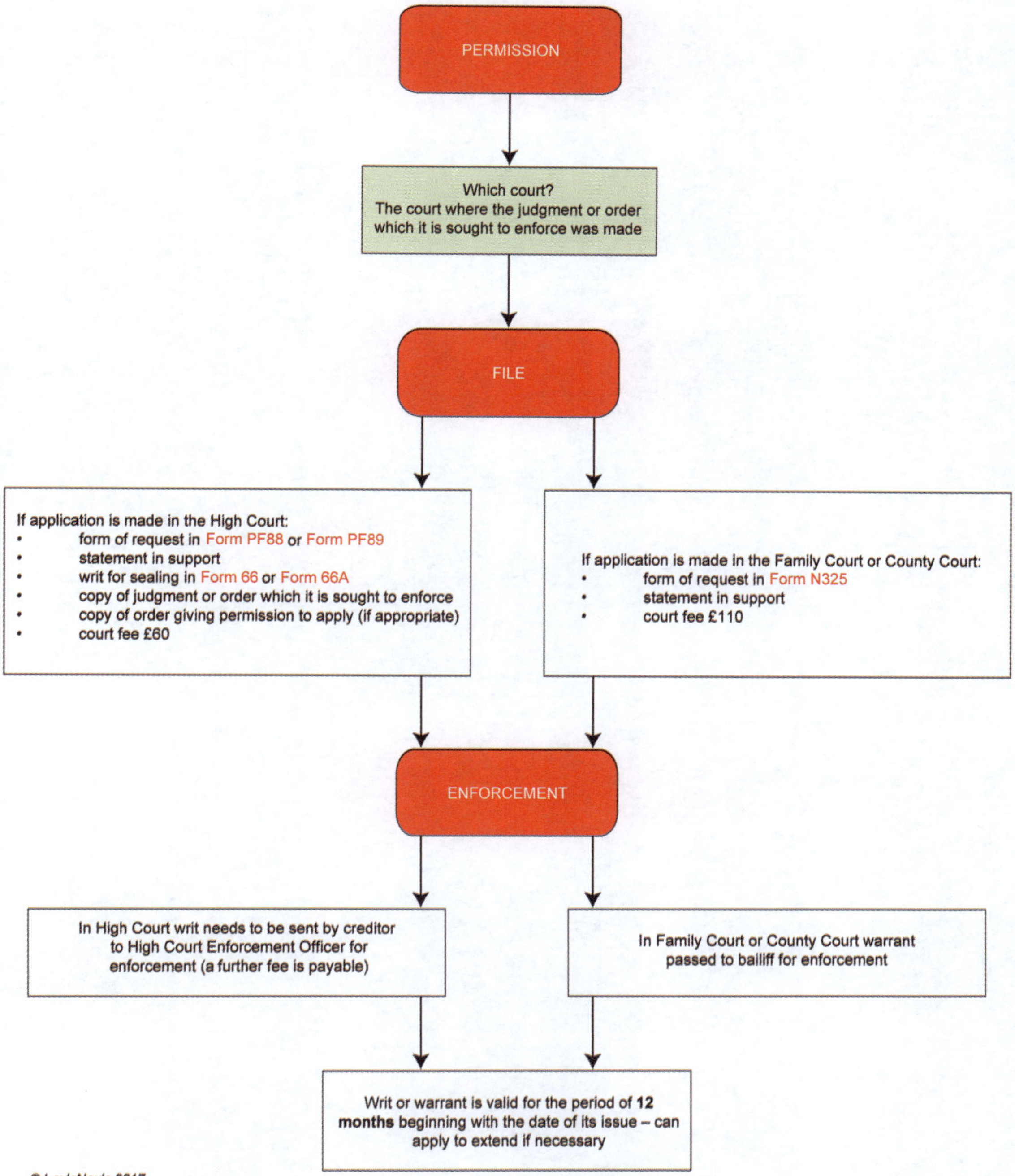

See also Procedural Guide (PG) C13 in Family Court Practice (The Red Book)

PART II

KEY LEGISLATION AND GUIDANCE

MATRIMONIAL CAUSES ACT 1973

SECTIONS 21A–25D

21A Pension sharing orders

(1) For the purposes of this Act, a pension sharing order is an order which –

(a) provides that one party's –

(i) shareable rights under a specified pension arrangement, or
(ii) shareable state scheme rights,

be subject to pension sharing for the benefit of the other party, and
(b) specifies the percentage value to be transferred.

(1A) Where section 25E(7) applies, the reference in subsection (1) –

(a) to shareable rights under a specified pension arrangement shall include a reference to entitlement to PPF compensation (as defined in section 25E(9)); and
(b) to pension sharing shall include a reference to sharing of that compensation.

(2) In subsection (1) above –

(a) the reference to shareable rights under a pension arrangement is to rights in relation to which pension sharing is available under Chapter I of Part IV of the Welfare Reform and Pensions Act 1999, or under corresponding Northern Ireland legislation,
(b) the reference to shareable state scheme rights is to rights in relation to which pension sharing is available under Chapter II of Part IV of the Welfare Reform and Pensions Act 1999, or under corresponding Northern Ireland legislation, and
(c) 'party' means a party to a marriage.

Amendments—Inserted by Welfare Reform and Pensions Act 1999, s 19, Sch 3, para 2.

21B Pension compensation sharing orders

(1) For the purposes of this Act, a pension compensation sharing order is an order which –

(a) provides that one party's shareable rights to PPF compensation that derive from rights under a specified pension scheme are to be subject to pension compensation sharing for the benefit of the other party, and
(b) specifies the percentage value to be transferred.

(2) In subsection (1) –

(a) the reference to shareable rights to PPF compensation is to rights in relation to which pension compensation sharing is available under Chapter 1 of Part 3 of the Pensions Act 2008 or under corresponding Northern Ireland legislation;
(b) 'party' means a party to a marriage;
(c) 'specified' means specified in the order.

Amendments—Inserted by Pensions Act 2008, Sch 6, Pt 1.

21C Pension compensation: interpretation

In this Part –

'PPF compensation' means compensation payable under the pension compensation provisions;
'the pension compensation provisions' means –

(a) Chapter 3 of Part 2 of the Pensions Act 2004 (pension protection) and any regulations or order made under it,
(b) Chapter 1 of Part 3 of the Pensions Act 2008 (pension compensation on divorce etc) and any regulations or order made under it, and
(c) any provision corresponding to the provisions mentioned in paragraph (a) or (b) in force in Northern Ireland.

Amendments—Inserted by Pensions Act 2008, Sch 6, Pt 1.

Ancillary relief in connection with divorce proceedings etc

22 Maintenance pending suit

(1) On a petition for divorce, nullity of marriage or judicial separation, the court may make an order for maintenance pending suit, that is to say, an order requiring either party to the marriage to make to the other such periodical payments for his or her maintenance and for such term, being a term beginning not earlier than the date of the presentation of the petition and ending with the date of the determination of the suit, as the court thinks reasonable.

(2) An order under this section may not require a party to a marriage to pay to the other party any amount in respect of legal services for the purposes of the proceedings.

(3) In subsection (2) 'legal services' has the same meaning as in section 22ZA.

Amendments—Legal Aid, Sentencing and Punishment of Offenders Act 2012, s 49.

22ZA Orders for payment in respect of legal services

(1) In proceedings for divorce, nullity of marriage or judicial separation, the court may make an order or orders requiring one party to the marriage to pay to the other ('the applicant') an amount for the purpose of enabling the applicant to obtain legal services for the purposes of the proceedings.

(2) The court may also make such an order or orders in proceedings under this Part for financial relief in connection with proceedings for divorce, nullity of marriage or judicial separation.

(3) The court must not make an order under this section unless it is satisfied that, without the amount, the applicant would not reasonably be able to obtain appropriate legal services for the purposes of the proceedings or any part of the proceedings.

(4) For the purposes of subsection (3), the court must be satisfied, in particular, that –

(a) the applicant is not reasonably able to secure a loan to pay for the services, and
(b) the applicant is unlikely to be able to obtain the services by granting a charge over any assets recovered in the proceedings.

(5) An order under this section may be made for the purpose of enabling the applicant to obtain legal services of a specified description, including legal services provided in a specified period or for the purposes of a specified part of the proceedings.

(6) An order under this section may –

(a) provide for the payment of all or part of the amount by instalments of specified amounts, and
(b) require the instalments to be secured to the satisfaction of the court.

(7) An order under this section may direct that payment of all or part of the amount is to be deferred.

(8) The court may at any time in the proceedings vary an order made under this section if it considers that there has been a material change of circumstances since the order was made.

(9) For the purposes of the assessment of costs in the proceedings, the applicant's costs are to be treated as reduced by any amount paid to the applicant pursuant to an order under this section for the purposes of those proceedings.

(10) In this section 'legal services', in relation to proceedings, means the following types of services –

(a) providing advice as to how the law applies in the particular circumstances,
(b) providing advice and assistance in relation to the proceedings,
(c) providing other advice and assistance in relation to the settlement or other resolution of the dispute that is the subject of the proceedings, and
(d) providing advice and assistance in relation to the enforcement of decisions in the proceedings or as part of the settlement or resolution of the dispute,

and they include, in particular, advice and assistance in the form of representation and any form of dispute resolution, including mediation.

(11) In subsections (5) and (6) 'specified' means specified in the order concerned.

Amendments—Inserted by Legal Aid, Sentencing and Punishment of Offenders Act 2012, s 49.

22ZB Matters to which court is to have regard in deciding how to exercise power under section 22ZA

(1) When considering whether to make or vary an order under section 22ZA, the court must have regard to –

(a) the income, earning capacity, property and other financial resources which each of the applicant and the paying party has or is likely to have in the foreseeable future,
(b) the financial needs, obligations and responsibilities which each of the applicant and the paying party has or is likely to have in the foreseeable future,
(c) the subject matter of the proceedings, including the matters in issue in them,
(d) whether the paying party is legally represented in the proceedings,
(e) any steps taken by the applicant to avoid all or part of the proceedings, whether by proposing or considering mediation or otherwise,
(f) the applicant's conduct in relation to the proceedings,
(g) any amount owed by the applicant to the paying party in respect of costs in the proceedings or other proceedings to which both the applicant and the paying party are or were party, and
(h) the effect of the order or variation on the paying party.

(2) In subsection (1)(a) 'earning capacity', in relation to the applicant or the paying party, includes any increase in earning capacity which, in the opinion of the court, it would be reasonable to expect the applicant or the paying party to take steps to acquire.

(3) For the purposes of subsection (1)(h), the court must have regard, in particular, to whether the making or variation of the order is likely to –

(a) cause undue hardship to the paying party, or
(b) prevent the paying party from obtaining legal services for the purposes of the proceedings.

(4) The Lord Chancellor may by order amend this section by adding to, omitting or varying the matters mentioned in subsections (1) to (3).

(5) An order under subsection (4) must be made by statutory instrument.

(6) A statutory instrument containing an order under subsection (4) may not be made unless a draft of the instrument has been laid before, and approved by a resolution of, each House of Parliament.

(7) In this section 'legal services' has the same meaning as in section 22ZA.

Amendments—Inserted by Legal Aid, Sentencing and Punishment of Offenders Act 2012, s 50.

23 Financial provision orders in connection with divorce proceedings etc

(1) On granting a decree of divorce, a decree of nullity of marriage or a decree of judicial separation or at any time thereafter (whether, in the case of a decree of divorce or of nullity of marriage, before or after the decree is made absolute), the court may make any one or more of the following orders, that is to say –

(a) an order that either party to the marriage shall make to the other such periodical payments, for such term, as may be specified in the order;
(b) an order that either party to the marriage shall secure to the other to the satisfaction of the court such periodical payments, for such term, as may be so specified;
(c) an order that either party to the marriage shall pay to the other such lump sum or sums as may be so specified;
(d) an order that a party to the marriage shall make to such person as may be specified in the order for the benefit of a child of the family, or to such a child, such periodical payments, for such term, as may be so specified;
(e) an order that a party to the marriage shall secure to such person as may be so specified for the benefit of such a child, or to such a child, to the satisfaction of the court, such periodical payments, for such term, as may be so specified;
(f) an order that a party to the marriage shall pay to such person as may be so specified for the benefit of such a child, or to such a child, such lump sum as may be so specified;

subject, however, in the case of an order under paragraph (d), (e) or (f) above, to the restrictions imposed by section 29(1) and (3) below on the making of financial provision orders in favour of children who have attained the age of 18.

(2) The court may also, subject to those restrictions, make any one or more of the orders mentioned in subsection (1)(d), (e) and (f) above –

(a) in any proceedings for divorce, nullity of marriage or judicial separation, before granting a decree; and
(b) where any such proceedings are dismissed after the beginning of the trial, either forthwith or within a reasonable period after the dismissal.

(3) Without prejudice to the generality of subsection (1)(c) or (f) above –

(a) an order under this section that a party to a marriage shall pay a lump sum to the other party may be made for the purpose of enabling that other party to meet any liabilities or expenses reasonably incurred by him or her in maintaining himself or herself or any child of the family before making an application for an order under this section in his or her favour;

(b) an order under this section for the payment of a lump sum to or for the benefit of a child of the family may be made for the purpose of enabling any liabilities or expenses reasonably incurred by or for the benefit of that child before the making of an application for an order under this section in his favour to be met; and

(c) an order under this section for the payment of a lump sum may provide for the payment of that sum by instalments of such amount as may be specified in the order and may require the payment of the instalments to be secured to the satisfaction of the court.

(4) The power of the court under subsection (1) or (2)(a) above to make an order in favour of a child of the family shall be exercisable from time to time; and where the court makes an order in favour of a child under subsection (2)(b) above, it may from time to time, subject to the restrictions mentioned in subsection (1) above, make a further order in his favour of any of the kinds mentioned in subsection (1)(d), (e) or (f) above.

(5) Without prejudice to the power to give a direction under section 30 below for the settlement of an instrument by conveyancing counsel, where an order is made under subsection (1)(a), (b) or (c) above on or after granting a decree of divorce or nullity of marriage, neither the order nor any settlement made in pursuance of the order shall take effect unless the decree has been made absolute.

(6) Where the court –

(a) makes an order under this section for the payment of a lump sum; and

(b) directs –

(i) that payment of that sum or any part of it shall be deferred; or

(ii) that the sum or any part of it shall be paid by instalments,

the court may order that the amount deferred or the instalments shall carry interest at such rate as may be specified by the order from such date, not earlier than the date of the order, as may be so specified, until the date when payment of it is due.

Amendments—Access to Justice Act 1982, s 16.

24 Property adjustment orders in connection with divorce proceedings etc

(1) On granting a decree of divorce, a decree of nullity of marriage or a decree of judicial separation or at any time thereafter (whether, in the case of a decree of divorce or of nullity of marriage, before or after the decree is made absolute), the court may make any one or more of the following orders, that is to say –

(a) an order that a party to the marriage shall transfer to the other party, to any child of the family or to such person as may be specified in the order for the benefit of such a child such property as may be so specified, being property to which the first-mentioned party is entitled, either in possession or reversion;

(b) an order that a settlement of such property as may be so specified, being property to which a party to the marriage is so entitled, be made to the satisfaction of the court for the benefit of the other party to the marriage and of the children of the family or either or any of them;

(c) an order varying for the benefit of the parties to the marriage and of the children of the family or either or any of them any ante-nuptial or post-nuptial settlement (including such a settlement made by will or codicil) made on the parties to the marriage, other than one in the form of a pension arrangement (within the meaning of section 25D below);

(d) an order extinguishing or reducing the interest of either of the parties to the marriage under any such settlement, other than one in the form of a pension arrangement (within the meaning of section 25D below);

subject, however, in the case of an order under paragraph (a) above, to the restrictions imposed by section 29(1) and (3) below on the making of orders for a transfer of property in favour of children who have attained the age of 18.

(2) The court may make an order under subsection (1)(c) above notwithstanding that there are no children of the family.

(3) Without prejudice to the power to give a direction under section 30 below for the settlement of an instrument by conveyancing counsel, where an order is made under this section on or after granting a decree of divorce or nullity of marriage, neither the order nor any settlement made in pursuance of the order shall take effect unless the decree has been made absolute.

Amendments—Welfare Reform and Pensions Act 1999, s 19, Sch 3, para 3.

24A Orders for sale of property

(1) Where the court makes an order under section 22ZA or makes under section 23 or 24 of this Act a secured periodical payments order, an order for the payment of a lump sum or a property adjustment order, then, on making that order or at any time thereafter, the court may make a further order for the sale of such property as may be specified in the order, being property in which or in the proceeds of sale of which either or both of the parties to the marriage has or have a beneficial interest, either in possession or reversion.

(2) Any order made under subsection (1) above may contain such consequential or supplementary provisions as the court thinks fit and, without prejudice to the generality of the foregoing provision, may include –

(a) provision requiring the making of a payment out of the proceeds of sale of the property to which the order relates, and
(b) provision requiring any such property to be offered for sale to a person, or class of persons, specified in the order.

(3) Where an order is made under subsection (1) above on or after the grant of a decree of divorce or nullity of marriage, the order shall not take effect unless the decree has been made absolute.

(4) Where an order is made under subsection (1) above, the court may direct that the order, or such provision thereof as the court may specify, shall not take effect until the occurrence of an event specified by the court or the expiration of a period so specified.

(5) Where an order under subsection (1) above contains a provision requiring the proceeds of sale of the property to which the order relates to be used to secure periodical payments to a party to the marriage, the order shall cease to have effect on the death or re-marriage of, or formation of a civil partnership by, that person.

(6) Where a party to a marriage has a beneficial interest in any property, or in the proceeds of sale thereof, and some other person who is not a party to the marriage also has a beneficial interest in that property or in the proceeds of sale thereof, then, before deciding whether to make an order under this section in relation to that property, it shall be the duty of the court to give that other person an opportunity to make representations with respect to the order; and any representations made by that other person shall be included among the circumstances to which the court is required to have regard under section 25(1) below.

Amendments—Inserted by Matrimonial Homes and Property Act 1981, s 7. Amended by Matrimonial and Family Proceedings Act 1984, s 46(1), Sch 1, para 11; Civil Partnership Act 2004, s 261(1), Sch 27, para 42; Legal Aid, Sentencing and Punishment of Offenders Act 2012, s 51

24B Pension sharing orders in connection with divorce proceedings etc

(1) On granting a decree of divorce or a decree of nullity of marriage or at any time thereafter (whether before or after the decree is made absolute), the court may, on an application made under this section, make one or more pension sharing orders in relation to the marriage.

(2) A pension sharing order under this section is not to take effect unless the decree on or after which it is made has been made absolute.

(3) A pension sharing order under this section may not be made in relation to a pension arrangement which –

(a) is the subject of a pension sharing order in relation to the marriage, or
(b) has been the subject of pension sharing between the parties to the marriage.

(4) A pension sharing order under this section may not be made in relation to shareable state scheme rights if –

(a) such rights are the subject of a pension sharing order in relation to the marriage, or
(b) such rights have been the subject of pension sharing between the parties to the marriage.

(5) A pension sharing order under this section may not be made in relation to the rights of a person under a pension arrangement if there is in force a requirement imposed by virtue of section 25B or 25C below which relates to benefits or future benefits to which he is entitled under the pension arrangement.

Amendments—Welfare Reform and Pensions Act 1999, s 19, Sch 3, para 4.

24C Pension sharing orders: duty to stay

(1) No pension sharing order may be made so as to take effect before the end of such period after the making of the order as may be prescribed by regulations made by the Lord Chancellor.

(2) The power to make regulations under this section shall be exercisable by statutory instrument which shall be subject to annulment in pursuance of a resolution of either House of Parliament.

Amendments—Welfare Reform and Pensions Act 1999, s 19, Sch 3, para 3.

24D Pension sharing orders: apportionment of charges

If a pension sharing order relates to rights under a pension arrangement, the court may include in the order provision about the apportionment between the parties of any charge under section 41 of the Welfare Reform and Pensions Act 1999 (charges in respect of pension sharing costs), or under corresponding Northern Ireland legislation.

Amendments—Welfare Reform and Pensions Act 1999, s 19, Sch 3, para 3.

24E Pension compensation sharing orders in connection with divorce proceedings

(1) On granting a decree of divorce or a decree of nullity of marriage or at any time thereafter (whether before or after the decree is made absolute), the court may, on an application made under this section, make a pension compensation sharing order in relation to the marriage.

(2) A pension compensation sharing order under this section is not to take effect unless the decree on or after which it is made has been made absolute.

(3) A pension compensation sharing order under this section may not be made in relation to rights to PPF compensation that –

- (a) are the subject of pension attachment,
- (b) derive from rights under a pension scheme that were the subject of pension sharing between the parties to the marriage,
- (c) are the subject of pension compensation attachment, or
- (d) are or have been the subject of pension compensation sharing between the parties to the marriage.

(4) For the purposes of subsection (3)(a), rights to PPF compensation 'are the subject of pension attachment' if any of the following three conditions is met.

(5) The first condition is that –

- (a) the rights derive from rights under a pension scheme in relation to which an order was made under section 23 imposing a requirement by virtue of section 25B(4), and
- (b) that order, as modified under section 25E(3), remains in force.

(6) The second condition is that –

- (a) the rights derive from rights under a pension scheme in relation to which an order was made under section 23 imposing a requirement by virtue of section 25B(7), and
- (b) that order –
  - (i) has been complied with, or
  - (ii) has not been complied with and, as modified under section 25E(5), remains in force.

(7) The third condition is that –

- (a) the rights derive from rights under a pension scheme in relation to which an order was made under section 23 imposing a requirement by virtue of section 25C, and
- (b) that order remains in force.

(8) For the purposes of subsection (3)(b), rights under a pension scheme 'were the subject of pension sharing between the parties to the marriage' if the rights were at any time the subject of a pension sharing order in relation to the marriage or a previous marriage between the same parties.

(9) For the purposes of subsection (3)(c), rights to PPF compensation 'are the subject of pension compensation attachment' if there is in force a requirement imposed by virtue of section 25F relating to them.

(10) For the purposes of subsection (3)(d), rights to PPF compensation 'are or have been the subject of pension compensation sharing between the parties to the marriage' if they are or have ever been the subject of a pension compensation sharing order in relation to the marriage or a previous marriage between the same parties.

Amendments—Inserted by Pensions Act 2008, Sch 6, Pt 1.

24F Pension compensation sharing orders: duty to stay

(1) No pension compensation sharing order may be made so as to take effect before the end of such period after the making of the order as may be prescribed by regulations made by the Lord Chancellor.

(2) The power to make regulations under this section shall be exercisable by statutory instrument which shall be subject to annulment in pursuance of a resolution of either House of Parliament.

Amendments—Inserted by Pensions Act 2008, Sch 6, Pt 1.

24G Pension compensation sharing orders: apportionment of charges

The court may include in a pension compensation sharing order provision about the apportionment between the parties of any charge under section 117 of the Pensions Act 2008 (charges in respect of pension compensation sharing costs), or under corresponding Northern Ireland legislation.

Amendments—Inserted by Pensions Act 2008, Sch 6, Pt 1.

25 Matters to which court is to have regard in deciding how to exercise its powers under ss 23, 24, 24A, 24B and 24E

(1) It shall be the duty of the court in deciding whether to exercise its powers under section 23, 24, 24A, 24B and 24E above and, if so, in what manner, to have regard to all the circumstances of the case, first consideration being given to the welfare while a minor of any child of the family who has not attained the age of 18.

(2) As regards the exercise of the powers of the court under section 23(1)(a), (b) or (c), 24, 24A, 24B and 24E above in relation to a party to the marriage, the court shall in particular have regard to the following matters –

- (a) the income, earning capacity, property and other financial resources which each of the parties to the marriage has or is likely to have in the foreseeable future, including in the case of earning capacity any increase in that capacity which it would in the opinion of the court be reasonable to expect a party to the marriage to take steps to acquire;
- (b) the financial needs, obligations and responsibilities which each of the parties to the marriage has or is likely to have in the foreseeable future;
- (c) the standard of living enjoyed by the family before the breakdown of the marriage;
- (d) the age of each party to the marriage and the duration of the marriage;
- (e) any physical or mental disability of either of the parties to the marriage;
- (f) the contributions which each of the parties has made or is likely in the foreseeable future to make to the welfare of the family, including any contribution by looking after the home or caring for the family;
- (g) the conduct of each of the parties, if that conduct is such that it would in the opinion of the court be inequitable to disregard it;
- (h) in the case of proceedings for divorce or nullity of marriage, the value to each of the parties to the marriage of any benefit which, by reason of the dissolution or annulment of the marriage, that party will lose the chance of acquiring.

(3) As regards the exercise of the powers of the court under section 23(1)(d), (e) or (f), (2) or (4), 24 or 24A above in relation to a child of the family, the court shall in particular have regard to the following matters –

- (a) the financial needs of the child;
- (b) the income, earning capacity (if any), property and other financial resources of the child;
- (c) any physical or mental disability of the child;
- (d) the manner in which he was being and in which the parties to the marriage expected him to be educated or trained;
- (e) the considerations mentioned in relation to the parties to the marriage in paragraphs (a), (b), (c) and (e) of subsection (2) above.

(4) As regards the exercise of the powers of the court under section 23(1)(d), (e) or (f), (2) or (4), 24 or 24A above against a party to a marriage in favour of a child of the family who is not the child of that party, the court shall also have regard –

(a) to whether that party assumed any responsibility for the child's maintenance, and, if so, to the extent to which, and the basis upon which, that party assumed such responsibility and to the length of time for which that party discharged such responsibility;
(b) to whether in assuming and discharging such responsibility that party did so knowing that the child was not his or her own;
(c) to the liability of any other person to maintain the child.

Amendments—Matrimonial and Family Proceedings Act 1984, s 3; Pensions Act 1995, s 166; Welfare Reform and Pensions Act 1999, s 19, Sch 3, para 5; Pensions Act 2008, Sch 6, Pt 1.

25A Exercise of court's powers in favour of party to marriage on decree of divorce or nullity of marriage

(1) Where on or after the grant of a decree of divorce or nullity of marriage the court decides to exercise its powers under section 23(1)(a), (b) or (c), 24, 24A, 24B or 24E above in favour of a party to the marriage, it shall be the duty of the court to consider whether it would be appropriate so to exercise those powers that the financial obligations of each party towards the other will be terminated as soon after the grant of the decree as the court considers just and reasonable.

(2) Where the court decides in such a case to make a periodical payments or secured periodical payments order in favour of a party to the marriage, the court shall in particular consider whether it would be appropriate to require those payments to be made or secured only for such term as would in the opinion of the court be sufficient to enable the party in whose favour the order is made to adjust without undue hardship to the termination of his or her financial dependence on the other party.

(3) Where on or after the grant of a decree of divorce or nullity of marriage an application is made by a party to the marriage for a periodical payments or secured periodical payments order in his or her favour, then, if the court considers that no continuing obligation should be imposed on either party to make or secure periodical payments in favour of the other, the court may dismiss the application with a direction that the applicant shall not be entitled to make any future application in relation to that marriage for an order under section 23(1)(a) or (b) above.

Amendments—Inserted by Matrimonial and Family Proceedings Act 1984, s 3. Amended by Welfare Reform and Pensions Act 1999, s 19, Sch 3, para 6; Pensions Act 2008, Sch 6, Pt 1

25B Pensions

(1) The matters to which the court is to have regard under section 25(2) above include –

(a) in the case of paragraph (a), any benefits under a pension arrangement which a party to the marriage has or is likely to have, and
(b) in the case of paragraph (h), any benefits under a pension arrangement which, by reason of the dissolution or annulment of the marriage, a party to the marriage will lose the chance of acquiring,

and, accordingly, in relation to benefits under a pension arrangement, section 25(2)(a) above shall have effect as if 'in the foreseeable future' were omitted.

(2) (*repealed*)

(3) The following provisions apply where, having regard to any benefits under a pension arrangement, the court determines to make an order under section 23 above.

(4) To the extent to which the order is made having regard to any benefits under a pension arrangement, the order may require the person responsible for the pension arrangement in question, if at any time any payment in respect of any benefits under the arrangement becomes due to the party with pension rights, to make a payment for the benefit of the other party.

(5) The order must express the amount of any payment required to be made by virtue of subsection (4) above as a percentage of the payment which becomes due to the party with pension rights.

(6) Any such payment by the person responsible for the arrangement –

- (a) shall discharge so much of his liability to the party with pension rights as corresponds to the amount of the payment, and
- (b) shall be treated for all purposes as a payment made by the party with pension rights in or towards the discharge of his liability under the order.

(7) Where the party with pension rights has a right of commutation under the arrangement, the order may require him to exercise it to any extent; and this section applies to any payment due in consequence of commutation in pursuance of the order as it applies to other payments in respect of benefits under the arrangement.

(7A) The power conferred by subsection (7) above may not be exercised for the purpose of commuting a benefit payable to the party with pension rights to a benefit payable to the other party.

(7B) The power conferred by subsection (4) or (7) above may not be exercised in relation to a pension arrangement which –

- (a) is the subject of a pension sharing order in relation to the marriage, or
- (b) has been the subject of pension sharing between the parties to the marriage.

(7C) In subsection (1) above, references to benefits under a pension arrangement include any benefits by way of pension, whether under a pension arrangement or not.

Amendments—Inserted by Pensions Act 1995, s 166. Amended by Welfare Reform and Pensions Act 1999, ss 21, 88, Sch 4, para 1, Sch 13, Pt II.

25C Pensions: lump sums

(1) The power of the court under section 23 above to order a party to a marriage to pay a lump sum to the other party includes, where the benefits which the party with pension rights has or is likely to have under a pension arrangement include any lump sum payable in respect of his death, power to make any of the following provision by the order.

(2) The court may –

- (a) if the person responsible for the pension arrangement in question has power to determine the person to whom the sum, or any part of it, is to be paid, require him to pay the whole or part of that sum, when it becomes due, to the other party,
- (b) if the party with pension rights has power to nominate the person to whom the sum, or any part of it, is to be paid, require the party with pension rights to nominate the other party in respect of the whole or part of that sum,
- (c) in any other case, require the person responsible for the pension arrangement in question to pay the whole or part of that sum, when it becomes due, for the benefit of the other party instead of to the person to whom, apart from the order, it would be paid.

Key Legislation and Guidance

(3) Any payment by the person responsible for the pension arrangement under an order made under section 23 above by virtue of this section shall discharge so much of his liability in respect of the party with pension rights as corresponds to the amount of the payment.

(4) The powers conferred by this section may not be exercised in relation to a pension arrangement which –

(a) is the subject of a pension sharing order in relation to the marriage, or
(b) has been the subject of pension sharing between the parties to the marriage.

Amendments—Inserted by Pensions Act 1995, s 166. Amended by Welfare Reform and Pensions Act 1999, s 21, Sch 4, para 2.

25D Pensions: supplementary

(1) Where –

(a) an order made under section 23 above by virtue of section 25B or 25C above imposes any requirement on the person responsible for a pension arrangement ('the first arrangement') and the party with pension rights acquires rights under another pension arrangement ('the new arrangement') which are derived (directly or indirectly) from the whole of his rights under the first arrangement, and
(b) the person responsible for the new arrangement has been given notice in accordance with regulations made by the Lord Chancellor,

the order shall have effect as if it had been made instead in respect of the person responsible for the new arrangement.

(2) The Lord Chancellor may by regulations –

(a) in relation to any provision of sections 25B or 25C above which authorises the court making an order under section 23 above to require the person responsible for a pension arrangement to make a payment for the benefit of the other party, make provision as to the person to whom, and the terms on which, the payment is to be made,
(ab) make, in relation to payment under a mistaken belief as to the continuation in force of a provision included by virtue of section 25B or 25C above in an order under section 23 above, provision about the rights or liabilities of the payer, the payee or the person to whom the payment was due,
(b) require notices to be given in respect of changes of circumstances relevant to such orders which include provision made by virtue of sections 25B and 25C above,
(ba) make provision for the person responsible for a pension arrangement to be discharged in prescribed circumstances from a requirement imposed by virtue of section 25B or 25C above,
(c), (d) (*repealed*)
(e) make provision about calculation and verification in relation to the valuation of –

(i) benefits under a pension arrangement, or
(ii) shareable state scheme rights,

for the purposes of the court's functions in connection with the exercise of any of its powers under this Part of this Act.

(2A) Regulations under subsection (2)(e) above may include –

(a) provision for calculation or verification in accordance with guidance from time to time prepared by a prescribed person, and
(b) provision by reference to regulations under section 30 or 49(4) of the Welfare Reform and Pensions Act 1999.

(2B) Regulations under subsection (2) above may make different provision for different cases.

(2C) Power to make regulations under this section shall be exercisable by statutory instrument which shall be subject to annulment in pursuance of a resolution of either House of Parliament.

(3) In this section and sections 25B and 25C above –

'occupational pension scheme' has the same meaning as in the Pension Schemes Act 1993;
'the party with pension rights' means the party to the marriage who has or is likely to have benefits under a pension arrangement and 'the other party' means the other party to the marriage;
'pension arrangement' means –

(a) an occupational pension scheme,
(b) a personal pension scheme,
(c) a retirement annuity contract,
(d) an annuity or insurance policy purchased, or transferred, for the purpose of giving effect to rights under an occupational pension scheme or a personal pension scheme, and
(e) an annuity purchased, or entered into, for the purpose of discharging liability in respect of a pension credit under section 29(1)(b) of the Welfare Reform and Pensions Act 1999 or under corresponding Northern Ireland legislation;

'personal pension scheme' has the same meaning as in the Pension Schemes Act 1993;
'prescribed' means prescribed by regulations;
'retirement annuity contract' means a contract or scheme approved under Chapter III of Part XIV of the Income and Corporation Taxes Act 1988;
'shareable state scheme rights' has the same meaning as in section 21A(1) above; and
'trustees or managers', in relation to an occupational pension scheme or a personal pension scheme, means –

(a) in the case of a scheme established under a trust, the trustees of the scheme, and
(b) in any other case, the managers of the scheme.

(4) In this section and sections 25B and 25C above, references to the person responsible for a pension arrangement are –

(a) in the case of an occupational pension scheme or a personal pension scheme, to the trustees or managers of the scheme,
(b) in the case of a retirement annuity contract or an annuity falling within paragraph (d) or (e) of the definition of 'pension arrangement' above, the provider of the annuity, and
(c) in the case of an insurance policy falling within paragraph (d) of the definition of that expression, the insurer.

Amendments—Inserted by Pensions Act 1995, s 166. Amended by Welfare Reform and Pensions Act 1999, ss 21, 88, Sch 4, para 3, Sch 13, Pt II.

CHILDREN ACT 1989

SECTIONS 1, 2, 4, 8, 12

PART I

INTRODUCTORY

1 Welfare of the child

(1) When a court determines any question with respect to –

- (a) the upbringing of a child; or
- (b) the administration of a child's property or the application of any income arising from it,

the child's welfare shall be the court's paramount consideration.

(2) In any proceedings in which any question with respect to the upbringing of a child arises, the court shall have regard to the general principle that any delay in determining the question is likely to prejudice the welfare of the child.

(2A) A court, in the circumstances mentioned in subsection (4)(a) or (7), is as respects each parent within subsection (6)(a) to presume, unless the contrary is shown, that involvement of that parent in the life of the child concerned will further the child's welfare.

(2B) In subsection (2A) 'involvement' means involvement of some kind, either direct or indirect, but not any particular division of a child's time.

(3) In the circumstances mentioned in subsection (4), a court shall have regard in particular to –

- (a) the ascertainable wishes and feelings of the child concerned (considered in the light of his age and understanding);
- (b) his physical, emotional and educational needs;
- (c) the likely effect on him of any change in his circumstances;
- (d) his age, sex, background and any characteristics of his which the court considers relevant;
- (e) any harm which he has suffered or is at risk of suffering;
- (f) how capable each of his parents, and any other person in relation to whom the court considers the question to be relevant, is of meeting his needs;
- (g) the range of powers available to the court under this Act in the proceedings in question.

(4) The circumstances are that –

- (a) the court is considering whether to make, vary or discharge a section 8 order, and the making, variation or discharge of the order is opposed by any party to the proceedings; or
- (b) the court is considering whether to make, vary or discharge a special guardianship order or an order under Part IV.

(5) Where a court is considering whether or not to make one or more orders under this Act with respect to a child, it shall not make the order or any of the orders unless it considers that doing so would be better for the child than making no order at all.

(6) In subsection (2A) 'parent' means parent of the child concerned; and, for the purposes of that subsection, a parent of the child concerned –

(a) is within this paragraph if that parent can be involved in the child's life in a way that does not put the child at risk of suffering harm; and
(b) is to be treated as being within paragraph (a) unless there is some evidence before the court in the particular proceedings to suggest that involvement of that parent in the child's life would put the child at risk of suffering harm whatever the form of the involvement.

(7) The circumstances referred to are that the court is considering whether to make an order under section 4(1)(c) or (2A) or 4ZA(1)(c) or (5) (parental responsibility of parent other than mother).

Amendments—Adoption and Children Act 2002, s 115; Children and Families Act 2014, s 11.

2 Parental responsibility for children

(1) Where a child's father and mother were married to each other at the time of his birth, they shall each have parental responsibility for the child.

(1A) Where a child –

(a) has a parent by virtue of section 42 of the Human Fertilisation and Embryology Act 2008; or
(b) has a parent by virtue of section 43 of that Act and is a person to whom section 1(3) of the Family Law Reform Act 1987 applies,

the child's mother and the other parent shall each have parental responsibility for the child.

(2) Where a child's father and mother were not married to each other at the time of his birth –

(a) the mother shall have parental responsibility for the child;
(b) the father shall have parental responsibility for the child if he has acquired it (and has not ceased to have it) in accordance with the provisions of this Act.

(2A) Where a child has a parent by virtue of section 43 of the Human Fertilisation and Embryology Act 2008 and is not a person to whom section 1(3) of the Family Law Reform Act 1987 applies –

(a) the mother shall have parental responsibility for the child;
(b) the other parent shall have parental responsibility for the child if she has acquired it (and has not ceased to have it) in accordance with the provisions of this Act.

(3) References in this Act to a child whose father and mother were, or (as the case may be) were not, married to each other at the time of his birth must be read with section 1 of the Family Law Reform Act 1987 (which extends their meaning).

(4) The rule of law that a father is the natural guardian of his legitimate child is abolished.

(5) More than one person may have parental responsibility for the same child at the same time.

(6) A person who has parental responsibility for a child at any time shall not cease to have that responsibility solely because some other person subsequently acquires parental responsibility for the child.

(7) Where more than one person has parental responsibility for a child, each of them may act alone and without the other (or others) in meeting that responsibility; but nothing in this Part shall be taken to affect the operation of any enactment which requires the consent of more than one person in a matter affecting the child.

(8) The fact that a person has parental responsibility for a child shall not entitle him to act in any way which would be incompatible with any order made with respect to the child under this Act.

(9) A person who has parental responsibility for a child may not surrender or transfer any part of that responsibility to another but may arrange for some or all of it to be met by one or more persons acting on his behalf.

(10) The person with whom any such arrangement is made may himself be a person who already has parental responsibility for the child concerned.

(11) The making of any such arrangement shall not affect any liability of the person making it which may arise from any failure to meet any part of his parental responsibility for the child concerned.

Amendments—Adoption and Children Act 2002, s 111; Human Fertilisation and Embryology Act 2008, s 56, Sch 6, Pt 1, para 26(1)–(3).

4 Acquisition of parental responsibility by father

(1) Where a child's father and mother were not married to each other at the time of his birth, the father shall acquire parental responsibility for the child if –

(a) he becomes registered as the child's father under any of the enactments specified in subsection (1A);
(b) he and the child's mother make an agreement (a 'parental responsibility agreement') providing for him to have parental responsibility for the child; or
(c) the court, on his application, orders that he shall have parental responsibility for the child.

(1A) The enactments referred to in subsection (1)(a) are –

(a) paragraphs (a), (b) and (c) of section 10(1) and of section 10A(1) of the Births and Deaths Registration Act 1953;
(b) paragraphs (a), (b)(i) and (c) of section 18(1), and sections 18(2)(b) and 20(1)(a) of the Registration of Births, Deaths and Marriages (Scotland) Act 1965; and
(c) sub-paragraphs (a), (b) and (c) of Article 14(3) of the Births and Deaths Registration (Northern Ireland) Order 1976.

(1B) The Secretary of State may by order amend subsection (1A) so as to add further enactments to the list in that subsection.

(2) No parental responsibility agreement shall have effect for the purposes of this Act unless –

(a) it is made in the form prescribed by regulations made by the Lord Chancellor; and
(b) where regulations are made by the Lord Chancellor prescribing the manner in which such agreements must be recorded, it is recorded in the prescribed manner.

(2A) A person who has acquired parental responsibility under subsection (1) shall cease to have that responsibility only if the court so orders.

(3) The court may make an order under subsection (2A) on the application –

(a) of any person who has parental responsibility for the child; or

(b) with leave of the court, of the child himself,

subject, in the case of parental responsibility acquired under subsection (1)(c), to section 12(4).

(4) The court may only grant leave under subsection (3)(b) if it is satisfied that the child has sufficient understanding to make the proposed application.

Amendments—Adoption and Children Act 2002, s 111; SI 2003/3191.

PART II

ORDERS WITH RESPECT TO CHILDREN IN FAMILY PROCEEDINGS

General

8 Child arrangements orders and other orders with respect to children

(1) In this Act –

'child arrangements order' means an order regulating arrangements relating to any of the following –

(a) with whom a child is to live, spend time or otherwise have contact, and
(b) when a child is to live, spend time or otherwise have contact with any person;

...

'a prohibited steps order' means an order that no step which could be taken by a parent in meeting his parental responsibility for a child, and which is of a kind specified in the order, shall be taken by any person without the consent of the court;

... and

'a specific issue order' means an order giving directions for the purpose of determining a specific question which has arisen, or which may arise, in connection with any aspect of parental responsibility for a child.

(2) In this Act 'a section 8 order' means any of the orders mentioned in subsection (1) and any order varying or discharging such an order.

(3) For the purposes of this Act 'family proceedings' means any proceedings –

(a) under the inherent jurisdiction of the High Court in relation to children; and
(b) under the enactments mentioned in subsection (4),

but does not include proceedings on an application for leave under section 100(3).

(4) The enactments are –

(a) Parts I, II and IV of this Act;
(b) the Matrimonial Causes Act 1973;
(ba) Schedule 5 to the Civil Partnership Act 2004;
(c) (*repealed*)
(d) the Adoption Act and Children Act 2002;
(e) the Domestic Proceedings and Magistrates' Courts Act 1978;
(ea) Schedule 6 to the Civil Partnership Act 2004;
(f) (*repealed*)
(g) Part III of the Matrimonial and Family Proceedings Act 1984;
(h) the Family Law Act 1996.
(i) sections 11 and 12 of the Crime and Disorder Act 1998.

Amendments—Family Law Act 1996, s 66(1), (3), Sch 8, para 60(1), Sch 10; Crime and Disorder Act 1998, s 119, Sch 8, para 68; Adoption and Children 2002, Sch 3, para 55; Civil Partnership Act 2004, s 261(1), Sch 27, para 129(1)–(3); Children and Families 2014, ss 9, 12, Sch 2.

12 Child arrangements orders and parental responsibility

(1) Where –

(a) the court makes a child arrangements order with respect to a child,
(b) the father of the child, or a woman who is a parent of the child by virtue of section 43 of the Human Fertilisation and Embryology Act 2008, is named in the order as a person with whom the child is to live, and
(c) the father, or the woman, would not otherwise have parental responsibility for the child, the court must also make an order under section 4 giving the father, or under section 4ZA giving the woman, that responsibility.

(1A) Where –

(a) the court makes a child arrangements order with respect to a child,
(b) the father of the child, or a woman who is a parent of the child by virtue of section 43 of the Human Fertilisation and Embryology Act 2008, is named in the order as a person with whom the child is to spend time or otherwise have contact but is not named in the order as a person with whom the child is to live, and
(c) the father, or the woman, would not otherwise have parental responsibility for the child, the court must decide whether it would be appropriate, in view of the provision made in the order with respect to the father or the woman, for him or her to have parental responsibility for the child and, if it decides that it would be appropriate for the father or the woman to have that responsibility, must also make an order under section 4 giving him, or under section 4ZA giving her, that responsibility.

(2) Where the court makes a child arrangements order and a person who is not a parent or guardian of the child concerned is named in the order as a person with whom the child is to live, that person shall have parental responsibility for the child while the order remains in force so far as providing for the child to live with that person.

(2A) Where the court makes a child arrangements order and –

(a) a person who is not the parent or guardian of the child concerned is named in the order as a person with whom the child is to spend time or otherwise have contact, but
(b) the person is not named in the order as a person with whom the child is to live, the court may provide in the order for the person to have parental responsibility for the child while paragraphs (a) and (b) continue to be met in the person's case.

(3) Where a person has parental responsibility for a child as a result of subsection (2) or (2A), he shall not have the right –

(a) (*repealed*)
(b) to agree, or refuse to agree, to the making of an adoption order, or an order under section 84 of the Adoption and Children Act 2002, with respect to the child; or
(c) to appoint a guardian for the child.

(4) Where subsection (1) requires the court to make an order under section 4 or 4ZA in respect of a parent of a child, the court shall not bring that order to an end at any time while the child arrangements order concerned remains in force so far as providing for the child to live with that parent.

(5), (6) (*repealed*)

Amendments—Adoption and Children 2002, ss 114, 139, Sch 3, paras 54, 57; Children and Young Persons 2008, s 37(2); Human Fertilisation and Embryology Act 2008, s 56, Sch 6, Pt 1, para 28(1),(2); Children and Families 2014, s 12, Sch 2.

FAMILY PROCEDURE RULES 2010, SI 2010/2955, PART 3

NON-COURT DISPUTE RESOLUTION

Chapter 1

Interpretation

3.1 In this Part –

'allocation' means allocation of proceedings other than appeal proceedings to a level of judge;
'authorised family mediator' means a person identified by the Family Mediation Council as qualified to conduct a MIAM;
'domestic violence' means any incident, or pattern of incidents, of controlling, coercive or threatening behaviour, violence or abuse (whether psychological, physical, sexual, financial or emotional) between the prospective applicant and another prospective party;
'family mediation information and assessment meeting' has the meaning given to it in section 10(3) of the 2014 Act.
'harm' has the meaning given to it in section 31 of the Children Act 1989;
'mediator's exemption' has the meaning given to it in Rule 3.8(2);
'MIAM' means a family mediation information and assessment meeting;
'MIAM exemption' has the meaning given to it in Rule 3.8(1);
'MIAM requirement' is the requirement in section 10(1) of the 2014 Act for a person to attend a MIAM before making a relevant family application;
'private law proceedings' has the meaning given to it in Rule 12.2;
'prospective applicant' is the person who is considering making a relevant family application;
'prospective party' is a person who would be likely to be a party to the proceedings in the relevant family application;
'prospective respondent' is a person who would be a likely respondent to the proceedings in the relevant family application; and
'relevant family application' has the meaning given to it in section 10(3) of the 2014 Act.

Amendments—Substituted by SI 2014/843. Amended by SI 2015/1868.

Chapter 2

The Court's Duty and Powers Generally

3.2 Scope of this Chapter

This Chapter contains the court's duty and powers to encourage and facilitate the use of non-court dispute resolution.

Amendments—Substituted by SI 2014/843.

3.3 The court's duty to consider non-court dispute resolution

(1) The court must consider, at every stage in proceedings, whether non-court dispute resolution is appropriate.

(2) In considering whether non-court dispute resolution is appropriate in proceedings which were commenced by a relevant family application, the court must take into account –

(a) whether a MIAM took place;
(b) whether a valid MIAM exemption was claimed or mediator's exemption was confirmed; and
(c) whether the parties attempted mediation or another form of non-court dispute resolution and the outcome of that process.

Amendments—Substituted by SI 2014/843.

3.4 When the court will adjourn proceedings or a hearing in proceedings

(1) If the court considers that non-court dispute resolution is appropriate, it may direct that the proceedings, or a hearing in the proceedings, be adjourned for such specified period as it considers appropriate –

(a) to enable the parties to obtain information and advice about, and consider using, non-court dispute resolution; and
(b) where the parties agree, to enable non-court dispute resolution to take place.

(2) The court may give directions under this rule on an application or of its own initiative.

(3) Where the court directs an adjournment under this rule, it will give directions about the timing and method by which the parties must tell the court if any of the issues in the proceedings have been resolved.

(4) If the parties do not tell the court if any of the issues have been resolved as directed under paragraph (3), the court will give such directions as to the management of the case as it considers appropriate.

(5) The court or court officer will –

(a) record the making of an order under this rule; and
(b) arrange for a copy of the order to be served as soon as practicable on the parties.

(6) Where the court proposes to exercise its powers of its own initiative, the procedure set out in rule 4.3(2) to (6) applies.

Amendments—Substituted by SI 2014/843. Amended by SI 2014/3296.

Chapter 3

Family Mediation Information and Assessment Meetings (MIAMs)

3.5 Scope of this Chapter

This Chapter contains Rules about the requirement in section 10(1) of the 2014 Act to attend a MIAM.

3.6 Applications to which the MIAM requirement applies

(1) The MIAM requirement applies to any application to initiate the proceedings specified in paragraph (2), unless a MIAM exemption or a mediator's exemption applies.

(2) The specified proceedings are –

(a) the private law proceedings relating to children specified in Practice Direction 3A; and
(b) the proceedings for a financial remedy specified in Practice Direction 3A.

3.7 Making an application

An application to initiate any of the proceedings specified in Rule 3.8 must contain, or be accompanied by, a form containing, either –

(a) a confirmation from an authorised family mediator that the prospective applicant has attended a MIAM;
(b) a claim by the prospective applicant that one of the MIAM exemptions applies; or

(A list of MIAM exemptions is set out in Rule 3.8(1) below.)

(c) a confirmation from an authorised family mediator that a mediator's exemption applies.

(A list of mediator's exemptions is set out in Rule 3.8(2) below.)

3.8 Circumstances in which the MIAM requirement does not apply (MIAM exemptions and mediator's exemptions)

The MIAM requirement does not apply if –

(1) a prospective applicant claims in the relevant form that any of the following circumstances (a 'MIAM exemption') applies –

Domestic violence

(a) there is evidence of domestic violence, as specified in Practice Direction 3A; or

Child protection concerns

(b)

(i) a child would be the subject of the application; and
(ii) that child or another child of the family who is living with that child is currently –
(aa) the subject of enquiries by a local authority under section 47 of the 1989 Act; or
(ab) the subject of a child protection plan put in place by a local authority; or

Urgency

(c) the application must be made urgently because -

(i) there is risk to the life, liberty or physical safety of the prospective applicant or his or her family or his or her home; or
(ii) any delay caused by attending a MIAM would cause –
(aa) a risk of harm to a child;
(ab) a risk of unlawful removal of a child from the United Kingdom, or a risk of unlawful retention of a child who is currently outside England and Wales;
(ac) a significant risk of a miscarriage of justice;
(ad) unreasonable hardship to the prospective applicant; or
(ae) irretrievable problems in dealing with the dispute (including the irretrievable loss of significant evidence); or

(iii) there is a significant risk that in the period necessary to schedule and attend a MIAM, proceedings relating to the dispute will be brought in another state in which a valid claim to jurisdiction may exist, such that a court in that other state would be seised of the dispute before a court in England and Wales; or

Previous MIAM attendance or MIAM exemption

(d)

(i) in the 4 months prior to making the application, the person attended a MIAM or participated in another form of non-court dispute resolution relating to the same or substantially the same dispute; or
(ii) at the time of making the application, the person is participating in another form of non-court dispute resolution relating to the same or substantially the same dispute; or

(e)

(i) in the 4 months prior to making the application, the person filed a relevant family application confirming that a MIAM exemption applied; and
(ii) that application related to the same or substantially the same dispute; or

(f)

(i) the application would be made in existing proceedings which are continuing; and
(ii) the prospective applicant attended a MIAM before initiating those proceedings; or

(g)

(i) the application would be made in existing proceedings which are continuing; and
(ii) a MIAM exemption applied to the application for those proceedings; or

Other

(h)

(i) there is evidence that the prospective applicant is bankrupt, as specified in Practice Direction 3A; and
(ii) the proceedings would be for a financial remedy; or

(i) the prospective applicant does not have sufficient contact details for any of the prospective respondents to enable a family mediator to contact any of the prospective respondents for the purpose of scheduling the MIAM; or
(j) the application would be made without notice; or

(Paragraph 5.1 of Practice Direction 18A sets out the circumstances in which applications may be made without notice.)

(k)

(i) the prospective applicant is or all of the prospective respondents are subject to a disability or other inability that would prevent attendance at a MIAM unless appropriate facilities can be offered by an authorised mediator;
(ii) the prospective applicant has contacted as many authorised family mediators as have an office within fifteen miles of his or home (or three of them if there are three or more), and all have stated that they are unable to provide such facilities; and
(iii) the names, postal addresses and telephone numbers or e-mail addresses for such authorised family mediators, and the dates of contact, can be provided to the court if requested; or

(l) the prospective applicant or all of the prospective respondents cannot attend a MIAM because he or she is, or they are, as the case may be –

(i) in prison or any other institution in which he or she is or they are required to be detained;
(ii) subject to conditions of bail that prevent contact with the other person; or
(iii) subject to a licence with a prohibited contact requirement in relation to the other person; or

(m) the prospective applicant or all of the prospective respondents are not habitually resident in England and Wales; or
(n) a child is one of the prospective parties by virtue of Rule 12.3(1); or
(o)

(i) the prospective applicant has contacted as many authorised family mediators as have an office within fifteen miles of his or her home (or three of them if there are three or more), and all of them have stated that they are not available to conduct a MIAM within fifteen business days of the date of contact; and
(ii) the names, postal addresses and telephone numbers or e-mail addresses for such authorised family mediators, and the dates of contact, can be provided to the court if requested; or

(p) there is no authorised family mediator with an office within fifteen miles of the prospective applicant's home; or

(2) an authorised family mediator confirms in the relevant form (a 'mediator's exemption') that he or she is satisfied that –

(a) mediation is not suitable as a means of resolving the dispute because none of the respondents is willing to attend a MIAM; or
(b) mediation is not suitable as a means of resolving the dispute because all of the respondents failed without good reason to attend a MIAM appointment; or
(c) mediation is otherwise not suitable as a means of resolving the dispute.

3.9 Conduct of MIAMs

(1) Only an authorised family mediator may conduct a MIAM.

(2) At the MIAM, the authorised family mediator must –

(a) provide information about the principles, process and different models of mediation, and information about other methods of non-court dispute resolution;
(b) assess the suitability of mediation as a means of resolving the dispute;
(c) assess whether there has been, or is a risk of, domestic violence; and
(d) assess whether there has been, or is a risk of, harm by a prospective party to a child that would be a subject of the application.

3.10 MIAM exemption not validly claimed

(1) If a MIAM exemption has been claimed, the court will, if appropriate when making a decision on allocation, and in any event at the first hearing, inquire into whether the exemption was validly claimed.

(2) If a court finds that the MIAM exemption was not validly claimed, the court will -

(a) direct the applicant, or direct the parties to attend a MIAM; and
(b) if necessary, adjourn the proceedings to enable a MIAM to take place;

unless the court considers that in all the circumstances of the case, the MIAM requirement should not apply to the application in question.

(3) In making a decision under Rule 3.10(2), the court will have particular regard to –

(a) any applicable time limits;
(b) the reason or reasons why the MIAM exemption was not validly claimed;
(c) the applicability of any other MIAM exemptions; and

(d) the number and nature of issues that remain to be resolved in the proceedings.

****

PRACTICE DIRECTION 3A - FAMILY MEDIATION INFORMATION AND ASSESSMENT MEETINGS (MIAMS)

This Practice Direction supplements FPR Part 3

Summary

1 The purpose of this Practice Direction is to supplement the MIAM Rules in the Family Procedure Rules and to set out good practice to be followed by prospective respondents who are expected to also attend a MIAM.

2 Under section 10(1) of the Children and Families Act 2014, it is now a requirement for a person to attend a MIAM before making certain kinds of applications to obtain a court order. (A list of these applications is set out in Rule 3.6 and in paragraphs 12 and 13 below.) The person who would be the respondent to the application is expected to attend the MIAM. The court has a general power to adjourn proceedings in order for non-court dispute resolution to be attempted, including attendance at a MIAM to consider family mediation and other options.

3 A MIAM is a short meeting that provides information about mediation as a way of resolving disputes. A MIAM is conducted by a trained mediator who will assess whether mediation is appropriate in the circumstances. A MIAM should be held within 15 business days of contacting the mediator.

4 There are exemptions to the MIAM requirement. These are set out in the MIAM Rules (see Chapter 3 to Part 3 of the Family Procedure Rules), and are explained in more detail in this Practice Direction.

5 The effect of the MIAM requirement and accompanying Rules is that a person who wishes to make certain kinds of applications to the court must first attend a MIAM unless a 'MIAM exemption' or a 'mediator's exemption' applies. These exemptions are set out in Rule 3.8.

6 When making certain kinds of applications (see paragraphs 12 and 13 below), an applicant must therefore provide on the application form, or on a separate form, one of the following: (i) confirmation from a mediator that she or he has attended a MIAM; (ii) confirmation from a mediator that a 'mediator's exemption' applies; or (iii) a claim that a MIAM exemption applies. An applicant who claims an exemption from the MIAM requirement is not required to attach any supporting evidence with their application, but should bring any supporting evidence to the first hearing.

7 If an applicant claims a MIAM exemption, the court will issue proceedings but will inquire into the exemption claimed, either at the stage at which the case is allocated or at the first hearing. At the first hearing, the court may review any supporting evidence in order to ensure that the MIAM exemption was validly claimed. As set out in more detail below, if a MIAM exemption has not been validly claimed, the court may direct the applicant or the parties to attend a MIAM, and may adjourn proceedings for that purpose.

Background: Consideration of mediation and other non-court dispute resolution

8 The adversarial court process is not always best suited to the resolution of family disputes. Such disputes are often best resolved through discussion and agreement, where that can be managed safely and appropriately.

9 Family mediation is one way of settling disagreements. A trained mediator can help the parties to reach an agreement. A mediator who conducts a MIAM is a qualified independent facilitator who can also discuss other forms of dispute resolution if mediation is not appropriate.

10 Attendance at a MIAM provides an opportunity for the parties to a dispute to receive information about the process of mediation and to understand the benefits it can offer as a way to resolve disputes. At that meeting, a trained mediator will discuss with the parties the nature of their dispute and will explore with them whether mediation would be a suitable way to resolve the issues on which there is disagreement.

The applications to which the MIAM requirement applies

11 In accordance with section 10 of the 2014 Act, and Rule 3.6, the proceedings to which the MIAM requirement applies are the private law proceedings relating to children listed in paragraph 12 and the proceedings for a financial remedy listed in paragraph 13 below.

Private law proceedings relating to children

12 (1) The private law proceedings relating to children referred to in paragraph 11 are proceedings for the following orders, unless one of the circumstances specified in sub-paragraph (2) applies –

- (a) a child arrangements order and other orders with respect to a child or children under section 8 of the Children Act 1989;
- (b) a parental responsibility order (under sections 4(1)(c), 4ZA(1)(c) or 4A(1)(b) of the Children Act 1989) or an order terminating parental responsibility (under sections 4(2A), 4ZA(5) or 4A(3) of that Act);
- (c) an order appointing a child's guardian (under section 5(1) of the Children Act 1989) or an order terminating the appointment (under section 6(7) of that Act);
- (d) an order giving permission to change a child's surname or remove a child from the United Kingdom (under sections 13(1) or 14C of the Children Act 1989);
- (e) a special guardianship order; and
- (f) an order varying or discharging such an order (under section 14D of the Children Act 1989).

(2) The circumstances referred to in sub-paragraph (1) are that the proceedings –

- (a) are for a consent order;
- (b) are for an order relating to a child or children in respect of whom there are ongoing emergency proceedings, care proceedings or supervision proceedings; or
- (c) are for an order relating to a child or children who are the subject of an emergency protection order, a care order or a supervision order.

Proceedings for a financial remedy

13 (1) The proceedings for a financial remedy referred to in paragraph 11 are proceedings for the following orders, unless one of the circumstances specified in sub-paragraph (2) applies –

- (a) the following financial orders:
  - (i) an order for maintenance pending suit;
  - (ii) an order for maintenance pending outcome of proceedings;

(iii) an order for periodical payments or lump sum provision as mentioned in section 21(1) of the Matrimonial Causes Act 1973, except an order under section 27(6) of that Act;
(iv) an order for periodical payments or lump sum provision as mentioned in paragraph 2(1) of Schedule 5 to the Civil Partnership Act 2004, made under Part 1 of Schedule 5 to that Act;
(v) a property adjustment order;
(vi) a variation order;
(vii) a pension sharing order; or
(viii) a pension compensation sharing order;

(b) an order for financial provision for children (under Schedule 1 to the Children Act 1989);
(c) an order for financial provision in a case of neglect to maintain (under section 27 of the Matrimonial Causes Act 1973 or under Part 9 of Schedule 5 to the Civil Partnership Act 2004);
(d) an order for alteration of a maintenance agreement (under section 35 of the Matrimonial Causes Act 1973 or under paragraph 69 of Schedule 5 to the 2004 Act);
(e) an order for financial provision for failure to maintain for parties to a marriage and children of the family (under Part 1 of the Domestic Proceedings and Magistrates' Courts Act 1978 or an order under Schedule 6 to the Civil Partnership Act 2004); and
(f) an order for special protection for respondent in certain separation cases (under section 10(2) of the Matrimonial Causes Act 1973 or under section 48(2) of the Civil Partnership Act 2004).

(2) The circumstances referred to in sub-paragraph (1) are that the proceedings –

(a) are for a consent order; or
(b) are for enforcement of any order made in proceedings for a financial remedy or of any agreement made in or in contemplation of proceedings for a financial remedy.

Making an application

14 An application to the court in any of the proceedings specified above must be on the relevant court form which must contain either: (a) a confirmation from a mediator that the applicant has attended a MIAM; (b) a claim by the applicant that a MIAM exemption applies (the list of MIAM exemptions is set out in Rule 3.8(1)); or (c) a confirmation from a mediator that a mediator's exemption applies (the list of circumstances that qualify for a mediator's exemption is in Rule 3.8(2)).

15 Relevant application forms are available from the HMCTS form finder service at www.justice.gov.uk/forms/hmcts. For matters concerning children you can find out which form to use by reading the leaflet CB1 – Making an application – Children and the Family Courts'. Leaflet CB7 – Guide for separated parents: children and the family courts also provides guidance on the court process.

16 The relevant form can be completed either by the applicant or his or her legal representative. Any reference in this Practice Direction or in the Rules to completion of the form by an applicant includes a reference to completion by a legal representative.

MIAM exemptions

17 FPR Rule 3.8(1) sets out the circumstances in which the MIAM requirement does not apply. These are called MIAM exemptions.

18 In order to claim that a MIAM exemption applies, an applicant will need to tick the appropriate MIAM exemption boxes on the relevant form.

19 Applicants should note that some of the MIAM exemptions require that certain evidence is available. The next section of the Practice Direction specifies those forms of evidence. This evidence does not need to be provided with the application but applicants should bring such evidence to the first hearing because the court will inquire into such evidence in order to determine whether the MIAM exemption has been validly claimed.

MIAM exemption – Domestic violence

20 (1) The forms of evidence referred to in Rule 3.8(1)(a) are –

(a) a relevant unspent conviction for a domestic violence offence;
(aa) a relevant conviction for a domestic violence offence where a prospective party was convicted of that offence within the sixty month period immediately preceding the date of the application;
(b) a relevant police caution for a domestic violence offence given within the sixty month period immediately preceding the date of the application;
(c) evidence of relevant criminal proceedings for a domestic violence offence which have not concluded;
(d) a relevant protective injunction which is in force or which was granted within the sixty month period immediately preceding the date of the application;
(e) an undertaking given in England and Wales under section 46 or 63E of the 1996 Act (or given in Scotland or Northern Ireland in place of a protection injunction –

    (i) by any prospective party in relation to another prospective party; and
    (ii) within the sixty month period immediately preceding the date of the application;

(f) evidence that a prospective party is on relevant police bail for a domestic violence offence;
(g) a letter from any person who is a member of a multi-agency risk assessment conference confirming that –

    (i) any prospective party was referred to the conference as a victim of domestic violence; and
    (ii) the conference has, within the sixty month period immediately preceding the date of the application, put in place a plan to protect that party from a risk of harm by another prospective party;

(h) a copy of a finding of fact, made in proceedings in the United Kingdom within the sixty month period immediately preceding the date of the application, that there has been domestic violence giving rise to a risk of harm by one prospective party to another prospective party;
(j) a letter or report from a health professional who has access to the medical records of a prospective party confirming that that professional, or another health professional –

    (i) has examined any prospective party in person within the sixty month period immediately preceding the date of the application; and
    (ii) was satisfied following that examination that that party had injuries or a condition consistent with those of a victim of domestic violence;

(ja) a letter from a social services department in England or Wales (or its equivalent in Scotland or Northern Ireland) confirming that, within the sixty month period immediately preceding the date of the application, any prospective party was assessed as being, or at risk of being, a victim of domestic violence by another prospective party;
(k) a letter or report from a domestic violence support organisation in the United Kingdom confirming –

    (i) that within the sixty month period immediately preceding the date of the application, any prospective party had been accommodated in a refuge;
    (ii) the dates on which that prospective party was admitted to and, if applicable, left the refuge; and

(iii) that that party was admitted to the refuge because of allegations by that party of domestic violence;

(l) a letter or report from a domestic violence support organisation in the United Kingdom confirming –

(i) that a prospective party was, within the sixty month period immediately preceding the date of the application, refused admission to a refuge on account of there being insufficient accommodation available in the refuge; and
(ii) the date on which that prospective party was refused admission to the refuge;

(m) a letter or report from –

(i) the person to whom the referral described below was made;
(ii) the health professional who made the referral described below; or
(iii) a health professional who has access to the medical records of a prospective party,

confirming that there was, within the sixty month period immediately preceding the date of the application, a referral by a health professional of a prospective party to a person who provides specialist support or assistance for victims of, or those at risk of, domestic violence;

(n) a relevant domestic violence protection notice issued under section 24 of the Crime and Security Act 2010, or a relevant domestic violence protection order made under section 28 of that Act, against a prospective party within the sixty month period immediately preceding the date of the application;
(o) evidence of a relevant court order binding over a prospective party in connection with a domestic violence offence, which is in force or which was granted within the sixty month period immediately preceding the date of the application; or
(p) evidence which demonstrates that a prospective party has been, or is at risk of being, the victim of domestic violence by another prospective party in the form of abuse which relates to financial matters, where that evidence dates within the sixty month period immediately preceding the date of the application.

MIAM exemption – Bankruptcy

21 The forms of evidence referred to in Rule 3.8(1)(h) are –

(a) application by the prospective applicant for a bankruptcy order;
(b) petition by a creditor of the prospective applicant for a bankruptcy order; or
(c) a bankruptcy order in respect of the prospective applicant.

Finding an authorised family mediator

22 As set out in Rule 3.9, a MIAM must be conducted by an authorised family mediator. Under that rule, an authorised family mediator is a person identified by the Family Mediation Council as qualified to conduct a MIAM.

23 A list of authorised family mediators, including their location, can be found using the 'Find your local mediator' search engine at: www.familymediationcouncil.org.uk

24 The expectation is that a prospective applicant should be able to find an authorised family mediator within 15 miles of his or her home. As stated in Rule 3.8(1)(o) a MIAM exemption is available if:

(i) the prospective applicant has contacted as many authorised family mediators as have an office within fifteen miles of his or her home (or three of them if there are three or more), and all of them have stated that they are not available to conduct a MIAM within fifteen business days of the date of contact; and

(ii) the names, postal addresses and telephone numbers or e-mail addresses for such authorised family mediators, and the dates of contact, can be provided to the court if requested.

25 Rule 3.8(1)(p) also provides an exemption if there is no authorised family mediator with an office within fifteen miles of the prospective applicant's home.

26 To determine whether a mediator is within the distance of 15 miles from their home, applicants can use the 'Find your local mediator' search engine to type in their own post code and then use the distance option to display only family mediators within a 15 mile distance.

27 The applicant will need to be prepared to produce at the first hearing the names, contact information and details of the dates of contact with the authorised family mediators.

28 Information about the Family Mediation Council, including its code of conduct can also be found at www.familymediationcouncil.org.uk

Funding attendance at a MIAM

29 The cost of attending a MIAM will depend on whether the prospective parties attend separately or together and whether at least one of the prospective parties is eligible for Legal Aid. If at least one party is eligible for Legal Aid then the total cost of MIAM attendance can be met by the Legal Aid Agency, whether the parties attend the same MIAM or separate MIAMs.

30 If neither party is eligible for Legal Aid then the mediator will agree with the prospective parties how the cost of MIAM attendance is to be met.

31 Parties can find out whether they are eligible for Legal Aid by using the calculator tool available at www.gov.uk/legal-aid

Attending a MIAM

32 Prospective respondents are expected to attend a MIAM, either with the prospective applicant or separately. A respondent may choose to attend a MIAM separately but this should usually be with the same authorised family mediator.

33 The prospective applicant should provide contact details for the prospective respondent to an authorised family mediator for the purpose of the mediator contacting them to discuss their willingness to attend a MIAM and, if appropriate, to schedule their attendance at a MIAM.

34 If the mediator contacts the prospective respondent and determines that he or she is unwilling to attend a MIAM, a prospective applicant should ask the mediator to confirm this as a ground for MIAM exemption in the relevant section of the application form, which should then be returned signed to the applicant.

MIAM exemption: Inquiries by the court

35 Where a MIAM exemption requires that certain evidence is available, the evidence does not need to be provided with the application form. Applicants should instead bring any such evidence to the first hearing because the court will inquire into such evidence in order to determine whether the MIAM exemption was validly claimed.

36 The court may if appropriate adjourn proceedings where such evidence is not available or may give directions about how and when such evidence is to be filed with the court.

37 If the court determines that the MIAM exemption was not validly claimed, the court may direct the applicant, or the parties, to attend a MIAM and may adjourn proceedings pending MIAM attendance.

Definitions

38 For the purpose of this Practice Direction –

'accommodated' [in paragraph 20(1)(k)(i)] does not require a stay of a minimum time period;
'care order' has the meaning given to it in Rule 2.3 of the FPR;
'care proceedings' has the meaning given to it in Rule 12.2 of the FPR;
'consent order' has the meaning given to it in Rule 2.3 of the FPR;
'emergency proceedings' has the meaning given to it in Rule 12.2 of the FPR;
'emergency protection order' has the meaning given to it in Rule 12.2 of the FPR;
'FPR' means the Family Procedure Rules 2010;
'financial order' has the meaning given to it in Rule 2.3 of the FPR;
'financial remedy' has the meaning given to it in Rule 2.3 of the FPR;
'health professional' means a registered -

- (a) medical practitioner who holds a licence to practise;
- (b) nurse;
- (c) midwife; or
- (d) practitioner psychologist who holds a licence to practise;

'mediator's exemption' has the meaning given to it in Rule 3.1 of the FPR;
'MIAM' means a family mediation information and assessment meeting;
'MIAM exemption' has the meaning given to it in Rule 3.1 of the FPR;
'MIAM requirement' has the meaning given to it in Rule 3.1 of the FPR;
'non-court dispute resolution' has the meaning given to it in Rule 2.3 of the FPR;
'pension compensation sharing order' has the meaning given in Rule 9.3 of the FPR;
'pension sharing order' has the meaning given in Rule 9.3 of the FPR;
'private law proceedings' has the meaning given to it in Rule 12.2 of the FPR;
'prospective applicant' has the meaning given to it in Rule 3.1 of the FPR;
'prospective party' has the meaning given to it in Rule 3.1 of the FPR;
'prospective respondent' has the meaning given to it in Rule 3.1 of the FPR;
'protective injunction' means -

- (a) a non-molestation order under section 42 of the 1996 Act or article 20 of the Family Homes and Domestic Violence (Northern Ireland) Order 1998;
- (b) an occupation order under section 33, 35, 36, 37 or 38 of the 1996 Act or article 11, 13, 14, 15 or 16 of the Family Homes and Domestic Violence (Northern Ireland) Order 1998;
- (c) an exclusion order under section 4 of the Matrimonial Homes (Family Protection) (Scotland) Act 1981 or section 104 of the 2004 Act;
- (d) a forced marriage protection order or interim forced marriage protection order under any of the following provisions –
  - (i) Part 4A of the 1996 Act;
  - (ii) section 2 of, and paragraph 1 of Schedule 1 to, the Forced Marriage (Civil Protection) Act 2007;
  - (iii) section 1 of the Forced Marriage etc. (Protection & Jurisdiction) (Scotland) Act 2011; and
  - (iv) section 5 of the Forced Marriage etc. (Protection & Jurisdiction) (Scotland) Act 2011;
- (da) an injunction under section 3A of the Protection from Harassment Act 1997;
- (e) a restraining order under section 5 or 5A of the Protection from Harassment Act 1997;

Key Legislation and Guidance

(f) a restraining injunction under article 5 or a restraining order under article 7 or 7A of the Protection from Harassment (Northern Ireland) Order 1997;

(g) a non-harassment order under section 234A of the Criminal Procedure (Scotland) Act 1995 or section 8 or 8A of the Protection from Harassment Act 1997;

(h) a common law injunction;

(i) any of the following interdicts –
   (i) a matrimonial interdict within the meaning of section 14 of the Matrimonial Homes (Family Protection) (Scotland) Act 1981;
   (ii) a domestic interdict within the meaning of section 18A of the Matrimonial Homes (Family Protection) (Scotland) Act 1981;
   (iii) an interdict for civil partners within the meaning of section 113 of the Civil Partnership Act 2004;
   (iv) an interdict that has been determined to be a domestic abuse interdict within the meaning of section 3 of the Domestic Abuse (Scotland) Act 2001; and
   (v) a common law interdict;

(i) a female genital mutilation protection order under paragraph 1 or 18 of Schedule 2 to the Female Genital Mutilation Act 2003;

(j) a violent offender order within the meaning of section 98 of the Criminal Justice and Immigration Act 2008;

'refuge' means a refuge established for the purpose of providing accommodation for victims of, or those at risk of, domestic violence;

'relevant' in paragraph 20 of this Practice Direction means that the evidence -

(a) identifies a prospective party as being, or at risk of being, the victim of domestic violence unless the evidence -
   (i) is in a form described in paragraph 20 (1)(a) to (c), (f), (n) or (o); and
   (ii) relates to a domestic violence offence which does not identify the victim; and

(b) identifies another party as being -
   (i) for evidence described in paragraph 20(1)(a) to (c) and (f), convicted of, cautioned with, on police bail for, or charged with the domestic violence offence; and
   (ii) for evidence described in paragraph 20(1)(d), the respondent to the protective injunction;
   (iii) for evidence described in paragraph 20(1)(n), the person against whom the notice or order has been issued or made; and
   (iv) for evidence described in paragraph 20(1)(o), the person against whom the order binding over has been made.

'supervision order' has the meaning given to it in Rule 12.2 of the FPR;

'supervision proceedings' has the meaning given to it in Rule 12.2 of the FPR; and

'variation order' has the meaning given to it in Rule 9.3 of the FPR.

****

FAMILY PROCEDURE RULES 2010, SI 2010/2955, PART 9

APPLICATIONS FOR A FINANCIAL REMEDY

Chapter 1

Application and Interpretation

9.1 Application

The rules in this Part apply to an application for a financial remedy.

('Financial remedy' and 'financial order' are defined in rule 2.3)

9.2 *(revoked)*

9.3 Interpretation

(1) In this Part –

'avoidance of disposition order' means –

(a) in proceedings under the 1973 Act, an order under section 37(2)(b) or (c) of that Act;
(b) in proceedings under the 1984 Act, an order under section 23(2)(b) or 23(3) of that Act;
(c) in proceedings under Schedule 5 to the 2004 Act, an order under paragraph 74(3) or (4); or
(d) in proceedings under Schedule 7 to the 2004 Act, an order under paragraph 15(3) or (4);

'the Board' means the Board of the Pension Protection Fund;

'FDR appointment' means a Financial Dispute Resolution appointment in accordance with rule 9.17;

'Financial Circumstances Form' means the Financial Circumstances Form published by the Permanent Bureau of the Hague Conference under Article 11(4) of the 2007 Hague Convention for use in relation to applications under Article 10 of that Convention;

'order preventing a disposition' means –

(a) in proceedings under the 1973 Act, an order under section 37(2)(a) of that Act;
(b) in proceedings under the 1984 Act, an order under section 23(2)(a) of that Act;
(c) in proceedings under Schedule 5 to the 2004 Act, an order under paragraph 74(2); or
(d) in proceedings under Schedule 7 to the 2004 Act, an order under paragraph 15(2);

'pension arrangement' means –

(a) an occupational pension scheme;
(b) a personal pension scheme;
(c) shareable state scheme rights;
(d) a retirement annuity contract;

(e) an annuity or insurance policy purchased, or transferred, for the purpose of giving effect to rights under an occupational pension scheme or a personal pension scheme; and
(f) an annuity purchased, or entered into, for the purpose of discharging liability in respect of a pension credit under section 29(1)(b) of the Welfare Reform and Pensions Act 1999 or under corresponding Northern Ireland legislation;

'pension attachment order' means –

(a) in proceedings under the 1973 Act, an order making provision under section 25B or 25C of that Act;
(b) in proceedings under the 1984 Act, an order under section 17(1)(a)(i) of that Act making provision equivalent to an order referred to in paragraph (a);
(c) in proceedings under Schedule 5 to the 2004 Act, an order making provision under paragraph 25 or paragraph 26; or
(d) in proceedings under Schedule 7 to the 2004 Act, an order under paragraph 9(2) or (3) making provision equivalent to an order referred to in paragraph (c);

'pension compensation attachment order' means –

(a) in proceedings under the 1973 Act, an order making provision under section 25F of that Act;
(b) in proceedings under the 1984 Act, an order under section 17(1)(a)(i) of that Act making provision equivalent to an order referred in to paragraph (a);
(c) in proceedings under Schedule 5 to the 2004 Act, an order under paragraph 34A; and
(d) in proceedings under Schedule 7 to the 2004 Act, an order under paragraph 9(2) or (3) making provision equivalent to an order referred to in paragraph (c);

'pension compensation sharing order' means –

(a) in proceedings under the 1973 Act, an order under section 24E of that Act;
(b) in proceedings under the 1984 Act, an order under section 17(1)(c) of that Act;
(c) in proceedings under Schedule 5 to the 2004 Act, an order under paragraph 19A; and
(d) in proceedings under Schedule 7 to the 2004 Act, an order under paragraph 9(2) or (3) making provision equivalent to an order referred to in paragraph (c);

'pension sharing order' means –

(a) in proceedings under the 1973 Act, an order making provision under section 24B of that Act;
(b) in proceedings under the 1984 Act, an order under section 17(1)(b) of that Act;
(c) in proceedings under Schedule 5 to the 2004 Act, an order under paragraph 15; or
(d) in proceedings under Schedule 7 to the 2004 Act, an order under paragraph 9(2) or (3) making provision equivalent to an order referred to in paragraph (c);

'pension scheme' means, unless the context otherwise requires, a scheme for which the Board has assumed responsibility in accordance with Chapter 3 of Part 2 of the Pensions Act 2004 (pension protection) or any provision in force in Northern Ireland corresponding to that Chapter;

'PPF compensation' has the meaning given to it –

(a) in proceedings under the 1973 Act, by section 21C of the 1973 Act;
(b) in proceedings under the 1984 Act, by section 18(7) of the 1984 Act; and
(c) in proceedings under the 2004 Act, by paragraph 19F of Schedule 5 to the 2004 Act;

'relevant valuation' means a valuation of pension rights or benefits as at a date not more than 12 months earlier than the date fixed for the first appointment which has been furnished or requested for the purposes of any of the following provisions –

(a) the Pensions on Divorce etc (Provision of Information) Regulations 2000;
(b) regulation 5 of and Schedule 2 to the Occupational Pension Schemes (Disclosure of Information) Regulations 1996 and regulation 11 of and Schedule 1 to the Occupational Pension Schemes (Transfer Value) Regulations 1996;
(c) section 93A or 94(1)(a) or (aa) of the Pension Schemes Act 1993;
(d) section 94(1)(b) of the Pension Schemes Act 1993 or paragraph 2(a) (or, where applicable, 2(b)) of Schedule 2 to the Personal Pension Schemes (Disclosure of Information) Regulations 1987;
(e) the Dissolution etc. (Pensions) Regulations 2005;

'variation order' means –

(a) in proceedings under the 1973 Act, an order under section 31 of that Act; or
(b) in proceedings under the 2004 Act, an order under Part 11 of Schedule 5 to that Act.

(2) (*revoked*)

(3)

(a) Where an application is made under Article 56 of, and using the form in Annex VII to, the Maintenance Regulation, references in this Part to 'financial statement' apply to the applicant as if for the words 'financial statement' were substituted 'the form in Annex VII to the Maintenance Regulation';
(aa) where an application for establishment or modification of maintenance is made under Article 10 of the 2007 Hague Convention, references in this Part to 'financial statement' apply to the applicant as if for 'financial statement' there were substituted 'Financial Circumstances Form;
(b) Sub-paragraphs (a) and (aa) do not apply where the relief sought includes relief which is of a type to which the Maintenance Regulation or the 2007 Hague Convention, as the case may be, does not apply.

Amendments—SI 2011/1328; SI 2012/2806; SI 2013/3204.

Chapter 2

Procedure for Applications

9.4 When an application for a financial order may be made

An application for a financial order may be made –

(a) in an application for a matrimonial or civil partnership order; or
(b) at any time after an application for a matrimonial or civil partnership order has been made.

9.5 Where to start proceedings

(1) An application for a financial remedy must be filed –

(a) if there are proceedings for a matrimonial order or a civil partnership order which are proceeding in the family court, in that court; or
(b) if there are proceedings for a matrimonial order or a civil partnership order which are proceeding in the High Court, in the registry in which those proceedings are taking place.

(2) (*revoked*)

(3) An application for a financial remedy under Part 3 of the 1984 Act or Schedule 7 to the 2004 Act which is proceeding in the High Court must be heard by a judge, but not a district judge, of that court unless a direction has been made that the application may be heard by a district judge of the principal registry.

(Rule 8.28 enables a judge to direct that an application for a financial remedy under Part 3 of the 1984 Act or Schedule 7 to the 2004 Act which is proceeding in the High Court may be heard by a district judge of the principal registry.)

Amendments—SI 2013/3204.

9.6 Application for an order preventing a disposition

(1) The Part 18 procedure applies to an application for an order preventing a disposition.

(2) An application for an order preventing a disposition may be made without notice to the respondent.

('Order preventing a disposition' is defined in rule 9.3.)

9.7 Application for interim orders

(1) A party may apply at any stage of the proceedings for –

- (a) an order for maintenance pending suit;
- (b) an order for maintenance pending outcome of proceedings;
- (c) an order for interim periodical payments;
- (d) an interim variation order;
- (da) an order for payment in respect of legal services; or
- (e) any other form of interim order.

(2) An application for an order mentioned in paragraph (1) shall be made using the Part 18 procedure.

(3) Where a party makes an application before filing a financial statement, the written evidence in support must –

- (a) explain why the order is necessary; and
- (b) give up to date information about that party's financial circumstances.

(4) Unless the respondent has filed a financial statement, the respondent must, at least 7 days before the court is to deal with the application, file a statement of his means and serve a copy on the applicant.

(5) An application for an order mentioned in paragraph (1)(e) may be made without notice.

Amendments—SI 2013/1472.

9.8 Application for periodical payments order at same rate as an order for maintenance pending suit

(1) This rule applies where there are matrimonial proceedings and –

- (a) a decree nisi of divorce or nullity of marriage has been made;
- (b) at or after the date of the decree nisi an order for maintenance pending suit is in force; and
- (c) the spouse in whose favour the decree nisi was made has made an application for an order for periodical payments.

(2) The spouse in whose favour the decree nisi was made may apply, using the Part 18 procedure, for an order providing for payments at the same rate as those provided for by the order for maintenance pending suit.

9.9 Application for periodical payments order at same rate as an order for maintenance pending outcome of proceedings

(1) This rule applies where there are civil partnership proceedings and –

(a) a conditional order of dissolution or nullity of civil partnership has been made;
(b) at or after the date of the conditional order an order for maintenance pending outcome of proceedings is in force;
(c) the civil partner in whose favour the conditional order was made has made an application for an order for periodical payments.

(2) The civil partner in whose favour the conditional order was made may apply, using the Part 18 procedure, for an order providing for payments at the same rate as those provided for by, the order for maintenance pending the outcome of proceedings.

9.9A Application to set aside a financial remedy order

(1) In this rule –

(a) 'financial remedy order' means an order or judgment that is a financial remedy, and includes –

  (i) part of such an order or judgment; or
  (ii) a consent order; and

(b) 'set aside' means –

  (i) in the High Court, to set aside a financial remedy order pursuant to section 17(2) of the Senior Courts Act 1981 and this rule;
  (ii) in the family court, to rescind or vary a financial remedy order pursuant to section 31F(6) of the 1984 Act.

(2) A party may apply under this rule to set aside a financial remedy order where no error of the court is alleged.

(3) An application under this rule must be made within the proceedings in which the financial remedy order was made.

(4) An application under this rule must be made in accordance with the Part 18 procedure, subject to the modifications contained in this rule.

(5) Where the court decides to set aside a financial remedy order, it shall give directions for the rehearing of the financial remedy proceedings or make such other orders as may be appropriate to dispose of the application.

Amendments—Inserted by SI 2016/901.

Chapter 3

Applications for Financial Remedies for Children

9.10 Application by parent, guardian etc for financial remedy in respect of children

(1) The following people may apply for a financial remedy in respect of a child –

(a) a parent, guardian or special guardian of any child of the family;
(b) any person who is named in a child arrangements order as a person with whom a child of the family is to live, and any applicant for such an order;
(c) any other person who is entitled to apply for a child arrangements order which names that person as a person with whom a child is to live;
(d) a local authority, where an order has been made under section 31(1)(a) of the 1989 Act placing a child in its care;
(e) the Official Solicitor, if appointed the children's guardian of a child of the family under rule 16.24; and
(f) subject to paragraph (1A), a child of the family who has been given permission to apply for a financial remedy.

(1A) Where the application is –

(a) for the variation of an order under section 2(1)(c), 6 or 7 of the 1978 Act or paragraph 2(1)(c) of, or Part 2 or 3 of, Schedule 6 to the 2004 Act for periodical payments in respect of a child;
(b) the application is made by the child in question; and
(c) the child in question is aged 16 or over,

the child does not require permission to make the application.

(2) (*revoked*)

Amendments—SI 2013/3204; SI 2014/843.

9.11 Children to be separately represented on certain applications

(1) Where an application for a financial remedy includes an application for an order for a variation of settlement, the court must, unless it is satisfied that the proposed variation does not adversely affect the rights or interests of any child concerned, direct that the child be separately represented on the application.

(2) On any other application for a financial remedy the court may direct that the child be separately represented on the application.

(3) Where a direction is made under paragraph (1) or (2), the court may if the person to be appointed so consents, appoint –

(a) a person other than the Official Solicitor; or
(b) the Official Solicitor,

to be a children's guardian and rule 16.24(5) and (6) and rules 16.25 to 16.28 apply as appropriate to such an appointment.

Chapter 4

Procedure after Filing an Application

Amendments—SI 2013/3204.

9.12 Duties of the court and the applicant upon issuing an application

(1) When an application under this Part is issued, except where Chapter 5 of this Part applies –

- (a) the court will fix a first appointment not less than 12 weeks and not more than 16 weeks after the date of the filing of the application; and
- (b) subject to paragraph (2), within 4 days beginning with the date on which the application was filed, a court officer will –
  - (i) serve a copy of the application on the respondent; and
  - (ii) give notice of the date of the first appointment to the applicant and the respondent.

(2) Where the applicant wishes to serve a copy of the application on the respondent and on filing the application so notifies the court –

- (a) paragraph (1)(b) does not apply;
- (b) a court officer will return to the applicant the copy of the application and the notice of the date of the first appointment; and
- (c) the applicant must, –
  - (i) within 4 days beginning with the date on which the copy of the application is received from the court, serve the copy of the application and notice of the date of the first appointment on the respondent; and
  - (ii) file a certificate of service at or before the first appointment.

(Rule 6.37 sets out what must be included in a certificate of service)

(3) The date fixed under paragraph (1), or for any subsequent appointment, must not be cancelled except with the court's permission and, if cancelled, the court must immediately fix a new date.

(4) In relation to an application to which the Maintenance Regulation or the 2007 Hague Convention applies, where the applicant does not already know the address of the respondent at the time the application is issued, paragraph (2) does not apply and the court will serve the application in accordance with paragraph (1).

Amendments—SI 2011/1328; SI 2012/2806; SI 2013/3204.

9.13 Service of application on mortgagees, trustees etc

(1) Where an application for a financial remedy includes an application for an order for a variation of settlement, the applicant must serve copies of the application on –

- (a) the trustees of the settlement;
- (b) the settlor if living; and
- (c) such other persons as the court directs.

(2) In the case of an application for an avoidance of disposition order, the applicant must serve copies of the application on the person in whose favour the disposition is alleged to have been made.

(3) Where an application for a financial remedy includes an application relating to land, the applicant must serve a copy of the application on any mortgagee of whom particulars are given in the application.

(4) Any person served under paragraphs (1), (2) or (3) may make a request to the court in writing, within 14 days beginning with the date of service of the application, for a copy of the applicant's financial statement or any relevant part of that statement.

(5) Any person who –

(a) is served with copies of the application in accordance with paragraphs (1), (2) or (3); or
(b) receives a copy of a financial statement, or a relevant part of that statement, following an application made under paragraph (4),

may within 14 days beginning with the date of service or receipt file a statement in answer.

(6) Where a copy of an application is served under paragraphs (1), (2) or (3), the applicant must file a certificate of service at or before the first appointment.

(7) A statement in answer filed under paragraph (5) must be verified by a statement of truth.

9.14 Procedure before the first appointment

(1) Not less than 35 days before the first appointment both parties must simultaneously exchange with each other and file with the court a financial statement in the form referred to in Practice Direction 5A.

(2) The financial statement must –

(a) be verified by a statement of truth; and
(b) accompanied by the following documents only –
    (i) any documents required by the financial statement;
    (ii) any other documents necessary to explain or clarify any of the information contained in the financial statement; and
    (iii) any documents provided to the party producing the financial statement by a person responsible for a pension arrangement, either following a request under rule 9.30 or as part of a relevant valuation; and
    (iv) any notification or other document referred to in rule 9.37(2), (4) or (5) which has been received by the party producing the financial statement.

(2ZA) Paragraph (2A) applies where the court has determined that the procedure in this Chapter should apply to an application under Article 56 of the Maintenance Regulation or Article 10 of the 2007 Hague Convention.

(2A) The requirement of paragraph (2)(a) relating to verification by a statement of truth does not apply to the financial statement of either party where the application has been made under –

(a) Article 56 of the Maintenance Regulation, using the form in Annex VII to that Regulation; or
(b) Article 10 of the 2007 Hague Convention, using the Financial Circumstances Form,

and the relief sought is limited to a type to which that Regulation or that Convention, as appropriate, applies, but the court may at any time direct that the financial statement of either party shall be verified by a statement of truth.

(3) Where a party was unavoidably prevented from sending any document required by the financial statement, that party must at the earliest opportunity –

(a) serve a copy of that document on the other party; and

(b) file a copy of that document with the court, together with a written explanation of the failure to send it with the financial statement.

(4) No disclosure or inspection of documents may be requested or given between the filing of the application for a financial remedy and the first appointment, except –

(a) copies sent with the financial statement, or in accordance with paragraph (3); or
(b) in accordance with paragraphs (5) and (6).

(Rule 21.1 explains what is meant by disclosure and inspection.)

(5) Not less than 14 days before the hearing of the first appointment, each party must file with the court and serve on the other party –

(a) a concise statement of the issues between the parties;
(b) a chronology;
(c) a questionnaire setting out by reference to the concise statement of issues any further information and documents requested from the other party or a statement that no information and documents are required; and
(d) a notice stating whether that party will be in a position at the first appointment to proceed on that occasion to a FDR appointment.

(6) Not less than 14 days before the hearing of the first appointment, the applicant must file with the court and serve on the respondent confirmation –

(a) of the names of all persons served in accordance with rule 9.13(1) to (3); and
(b) that there are no other persons who must be served in accordance with those paragraphs.

Amendments—SI 2011/1328; SI 2012/679; SI 2012/2806; SI 2014/667.

9.15 Duties of the court at the first appointment

(1) The first appointment must be conducted with the objective of defining the issues and saving costs.

(2) At the first appointment the court must determine –

(a) the extent to which any questions seeking information under rule 9.14(5)(c) must be answered; and
(b) what documents requested under rule 9.14(5)(c) must be produced,

and give directions for the production of such further documents as may be necessary.

(3) The court must give directions where appropriate about –

(a) the valuation of assets (including the joint instruction of joint experts);
(b) obtaining and exchanging expert evidence, if required;
(c) the evidence to be adduced by each party; and
(d) further chronologies or schedules to be filed by each party.

(4) If the court decides that a referral to a FDR appointment is appropriate it must direct that the case be referred to a FDR appointment.

(5) If the court decides that a referral to a FDR appointment is not appropriate it must direct one or more of the following –

(a) that a further directions appointment be fixed;
(b) that an appointment be fixed for the making of an interim order;

(c) that the case be fixed for a final hearing and, where that direction is given, the court must determine the judicial level at which the case should be heard.

(Under Part 3 the court may also direct that the case be adjourned if it considers that non-court dispute resolution is appropriate.)

(6) In considering whether to make a costs order under rule 28.3(5), the court must have particular regard to the extent to which each party has complied with the requirement to send documents with the financial statement and the explanation given for any failure to comply.

(7) The court may –

(a) where an application for an interim order has been listed for consideration at the first appointment, make an interim order;
(b) having regard to the contents of the notice filed by the parties under rule 9.14(5)(d), treat the appointment (or part of it) as a FDR appointment to which rule 9.17 applies;
(c) in a case where a pension sharing order or a pension attachment order is requested, direct any party with pension rights to file and serve a Pension Inquiry Form, completed in full or in part as the court may direct; and
(d) in a case where a pension compensation sharing order or a pension compensation attachment order is requested, direct any party with PPF compensation rights to file and serve a Pension Protection Fund Inquiry Form, completed in full or in part as the court may direct.

(8) Both parties must personally attend the first appointment unless the court directs otherwise.

Amendments—SI 2014/843.

9.16 After the first appointment

(1) Between the first appointment and the FDR appointment, a party is not entitled to the production of any further documents except –

(a) in accordance with directions given under rule 9.15(2); or
(b) with the permission of the court.

(2) At any stage –

(a) a party may apply for further directions or a FDR appointment;
(b) the court may give further directions or direct that parties attend a FDR appointment.

9.17 The FDR appointment

(1) The FDR appointment must be treated as a meeting held for the purposes of discussion and negotiation.

(2) The judge hearing the FDR appointment must have no further involvement with the application, other than to conduct any further FDR appointment or to make a consent order or a further directions order.

(3) Not less than 7 days before the FDR appointment, the applicant must file with the court details of all offers and proposals, and responses to them.

(4) Paragraph (3) includes any offers, proposals or responses made wholly or partly without prejudice, but paragraph (3) does not make any material admissible as evidence if, but for that paragraph, it would not be admissible.

(5) At the conclusion of the FDR appointment, any documents filed under paragraph (3), and any filed documents referring to them, must, at the request of the party who filed them, be returned to that party and not retained on the court file.

(6) Parties attending the FDR appointment must use their best endeavours to reach agreement on matters in issue between them.

(7) The FDR appointment may be adjourned from time to time.

(8) At the conclusion of the FDR appointment, the court may make an appropriate consent order.

(9) If the court does not make an appropriate consent order as mentioned in paragraph (8), the court must give directions for the future course of the proceedings including, where appropriate –

- (a) the filing of evidence, including up to date information; and
- (b) fixing a final hearing date.

(10) Both parties must personally attend the FDR appointment unless the court directs otherwise.

Chapter 5

Procedure after Filing Particular Applications

Amendments—SI 2013/3204.

9.18 Duties of the court and the applicant upon filing an application

(A1) This Chapter applies where an application is made –

- (a) under –
  - (i) the 1978 Act;
  - (ii) Schedule 6 to the 2004 Act;
  - (iii) Schedule 1 to the 1989 Act;
  - (iv) Article 56 of the Maintenance Regulation; or
  - (v) Article 10 of the 2007 Hague Convention.
- (b) for the variation of an order for a financial remedy.

(1) Where an application is issued –

- (a) the court will fix a first hearing date not less than 4 weeks and not more than 8 weeks after the date of the filing of the application; and
- (b) subject to paragraph (2), within 4 days beginning with the date on which the application was filed, a court officer will -
  - (i) serve a copy of the application on the respondent;
  - (ii) give notice of the date of the first hearing to the applicant and the respondent; and
  - (iii) send a blank financial statement to both the applicant and the respondent.

(2) Where the applicant wishes to serve a copy of the application on the respondent and, on filing the application, so notifies the court –

- (a) paragraph (1)(b) does not apply;
- (b) a court officer will return to the applicant the copy of the application and the notice of the date of the first hearing; and
- (c) the applicant must –

(i) within 4 days beginning with the date on which the copy of the application is received from the court, serve the copy of the application and notice of the date of the first hearing on the respondent;
(ii) send a blank financial statement to the respondent; and
(iii) file a certificate of service at or before the first hearing.

(3) The date fixed under paragraph (1), or for any other subsequent hearing or appointment must not be cancelled except with the court's permission and, if cancelled, the court must immediately fix a new date.

(4) The requirement in paragraph (1)(b)(iii) for the court officer to send a blank financial statement to the applicant does not apply where the application has been made under –

(a) Article 56 of the Maintenance Regulation, using the form in Annex VII to that Regulation; or
(b) Article 10 of the 2007 Hague Convention, using the Financial Circumstances Form.

(5) In relation to an application to which the Maintenance Regulation or the 2007 Hague Convention applies, where the applicant does not already know the address of the respondent at the time the application is issued, paragraph (2) does not apply and the court will serve the application in accordance with paragraph (1).

Amendments—SI 2011/1328; SI 2012/2806; SI 2013/3204; SI 2014/667.

9.18A Request for change of procedure

(1) This rule applies if the applicant wishes to seek a direction from the court that the procedure in Chapter 4 of this Part should apply to an application for an order in proceedings referred to in rule 9.18(A1).

(2) The application for the order must state –

(a) that the applicant seeks a direction that the procedure in Chapter 4 of this Part should apply; and
(b) the applicant's reasons for seeking such a direction.

(3) The court will –

(a) determine without notice to the parties and before the first hearing whether the procedure in Chapter 4 or Chapter 5 of this Part should apply to the application; and
(b) notify the parties of its determination and any directions made in consequence of that determination.

Amendments—Inserted by SI 2013/3204.

9.19 Procedure before the first hearing

(1) Not more than 14 days after the date of the issue of the application both parties must simultaneously exchange with each other and file with the court a financial statement referred to in Practice Direction 5A.

(2) The financial statement must –

(a) be verified by a statement of truth; and
(b) contain the following documents only –

(i) any documents required by the financial statement; and

(ii) any other documents necessary to explain or clarify any of the information contained in the financial statement.

(2A) The requirement of paragraph (2)(a) relating to verification by statement of truth does not apply to the financial statement of either party where the application has been made under –

(a) Article 56 of the Maintenance Regulation, using the form in Annex VII to that Regulation; or

(b) Article 10 of the 2007 Hague Convention, using the Financial Circumstances Form, but the court may at any time direct that the financial statement of either party shall be verified by a statement of truth.

(3) Where a party was unavoidably prevented from sending any document required by the financial statement, that party must at the earliest opportunity –

(a) serve a copy of that document on the other party; and

(b) file a copy of that document with the court, together with a statement explaining the failure to send it with the financial statement.

(4) No disclosure or inspection of documents may be requested or given between the filing of the application for a financial remedy and the first hearing except copies sent with the financial statement or in accordance with paragraph (3).

(Rule 21.1 explains what is meant by disclosure and inspection.)

Amendments—SI 2011/1328; SI 2012/679; SI 2012/2806.

9.20 Power of the court to direct filing of evidence and set dates for further hearings

Unless the court is able to determine the application at the first hearing the court may direct that further evidence be filed and set a date for a directions hearing or appointment or final hearing.

9.21 Who the respondent is on an application under section 20 or section 20A of the 1978 Act or Part 6 of Schedule 6 to the 2004 Act

In relation to proceedings set out in column 1 of the following table, column 2 sets out who the respondents to those proceedings will be.

Proceedings	*Respondent*
Application under section 20 of the 1978 Act.	The other party to the marriage; and where the order to which the application relates requires periodical payments to be made to, or in respect of, a child who is 16 years of age or over, that child.
Application under paragraphs 30 to 34 of Schedule 6 to the 2004 Act.	The other party to the civil partnership; and where the order to which the application relates requires periodical payments to be made to, or in respect of, a child who is 16 years of age or over, that child.
Application for the revival of an order under section 20A of the 1978 Act or paragraph 40 of Schedule 6 to the 2004 Act.	The parties to the proceedings leading to the order which it is sought to have revived.

Amendments—SI 2013/3204.

9.21A Duty to make entries in the court's register

Where a court officer receives notice of any direction made in the High Court or family court under section 28 of the 1978 Act by virtue of which an order made under that Act or the 2004 Act ceases to have effect, particulars of the direction must be noted in the court's records.

Amendments—Inserted by SI 2014/667.

Chapter 5A

Certain Applications

Amendments—Inserted by SI 2014/667.

9.22 Application for a maintenance order, or revocation of a maintenance order to which the 1982 Act, the Lugano Convention, the 1988 Convention or the Maintenance Regulation applies

(1) This rule applies where a person makes an application for a maintenance order, or for the variation or the revocation of a maintenance order, in relation to which the court has jurisdiction by virtue of the 1982 Act, the Lugano Convention, the 1988 Convention or the Maintenance Regulation, and the respondent is outside the United Kingdom.

(2) Where the respondent does not enter an appearance and is not represented at the hearing –

- (a) the court will apply the provisions of Article 20 of the 1968 Convention, Article 20 of the 1988 Convention, Article 26 of the Lugano Convention, or Article 11 of the Maintenance Regulation as appropriate;
- (b) where the court proceeds to hear the application having applied the appropriate provision referred to in sub-paragraph (a), the court will take into account any written representations made and any evidence given by the respondent under these rules.

(3) *(revoked)*

(4) In this rule –

- (a) 'the 1982 Act', 'the Lugano Convention' and 'the 1988 Convention' have the meanings given to them in rule 34.1(2);
- (b) 'the 1968 Convention' has the meaning given to it in the Civil Jurisdiction and Judgments Act 1982.

Amendments—Substituted by SI 2011/1328. Amended by SI 2013/3204.

9.23 *(revoked)*

Chapter 6

General Procedure

9.24 Power to order delivery up of possession etc.

(1) This rule applies where the court has made an order under –

- (a) section 24A of the 1973 Act;
- (b) section 17(2) of the 1984 Act;
- (c) Part 3 of Schedule 5 to the 2004 Act; or
- (d) paragraph 9(4) of Schedule 7 to the 2004 Act.

(2) When the court makes an order mentioned in paragraph (1), it may order any party to deliver up to the purchaser or any other person –

(a) possession of the land, including any interest in, or right over, land;
(b) receipt of rents or profits relating to it; or
(c) both.

9.25 Where proceedings may be heard

(1) Paragraph (2) applies to an application –

(a) for a financial order;
(b) under Part 3 of the 1984 Act; or
(c) under Schedule 7 to the 2004 Act.

(2) An application mentioned in paragraph (1) must be heard –

(a) *(revoked)*
(b) where the case is proceeding in the High Court –

(i) at the Royal Courts of Justice; or
(ii) in matrimonial or civil partnership proceedings, any court at which sittings of the High Court are authorised.

(3)–(5) *(revoked)*

Amendments—SI 2013/3204.

9.26 Applications for consent orders for financial remedy

(1) Subject to paragraph (5) and to rule 35.2 in relation to an application for a consent order –

(a) the applicant must file two copies of a draft of the order in the terms sought, one of which must be endorsed with a statement signed by the respondent to the application signifying agreement; and
(b) each party must file with the court and serve on the other party, a statement of information in the form referred to in Practice Direction 5A.

(2) Where each party's statement of information is contained in one form, it must be signed by both the applicant and respondent to certify that they have read the contents of the other party's statement.

(3) Where each party's statement of information is in a separate form, the form of each party must be signed by the other party to certify that they have read the contents of the statement contained in that form.

(4) Unless the court directs otherwise, the applicant and the respondent need not attend the hearing of an application for a consent order.

(5) Where all or any of the parties attend the hearing of an application for a financial remedy the court may –

(a) dispense with the filing of a statement of information; and
(b) give directions for the information which would otherwise be required to be given in such a statement in such a manner as it thinks fit.

(6) In relation to an application for a consent order under Part 3 of the 1984 Act or Schedule 7 to the 2004 Act, the application for permission to make the application may be heard at the same time as the application for a financial remedy if evidence of the respondent's consent to the order is filed with the application.

(The following rules contain provision in relation to applications for consent orders – rule 9.32 (pension sharing order), rule 9.34 (pension attachment order), rule 9.41 (pension compensation sharing orders) and rule 9.43 (pension compensation attachment orders).

9.26A Questions as to the court's jurisdiction or whether the proceedings should be stayed

(1) This rule applies to applications for maintenance where a question as to jurisdiction arises under –

- (a) the 1968 Convention;
- (b) the 1988 Convention;
- (c) the Lugano Convention;
- (d) the Maintenance Regulation; or
- (e) Article 18 of the 2007 Hague Convention.

(2) If at any time after the issue of the application it appears to the court that it does not or may not have jurisdiction to hear an application, or that under the instruments referred to in paragraph (1) it is or may be required to stay the proceedings or to decline jurisdiction, the court must –

- (a) stay the proceedings, and
- (b) fix a date for a hearing to determine jurisdiction or whether there should be a stay or other order.

(3) The court officer will serve notice of the hearing referred to at paragraph (2)(b) on the parties to the proceedings.

(4) The court must, in writing –

- (a) give reasons for its decision under paragraph (2), and
- (b) where it makes a finding of fact, state such finding.

(5) The court may with the consent of all the parties deal with any question as to the jurisdiction of the court, or as to whether the proceedings should be stayed, without a hearing.

(6) In this rule –

- (a) 'the 1968 Convention' has the meaning given to it in the Civil Jurisdiction and Judgments Act 1982;
- (b) 'the 1988 Convention' and 'the Lugano Convention' have the meanings given to them in rule 34.1(2).

Amendments—Inserted by SI 2011/1328. Amended by SI 2012/2806.

9.26AA International Maintenance Obligations: Communication with the Central Authority for England and Wales

(1) Where the Lord Chancellor requests information or a document from the court officer for the relevant court for the purposes of Article 58 of the Maintenance Regulation or Articles 12 or 25(2) of the 2007 Hague Convention, the court officer shall provide the requested information or document to the Lord Chancellor forthwith.

(2) In this rule, 'relevant court' means the court at which an application under Article 56 of the Maintenance Regulation or Article 10 of the 2007 Hague Convention has been filed.

[The Lord Chancellor is the Central Authority for England and Wales in relation to the 2007 Hague Convention and the Maintenance Regulation]

Amendments—Inserted by SI 2012/2806.

9.26B Adding or removing parties

(1) The court may direct that a person or body be added as a party to proceedings for a financial remedy if –

(a) it is desirable to add the new party so that the court can resolve all the matters in dispute in the proceedings; or
(b) there is an issue involving the new party and an existing party which is connected to the matters in dispute in the proceedings, and it is desirable to add the new party so that the court can resolve that issue.

(2) The court may direct that any person or body be removed as a party if it is not desirable for that person or body to be a party to the proceedings.

(3) If the court makes a direction for the addition or removal of a party under this rule, it may give consequential directions about –

(a) the service of a copy of the application form or other relevant documents on the new party; and
(b) the management of the proceedings.

(4) The power of the court under this rule to direct that a party be added or removed may be exercised either on the court's own initiative or on the application of an existing party or a person or body who wishes to become a party.

(5) An application for an order under this rule must be made in accordance with the Part 18 procedure and, unless the court directs otherwise, must be supported by evidence setting out the proposed new party's interest in or connection with the proceedings or, in the case of removal of a party, the reasons for removal.

Amendments—Inserted by SI 2012/679.

9.26C Method of making periodical payments

(1) This rule applies where under section 1(4) or (4A) of the Maintenance Enforcement Act 1991 the court orders that payments under a qualifying periodical maintenance order are to be made by a particular means.

(2) The court officer will record on a copy of the order the means of payment that the court has ordered.

(3) The court officer will notify in writing the person liable to make payments under the order how the payments are to be made.

(4) Where under section 1(4A) of the Maintenance Enforcement Act 1991 the court orders payment to the court by a method of payment under section 1(5) of that Act, the court officer will notify the person liable to make payments under the order of sufficient details of the account into which payments should be made to enable payments to be made into that account.

(5) Where payments are made to the court, the court officer will give or send a receipt to any person who makes such a payment and who asks for a receipt.

(6) Where payments are made to the court, the court officer will make arrangements to make the payments to –

- (a) the person entitled to them; or
- (b) if the person entitled to them is a child, to the child or to the person with whom the child has his or her home.

(7) The Part 18 procedure applies to an application under section 1(7) of the Maintenance Enforcement Act 1991 (application from an interested party to revoke, suspend, revive or vary the method of payment).

(8) Where the court makes an order under section 1(7) of the Maintenance Enforcement Act 1991 or dismisses an application for such an order, the court officer will, as far as practicable, notify in writing all interested parties of the effect of the order and will take the steps set out in paragraphs (2), (3) and (4), as appropriate..

(9) In this rule, 'interested party' and 'qualifying periodical maintenance order' have the meanings given in section 1(10) of the Maintenance Enforcement Act 1991.

Amendments—Inserted by SI 2014/667.

9.26D Court officer to notify subsequent marriage or formation of civil partnership of a person entitled to payments under a maintenance order

(1) This rule applies where –

- (a) there is an order of a type referred to in paragraph (4) which requires payments to be made to the court or to an officer of the court; and
- (b) the court is notified in writing by –
  - (i) the person entitled to receive payments under the order;
  - (ii) the person required to make payments under the order; or
  - (iii) the personal representative of such a person,

that the person entitled to receive payments under the order has subsequently married or formed a civil partnership.

(2) The court officer will, where practicable, notify in writing the courts referred to in paragraph (3) of the notification of the subsequent marriage or formation of a civil partnership.

(3) The courts to be notified are –

- (a) any other court which has made an order of a type referred to in paragraph (4);
- (b) in the case of a provisional order made under section 3 of the 1920 Act or section 3 of the 1972 Act, the court which confirmed the order;
- (c) if an order of a type referred to in paragraph (4) has been transmitted abroad for registration under section 2 of the 1920 Act or section 2 of the 1972 Act, the court in which the order is registered; and
- (d) any other court in which an application to enforce the order has been made.

(4) The orders are –

- (a) those to which the following provisions apply –
  - (i) section 38 of the 1973 Act;

(ii) section 4(2) of the 1978 Act;
(iii) paragraph 65 of Schedule 5 to the 2004 Act; and
(iv) paragraph 26(2) of Schedule 6 to the 2004 Act; and

(b) an attachment of earnings order made to secure payments under an order referred to in sub-paragraph (a).

(5) In this rule –

'the 1920 Act' means the Maintenance Orders (Facilities for Enforcement) Act 1920; and
'the 1972 Act' means the Maintenance Orders (Reciprocal Enforcement) Act 1972.

Amendments—Inserted by SI 2014/667.

9.26E Enforcement and apportionment where periodical payments are made under more than one order

(1) This rule applies where periodical payments are required to be made by a payer to a payee under more than one periodical payments order.

(2) Proceedings for the recovery of payments under more than one order may be made in one application by the payee, which must indicate the payments due under each order.

(3) Paragraphs (4) and (5) apply where any sum paid to the court on any date by a payer who is liable to make payments to the court under two or more periodical payments orders is less than the total sum that the payer is required to pay to the court on that date in respect of those orders.

(4) The payment made will be apportioned between the orders in proportion to the amounts due under each order over a period of one year.

(5) If, as a result of the apportionment referred to in paragraph (4), the payments under any periodical payments order are no longer in arrears, the residue shall be applied to the amount due under the other order or, if there is more than one other order, shall be apportioned between the other orders in accordance with paragraph (4).

(6) In this rule –

'payee' means a person entitled to receive payments under a periodical payments order; and
'payer' means a person required to make payments under a periodical payments order.

Amendments—Inserted by SI 2014/667.

Chapter 7

Estimates of Costs

9.27 Estimates of Costs

(1) Subject to paragraph (2), at every hearing or appointment each party must produce to the court an estimate of the costs incurred by that party up to the date of that hearing or appointment.

(2) Not less than 14 days before the date fixed for the final hearing of an application for a financial remedy, each party ('the filing party') must (unless the court directs otherwise) file with the court and serve on each other party a statement giving full particulars of all costs in respect of the proceedings which the filing party has incurred or expects to incur, to enable the court to take account of the parties' liabilities for costs when deciding what order (if any) to make for a financial remedy.

(3) (*revoked*)

(Rule 28.3 makes provision for orders for costs in financial remedy proceedings.)

Amendments—SI 2013/3204.

9.28 Duty to make open proposals

(1) Not less than 14 days before the date fixed for the final hearing of an application for a financial remedy, the applicant must (unless the court directs otherwise) file with the court and serve on the respondent an open statement which sets out concise details, including the amounts involved, of the orders which the applicant proposes to ask the court to make.

(2) Not more than 7 days after service of a statement under paragraph (1), the respondent must file with the court and serve on the applicant an open statement which sets out concise details, including the amounts involved, of the orders which the respondent proposes to ask the court to make.

Chapter 8

Pensions

9.29 Application and interpretation of this Chapter

(1) This Chapter applies

(a) where an application for a financial remedy has been made; and
(b) the applicant or respondent is the party with pension rights.

(2) In this Chapter –

(a) in proceedings under the 1973 Act and the 1984 Act, all words and phrases defined in sections 25D(3) and (4) of the 1973 Act have the meaning assigned by those subsections;
(b) in proceedings under the 2004 Act –

all words and phrases defined in paragraphs 16(4) to (5) and 29 of Schedule 5 to that Act have the meanings assigned by those paragraphs; and
'the party with pension rights' has the meaning given to 'civil partner with pension rights' by paragraph 29 of Schedule 5 to the 2004 Act;

(c) all words and phrases defined in section 46 of the Welfare Reform and Pensions Act 1999 have the meanings assigned by that section.

9.30 What the party with pension rights must do when the court fixes a first appointment

(1) Where the court fixes a first appointment as required by rule 9.12(1)(a) the party with pension rights must request the person responsible for each pension arrangement under which the party has or is likely to have benefits to provide the information referred to in regulation 2(2) of the Pensions on Divorce etc (Provision of Information) Regulations 2000.

(The information referred to in regulation 2 of the Pensions on Divorce etc (Provision of Information) Regulations 2000 relates to the valuation of pension rights or benefits.)

(2) The party with pension rights must comply with paragraph (1) within 7 days beginning with the date on which that party receives notification of the date of the first appointment.

(3) Within 7 days beginning with the date on which the party with pension rights receives the information under paragraph (1) that party must send a copy of it to the other party, together with the name and address of the person responsible for each pension arrangement.

(4) A request under paragraph (1) need not be made where the party with pension rights is in possession of, or has requested, a relevant valuation of the pension rights or benefits accrued under the pension arrangement in question.

9.31 Applications for pension sharing orders

Where an application for a financial remedy includes an application for a pension sharing order, or where a request for such an order is added to an existing application for a financial remedy, the applicant must serve a copy of the application on the person responsible for the pension arrangement concerned.

9.32 Applications for consent orders for pension sharing

(1) This rule applies where –

- (a) the parties have agreed on the terms of an order and the agreement includes a pension sharing order;
- (b) service has not been effected under rule 9.31; and
- (c) the information referred to in paragraph (2) has not otherwise been provided.

(2) The party with pension rights must –

- (a) request the person responsible for the pension arrangement concerned to provide the information set out in Section C of the Pension Inquiry Form; and
- (b) on receipt, send a copy of the information referred to in sub-paragraph (a) to the other party.

9.33 Applications for pension attachment orders

(1) Where an application for a financial remedy includes an application for a pension attachment order, or where a request for such an order is added to an existing application for a financial remedy, the applicant must serve a copy of the application on the person responsible for the pension arrangement concerned and must at the same time send –

- (a) an address to which any notice which the person responsible is required to serve on the applicant is to be sent;
- (b) an address to which any payment which the person responsible is required to make to the applicant is to be sent; and
- (c) where the address in sub-paragraph (b) is that of a bank, a building society or the Department of National Savings, sufficient details to enable the payment to be made into the account of the applicant.

(2) A person responsible for a pension arrangement who receives a copy of the application under paragraph (1) may, within 21 days beginning with the date of service of the application, request the party with the pension rights to provide that person with the information disclosed in the financial statement relating to the party's pension rights or benefits under that arrangement.

(3) If the person responsible for a pension arrangement makes a request under paragraph (2), the party with the pension rights must provide that person with a copy of the section of that party's financial statement that relates to that party's pension rights or benefits under that arrangement.

(4) The party with the pension rights must comply with paragraph (3) –

(a) within the time limited for filing the financial statement by rule 9.14(1); or
(b) within 21 days beginning with the date on which the person responsible for the pension arrangement makes the request,

whichever is the later.

(5) A person responsible for a pension arrangement who receives a copy of the section of a financial statement as required pursuant to paragraph (4) may, within 21 days beginning with the date on which that person receives it, send to the court, the applicant and the respondent a statement in answer.

(6) A person responsible for a pension arrangement who files a statement in answer pursuant to paragraph (5) will be entitled to be represented at the first appointment, or such other hearing as the court may direct, and the court must within 4 days, beginning with the date on which that person files the statement in answer, give the person notice of the date of the first appointment or other hearing as the case may be.

9.34 Applications for consent orders for pension attachment

(1) This rule applies where service has not been effected under rule 9.33(1).

(2) Where the parties have agreed on the terms of an order and the agreement includes a pension attachment order, then they must serve on the person responsible for the pension arrangement concerned –

(a) a copy of the application for a consent order;
(b) a draft of the proposed order, complying with rule 9.35; and
(c) the particulars set out in rule 9.33(1).

(3) No consent order that includes a pension attachment order must be made unless either –

(a) the person responsible for the pension arrangement has not made any objection within 21 days beginning with the date on which the application for a consent order was served on that person; or
(b) the court has considered any such objection, and for the purpose of considering any objection the court may make such direction as it sees fit for the person responsible to attend before it or to furnish written details of the objection.

9.35 Pension sharing orders or pension attachment orders

An order for a financial remedy, whether by consent or not, which includes a pension sharing order or a pension attachment order, must –

(a) in the body of the order, state that there is to be provision by way of pension sharing or pension attachment in accordance with the annex or annexes to the order; and
(b) be accompanied by a pension sharing annex or a pension attachment annex as the case may require, and if provision is made in relation to more than one pension arrangement there must be one annex for each pension arrangement.

9.36 Duty of the court upon making a pension sharing order or a pension attachment order

(1) A court which varies or discharges a pension sharing order or a pension attachment order, must send, or direct one of the parties to send –

(a) to the person responsible for the pension arrangement concerned; or
(b) where the Board has assumed responsibility for the pension scheme or part of it, the Board;

the documents referred to in paragraph (4).

(2) A court which makes a pension sharing order or pension attachment order, must send, or direct one of the parties to send to the person responsible for the pension arrangement concerned, the documents referred to in paragraph (4).

(3) Where the Board has assumed responsibility for the pension scheme or part of it after the making of a pension sharing order or attachment order but before the documents have been sent to the person responsible for the pension arrangement in accordance with paragraph (2), the court which makes the pension sharing order or the pension attachment order, must send, or direct one of the parties to send to the Board the documents referred to in paragraph (4).

(4) The documents to be sent in accordance with paragraph (1) to (3) are –

(a) in the case of –

(i) proceedings under the 1973 Act, a copy of the decree of judicial separation;
(ii) proceedings under Schedule 5 to the 2004 Act, a copy of the separation order;
(iii) proceedings under Part 3 of the 1984 Act, a copy of the document of divorce, annulment or legal separation;
(iv) proceedings under Schedule 7 to the 2004 Act, a copy of the document of dissolution, annulment or legal separation;

(b) in the case of divorce or nullity of marriage, a copy of the decree absolute under rule 7.31 or 7.32 or
(c) in the case of dissolution or nullity of civil partnership, a copy of the order making the conditional order final under rule 7.31 or 7.32; and
(d) a copy of the pension sharing order or the pension attachment order, or as the case may be of the order varying or discharging that order, including any annex to that order relating to that pension arrangement but no other annex to that order.

(5) The documents referred to in paragraph (4) must be sent –

(a) in proceedings under the 1973 Act and the 1984 Act, within 7 days beginning with the date on which –

(i) the relevant pension sharing or pension attachment order, or any order varying or discharging such an order, is made; or
(ii) the decree absolute of divorce or nullity or decree of judicial separation is made,
whichever is the later; and

(b) in proceedings under the 2004 Act, within 7 days beginning with the date on which –

(i) the relevant pension sharing or pension attachment order, or any order varying or discharging such an order, is made; or
(ii) the final order of dissolution or nullity or separation order is made,
whichever is the later.

Amendments—SI 2012/679.

Key Legislation and Guidance

9.37 Procedure where Pension Protection Fund becomes involved with the pension scheme

(1) This rule applies where –

(a) rules 9.30 to 9.34 or 9.36 apply; and
(a) the party with the pension rights ('the member') receives or has received notification in compliance with the Pension Protection Fund (Provision of Information) Regulations 2005 ('the 2005 Regulations') –

(i) from the trustees or managers of a pension scheme, that there is an assessment period in relation to that scheme; or
(ii) from the Board that it has assumed responsibility for the pension scheme or part of it.

(2) If the trustees or managers of the pension scheme notify or have notified the member that there is an assessment period in relation to that scheme, the member must send to the other party, all the information which the Board is required from time to time to provide to the member under the 2005 Regulations including –

(a) a copy of the notification; and
(b) a copy of the valuation summary,

in accordance with paragraph (3).

(3) The member must send the information or any part of it referred to in paragraph (2) –

(a) if available, when the member sends the information received under rule 9.30(1); or
(b) otherwise, within 7 days of receipt.

(4) If the Board notifies the member that it has assumed responsibility for the pension scheme, or part of it, the member must –

(a) send a copy of the notification to the other party within 7 days of receipt; and
(b) comply with paragraph (5).

(5) Where paragraph (4) applies, the member must –

(a) within 7 days of receipt of the notification, request the Board in writing to provide a forecast of the member's compensation entitlement as described in the 2005 Regulations; and
(b) send a copy of the forecast of the member's compensation entitlement to the other party within 7 days of receipt.

(6) In this rule –

'assessment period' means an assessment period within the meaning of Part 2 of the Pensions Act 2004; and
'valuation summary' has the meaning assigned to it by the 2005 Regulations.

Chapter 9

Pension Protection Fund Compensation

9.38 Application and interpretation of this Chapter

(1) This Chapter applies –

(a) where an application for a financial remedy has been made; and
(b) the applicant or respondent is, the party with compensation rights.

(2) In this Chapter 'party with compensation rights' –

(a) in proceedings under the 1973 Act and the 1984 Act, has the meaning given to it by section 25G(5) of the 1973 Act;
(b) in proceedings under the 2004 Act, has the meaning given to 'civil partner with compensation rights' by paragraph 37(1) of Schedule 5 to the 2004 Act.

9.39 What the party with compensation rights must do when the court fixes a first appointment

(1) Where the court fixes a first appointment as required by rule 9.12(1)(a) the party with compensation rights must request the Board to provide the information about the valuation of entitlement to PPF compensation referred to in regulations made by the Secretary of State under section 118 of the Pensions Act 2008.

(2) The party with compensation rights must comply with paragraph (1) within 7 days beginning with the date on which that party receives notification of the date of the first appointment.

(3) Within 7 days beginning with the date on which the party with compensation rights receives the information under paragraph (1) that party must send a copy of it to the other party, together with the name and address of the trustees or managers responsible for each pension scheme.

(4) Where the rights to PPF Compensation are derived from rights under more than one pension scheme, the party with compensation rights must comply with this rule in relation to each entitlement.

9.40 Applications for pension compensation sharing orders

Where an application for a financial remedy includes an application for a pension compensation sharing order or where a request for such an order is added to an existing application for a financial remedy, the applicant must serve a copy of the application on the Board.

9.41 Applications for consent orders for pension compensation sharing

(1) This rule applies where –

(a) the parties have agreed on the terms of an order and the agreement includes a pension compensation sharing order;
(b) service has not been effected under rule 9.40; and
(c) the information referred to in paragraph (2) has not otherwise been provided.

(2) The party with compensation rights must –

(a) request the Board to provide the information set out in Section C of the Pension Protection Fund Inquiry Form; and
(b) on receipt, send a copy of the information referred to in sub-paragraph (a) to the other party.

9.42 Applications for pension compensation attachment orders

Where an application for a financial remedy includes an application for a pension compensation attachment order or where a request for such an order is added to an existing application for a financial remedy, the applicant must serve a copy of the application on the Board and must at the same time send –

(a) an address to which any notice which the Board is required to serve on the applicant is to be sent;
(b) an address to which any payment which the Board is required to make to the applicant is to be sent; and
(c) where the address in sub-paragraph (b) is that of a bank, a building society or the Department of National Savings, sufficient details to enable the payment to be made into the account of the applicant.

9.43 Applications for consent orders for pension compensation attachment

(1) This rule applies where service has not been effected under rule 9.42.

(2) Where the parties have agreed on the terms of an order and the agreement includes a pension compensation attachment order, then they must serve on the Board –

(a) a copy of the application for a consent order;
(b) a draft of the proposed order, complying with rule 9.44; and
(c) the particulars set out in rule 9.42.

9.44 Pension compensation sharing orders or pension compensation attachment orders

An order for a financial remedy, whether by consent or not, which includes a pension compensation sharing order or a pension compensation attachment order, must –

(a) in the body of the order, state that there is to be provision by way of pension compensation sharing or pension compensation attachment in accordance with the annex or annexes to the order; and
(b) be accompanied by a pension compensation sharing annex or a pension compensation attachment annex as the case may require, and if provision is made in relation to entitlement to PPF compensation that derives from rights under more than one pension scheme there must be one annex for each such entitlement.

9.45 Duty of the court upon making a pension compensation sharing order or a pension compensation attachment order

(1) A court which makes, varies or discharges a pension compensation sharing order or a pension compensation attachment order, must send, or direct one of the parties to send, to the Board –

(a) in the case of –

   (i) proceedings under Part 3 of the 1984 Act, a copy of the document of divorce, annulment or legal separation;
   (ii) proceedings under Schedule 7 to the 2004 Act, a copy of the document of dissolution, annulment or legal separation;

(b) in the case of –

   (i) divorce or nullity of marriage, a copy of the decree absolute under rule 7.32 or 7.33;
   (ii) dissolution or nullity of civil partnership, a copy of the order making the conditional order final under rule 7.32 or 7.33;

(c) in the case of separation –

(i) in the matrimonial proceedings, a copy of the decree of judicial separation;
(ii) in civil partnership proceedings, a copy of the separation order; and

(d) a copy of the pension compensation sharing order or the pension compensation attachment order, or as the case may be of the order varying or discharging that order, including any annex to that order relating to that PPF compensation but no other annex to that order.

(2) The documents referred to in paragraph (1) must be sent –

(a) in proceedings under the 1973 Act and the 1984 Act, within 7 days beginning with the date on which –

(i) the relevant pension compensation sharing or pension compensation attachment order is made; or
(ii) the decree absolute of divorce or nullity or the decree of judicial separation is made, whichever is the later; and

(b) in proceedings under the 2004 Act, within 7 days beginning with the date on which –

(i) the relevant pension compensation sharing or pension compensation attachment order is made; or
(ii) the final order of dissolution or nullity or separation order is made, whichever is the later.

Chapter 10

Communication of Information from Financial Remedy Proceedings

Amendments—Chapter title inserted by SI 2015/1868.

9.46 Communication of information: Practice Direction 9B

(1) For the purposes of the law relating to contempt of court, information from financial remedy proceedings may be communicated in accordance with Practice Direction 9B.

(2) Paragraph (1) is subject to any direction of the court.

(3) Nothing in this rule permits the communication to the public at large, or any section of the public, of any information relating to the proceedings.

(Rule 29.2 makes provision about disclosure of information under the 1991 Act.)

Amendments—Inserted by SI 2015/1868.

PRACTICE DIRECTION 9A – APPLICATION FOR A FINANCIAL REMEDY

This Practice Direction supplements FPR Part 9

Introduction

1.1 Part 9 of the Family Procedure Rules sets out the procedure applicable to the financial proceedings that are included in the definition of a 'financial remedy'.

1.2 The shorter procedure set out in Chapter 5 of Part 9 of the Family Procedure Rules applies in respect of –

- proceedings under:
  - the 1978 Act,
  - Schedule 6 to the 2004 Act,
  - Schedule 1 to the 1989 Act;
  - Article 56 of the Maintenance Regulation; and
  - Article 10 of the 2007 Hague Convention
- any application for the variation of an order for a financial remedy.

The longer procedure set out in Chapter 4 of Part 9 applies in respect of all other applications for a financial remedy. In a case to which the shorter Chapter 5 procedure applies, the initial application can include a request for the court instead to apply the longer Chapter 4 procedure. Examples of cases in which it may be appropriate to make such a request include an application under Schedule 1 to the 1989 Act in which there are contested issues about the settlement of property, or a variation application in which a capital payment or pension sharing order is proposed.

1.3 Where an application for a financial remedy includes an application relating to land, details of any mortgagee must be included in the application.

Pre-application protocol

2.1 The 'pre-application protocol' annexed to this Direction outlines the steps parties should take to seek and provide information from and to each other prior to the commencement of any application for a financial remedy. The court will expect the parties to comply with the terms of the protocol.

Costs

3.1 Rule 9.27 requires each party to produce to the court, at every hearing or appointment, an estimate of the costs incurred by the party up to the date of that hearing or appointment.

3.2 The purpose of this rule is to enable the court to take account of the impact of each party's costs liability on their financial situations. Parties should ensure that the information contained in the estimate is as full and accurate as possible and that any sums already paid in respect of a party's financial remedy costs are clearly set out. Where relevant, any liability arising from the costs of other proceedings between the parties should continue to be referred to in the appropriate section of a party's financial statement; any such costs should not be included in the estimates under rule 9.27.

3.3 Rule 28.3 provides that the general rule in financial remedy proceedings is that the court will not make an order requiring one party to pay the costs of another party. However the court may make such an order at any stage of the proceedings where it considers it appropriate to do so because of the conduct of a party in relation to the proceedings.

3.4 Any breach of this practice direction or the pre-application protocol annexed to it will be taken into account by the court when deciding whether to depart from the general rule as to costs.

Amendments—FPR Update 9.

Procedure before the first appointment

4.1 In addition to the matters listed at rule 9.14(5), the parties should, if possible, with a view to identifying and narrowing any issues between the parties, exchange and file with the court –

(a) a summary of the case agreed between the parties;
(b) a schedule of assets agreed between the parties; and
(c) details of any directions that they seek, including, where appropriate, the name of any expert they wish to be appointed.

4.2 Where a party is prevented from sending the details referred to in (c) above, the party should make that information available at the first appointment.

Financial Statements and other documents

5.1 Practice Direction 22A (Written Evidence) applies to any financial statement filed in accordance with rules 9.14 or 9.19 and to any exhibits to a financial statement. In preparing a bundle of documents to be exhibited to or attached to a financial statement, regard must be had in particular to paragraphs 11.1 to 11.3 and 13.1 to 13.4 of that Direction. Where on account of their bulk, it is impracticable for the exhibits to a financial statement to be retained on the court file after the First Appointment, the court may give directions as to their custody pending further hearings.

5.2 Where the court directs a party to provide information or documents by way of reply to a questionnaire or request by another party, the reply must be verified by a statement of truth. Unless otherwise directed, a reply to a questionnaire or request for information and documents shall not be filed with the court.

(Part 17 and Practice Direction 17A make further provision about statements of truth)

Financial Dispute Resolution (FDR) Appointment

6.1 A key element in the procedure is the Financial Dispute Resolution (FDR) appointment. Rule 9.17 provides that the FDR appointment is to be treated as a meeting held for the purposes of discussion and negotiation. Such meetings have been developed as a means of reducing the tension which inevitably arises in family disputes and facilitating settlement of those disputes.

6.2 In order for the FDR to be effective, parties must approach the occasion openly and without reserve. Non-disclosure of the content of such meetings is vital and is an essential prerequisite for fruitful discussion directed to the settlement of the dispute between the parties. The FDR appointment is an important part of the settlement process. As a consequence of *Re D (Minors)*

(Conciliation: Disclosure of Information) [1993] Fam 231, evidence of anything said or of any admission made in the course of an FDR appointment will not be admissible in evidence, except at the trial of a person for an offence committed at the appointment or in the very exceptional circumstances indicated in *Re D*.

6.3 Courts will therefore expect –

(a) parties to make offers and proposals;
(b) recipients of offers and proposals to give them proper consideration; and
(c) (subject to paragraph 6.4), that parties, whether separately or together, will not seek to exclude from consideration at the appointment any such offer or proposal.

6.4 Paragraph 6.3(c) does not apply to an offer or proposal made during non-court dispute resolution.

6.5 In order to make the most effective use of the first appointment and the FDR appointment, the legal representatives attending those appointments will be expected to have full knowledge of the case.

6.6 (*omitted*)

(Provision relating to experts in financial remedy proceedings is contained in Practice Direction 25D (Financial Remedy Proceedings and Other Family Proceedings (Except Children Proceedings) – The Use of Single Joint Experts and the Process Leading to Expert Evidence Being Put Before The Court).)

Consent orders

7.1 Rule 9.26(1)(a) requires an application for a consent order to be accompanied by two copies of the draft order in the terms sought, one of which must be endorsed with a statement signed by the respondent to the application signifying the respondent's agreement. The rule is considered to have been properly complied with if the endorsed statement is signed by solicitors on record as acting for the respondent; but where the consent order applied for contains undertakings, it should be signed by the party giving the undertakings as well as by that party's solicitor.

(Provision relating to the enforcement of undertakings is contained in the Practice Direction 33A supplementing Part 33 of the FPR)

7.2 Rule 9.26(1)(b) requires each party to file with the court and serve on the other party a statement of information. Where this is contained in one form, both parties must sign the statement to certify that each has read the contents of the other's statement.

7.3 Rule 35.2 deals with applications for a consent order in respect of a financial remedy where the parties wish to have the content of a written mediation agreement to which the Mediation Directive applies made the subject of a consent order.

Section 10(2) of the Matrimonial Causes Act 1973 and section 48(2) of the Civil Partnership Act 2004

8.1 Where a respondent who has applied under section 10(2) of the Matrimonial Causes Act 1973, or section 48(2) of the Civil Partnership Act 2004, for the court to consider his or her financial position after a divorce or dissolution elects not to proceed with the application, a notice of withdrawal of the application signed by the respondent or by the respondent's solicitor may be filed without leave of the court. In this event a formal order dismissing or striking out the application is unnecessary. Notice of withdrawal should also be given to the applicant's solicitor.

8.2 An application under section 10(2) or section 48(2) which has been withdrawn is not a bar to making in matrimonial proceedings, the decree absolute and in civil partnership proceedings, the final order.

Maintenance Orders – registration in the family court

9.1 Where periodical payments are required to be made to a child under an order registered in the family court, section 31L(3) and (4) of the1984 Act permits the payments to be made instead to the person with whom the child has his home. That person may proceed in his own name for variation, revival or revocation of the order and may enforce payment in his own name.

9.2 The registration in the family court of an order made direct to a child entails a considerable amount of work. Accordingly, when the High Court is considering the form of an order where there are children, care should be taken not to make orders for payment direct where such orders would be of no benefit to the parties.

Amendments—FPR Update 9.

Pensions

10.1 The phrase 'party with pension rights' is used in FPR Part 9, Chapter 8. For matrimonial proceedings, this phrase has the meaning given to it by section 25D(3) of the Matrimonial Causes Act 1973 and means 'the party to the marriage who has or is likely to have benefits under a pension arrangement'. There is a definition of 'civil partner with pension rights' in paragraph 29 of Schedule 5 to the Civil Partnership Act 2004 which mirrors the definition of 'party with pension rights' in section 25D(3) of the 1973 Act. The phrase 'is likely to have benefits' in these definitions refers to accrued rights to pension benefits which are not yet in payment.

PPF Compensation

11.1 The phrase 'party with compensation rights' is used in FPR Part 9, Chapter 9. For matrimonial proceedings, the phrase has the meaning given to it by section 25G(5) of the Matrimonial Causes Act 1973 and means the party to the marriage who is or is likely to be entitled to PPF compensation. There is a definition of 'civil partner with compensation rights' in paragraph 37(1) of Schedule 5 to the Civil Partnership Act 2004 which mirrors the definition of 'party with compensation rights' in section 25G(5). The phrase 'is likely to be entitled to PPF Compensation' in those definitions refers to statutory entitlement to PPF Compensation which is not yet in payment.

Orders for payment in respect of legal services

12.1 An application for an order for payment in respect of legal services under section 22ZA of the 1973 Act or paragraph 38A of Part 8 of Schedule 5 to the 2004 Act must be made in accordance with FPR 9.7 using the Part 18 procedure. Where the application is made at the same time as an application for an order for maintenance pending suit or maintenance pending outcome, the applications may be included in one application notice, and evidence in support of or in response to the applications may be contained in one witness statement.

(Where an application is made for an order under FPR 9.7, a copy of the application notice must be served in accordance with the provisions of FPR Part 6 at least 14 days before the court is to deal with the application: FPR 18.8(1)(b).)

12.2 The evidence filed in support of an application for an order for payment in respect of legal services must, in addition to the matters referred to in rule 9.7(3), include a concise statement of the applicant's case on -

(a) the criteria set out in section 22ZA(3) and (4) of the 1974 Act or paragraph 38A(3) and (4) of Part 8 of Schedule 5 to the 2004 Act as applicable; and
(b) the matters set out in section 22ZB(1) of the 1973 Act or paragraph 38B(1) of Part 8 of Schedule 5 to the 2004 Act as applicable.

Applications to set aside a financial remedy

13.1 As set out in rule 9.9A(4), the Part 18 procedure applies to applications to set aside a financial remedy. Where such an application was made before rule 9.9A came into force, the Part 18 procedure will still apply subject to any directions that the court might make for the purpose of ensuring the proceedings are dealt with fairly (see the Family Procedure (Amendment No 2) Rules 2016, rule 5).

13.2 If the financial remedy order was made before 22 April 2014, by any court, an application to set it aside under rule 9.9A is to be made to the family court. This is the combined effect of rule 9.9A(3), which provides that the application is made within the original proceedings, and the Crime and Courts Act 2013 (Family Court: Transitional and Savings Provision) Order 2014, which provides that any such proceedings became family court proceedings as of 22 April 2014.

13.3 If the financial remedy order was made on or after 22 April 2014, an application to set it aside under rule 9.9A is to be made to the court that made the order.

13.4 An application under rule 9.9A is to be dealt with by the same level of judge that dealt with the original application, by virtue of rule 17 of the Family Court (Composition and Distribution of Business) Rules 2014. Where reasonably possible, the application will be dealt with by the same judge that dealt with the original application.

13.5 An application to set aside a financial remedy order should only be made where no error of the court is alleged. If an error of the court is alleged, an application for permission to appeal under Part 30 should be considered. The grounds on which a financial remedy order may be set aside are and will remain a matter for decisions by judges. The grounds include (i) fraud; (ii) material non-disclosure; (iii) certain limited types of mistake; (iv) a subsequent event, unforeseen and unforeseeable at the time the order was made, which invalidates the basis on which the order was made.

13.6 The effect of rules 9.9A(1)(a) and (2) is that an application may be made to set aside all or only part of a financial remedy order, including a financial remedy order that has been made by consent.

13.7 The family court has the power under section 31F(6) of the Matrimonial and Family Proceedings Act 1984 to vary or set aside a financial remedy order. The High Court has the power under rule 9.9A and section 17(2) of the Senior Courts Act 1981 to set aside a financial remedy order. The difference in the wording of the legislative provisions is the reason that 'set aside' has been defined as it has in rule 9.9A(1)(b).

13.8 In applications under rule 9.9A, the starting point is that the order which one party is seeking to have set aside was properly made. A mere allegation that it was obtained by, eg, non-disclosure, is not sufficient for the court to set aside the order. Only once the ground for setting aside the order has been established (or admitted) can the court set aside the order and rehear the original application for a financial remedy. The court has a full range of case management powers and considerable discretion as to how to determine an application to set aside a financial remedy order, including where appropriate the power to strike out or summarily dispose of an application to set aside. If and when a ground for setting aside has been established, the court may decide to set aside the whole or part of the order there and then, or may delay doing so, especially if there are third party claims to the parties' assets. Ordinarily, once the court has decided to set aside a financial remedy order, the court would give directions for a full rehearing to re-determine the original application. However, if the court is satisfied that it has sufficient information to do so, it may proceed to re-determine the original application at the same time as setting aside the financial remedy order.

13.9 The effect of rule 28.3(9) is that the Part 28 rules relating to costs do not apply to applications under rule 9.9A.

Annex – Pre-application protocol

Notes of guidance

Scope of the Protocol

1 This protocol is intended to apply to all applications for a financial remedy as defined by rule 2.3. It is designed to cover all classes of case, ranging from a simple application for periodical payments to an application for a substantial lump sum and property adjustment order. The protocol is designed to facilitate the operation of the procedure for financial remedy applications.

2 In considering the options of pre-application disclosure and negotiation, solicitors should bear in mind the advantage of having a court timetable and court managed process. There is sometimes an advantage in preparing disclosure before proceedings are commenced. However, solicitors should bear in mind the objective of controlling costs and in particular the costs of discovery and that the option of pre-application disclosure and negotiation has risks of excessive and uncontrolled expenditure and delay. This option should only be encouraged where both parties agree to follow this route and disclosure is not likely to be an issue or has been adequately dealt with in mediation or otherwise.

3 Solicitors should consider at an early stage and keep under review whether it would be appropriate to suggest mediation and/or collaborative law to the clients as an alternative to solicitor negotiation or court based litigation.

4 Making an application to the court should not be regarded as a hostile step or a last resort, rather as a way of starting the court timetable, controlling disclosure and endeavouring to avoid the costly final hearing and the preparation for it.

First letter

5 The circumstances of parties to an application for a financial remedy are so various that it would be difficult to prepare a specimen first letter. The request for information will be different in every case. However, the tone of the initial letter is important and the guidelines in paragraphs 14 and 15 should be followed. It should be approved in advance by the client. Solicitors writing to an unrepresented party should always recommend that he seeks independent legal advice and enclose a second copy of the letter to be passed to any solicitor instructed. A reasonable time limit for an answer may be 14 days.

Negotiation and settlement

6 In the event of pre-application disclosure and negotiation, as envisaged in paragraph 12 an application should not be issued when a settlement is a reasonable prospect.

Disclosure

7 The protocol underlines the obligation of parties to make full and frank disclosure of all material facts, documents and other information relevant to the issues. Solicitors owe their clients

a duty to tell them in clear terms of this duty and of the possible consequences of breach of the duty, which may include criminal sanctions under the Fraud Act 2006. This duty of disclosure is an ongoing obligation and includes the duty to disclose any material changes after initial disclosure has been given. Solicitors are referred to the Good Practice Guides available to Resolution members at www.resolution.org.uk and can also contact the Law Society's Practice Advice Service on 0870 606 2522.

The Protocol

General principles

8 All parties must always bear in mind the overriding objective set out at rules 1.1 to 1.4 and try to ensure that applications should be resolved and a just outcome achieved as speedily as possible without costs being unreasonably incurred. The needs of any children should be addressed and safeguarded. The procedures which it is appropriate to follow should be conducted with minimum distress to the parties and in a manner designed to promote as good a continuing relationship between the parties and any children affected as is possible in the circumstances.

9 The principle of proportionality must be borne in mind at all times. It is unacceptable for the costs of any case to be disproportionate to the financial value of the subject matter of the dispute.

10 Parties should be informed that where a court is considering whether to make an order requiring one party to pay the costs of another party, it will take into account pre-application offers to settle and conduct of disclosure.

Identifying the issues

11 Parties must seek to clarify their claims and identify the issues between them as soon as possible. So that this can be achieved, they must provide full, frank and clear disclosure of facts, information and documents, which are material and sufficiently accurate to enable proper negotiations to take place to settle their differences. Openness in all dealings is essential.

Disclosure

12 If parties carry out voluntary disclosure before the issue of proceedings the parties should exchange schedules of assets, income, liabilities and other material facts, using the financial statement as a guide to the format of the disclosure. Documents should only be disclosed to the extent that they are required by the financial statement. Excessive or disproportionate costs should not be incurred.

Correspondence

13 Any first letter and subsequent correspondence must focus on the clarification of claims and identification of issues and their resolution. Protracted and unnecessary correspondence and 'trial by correspondence' must be avoided.

14 The impact of any correspondence upon the reader and in particular the parties must always be considered. Any correspondence which raises irrelevant issues or which might cause the other party to adopt an entrenched, polarised or hostile position is to be discouraged.

Summary

15 The aim of all pre-application proceedings steps must be to assist the parties to resolve their differences speedily and fairly or at least narrow the issues and, should that not be possible, to assist the court to do so.

PRACTICE DIRECTION 9B – COMMUNICATION OF INFORMATION FROM FINANCIAL REMEDY PROCEEDINGS

This Practice Direction supplements FPR rule 9.46

1.1 Subject to any direction of the court, information from financial remedy proceedings may be communicated for the purposes of the law relating to contempt of court in accordance with this Practice Direction.

Communication of information by a party etc. for purposes relating to appeals under the Child Support Act 1991

2.1 A person specified in the first column of the following table may communicate to a person listed in the second column such information as is specified in the third column for the purpose specified in the fourth column –

A party	The Secretary of State, a McKenzie Friend, a lay adviser or the First-tier Tribunal dealing with an appeal under section 20 of the Child Support Act 1991	Any information relating to financial remedy proceedings	For the purposes of making or responding to an appeal under section 20 of the Child Support Act 1991 or the determination of such an appeal
A party or any other person lawfully in receipt of information	The Secretary of State, a McKenzie Friend, a lay adviser or the Upper Tier Tribunal dealing with an appeal under section 24 of the Child Support Act 1991 in respect of a decision of the First-tier Tribunal that was made under section 20 of that Act	Any information relating to financial remedy proceedings	For a purpose connected with an appeal under section 24 of the Child Support Act 1991 in respect of a decision of the First-tier Tribunal that was made under section 20 of that Act

Onward communication

3.1 A person in the second column of the table at paragraph 2.1 may only communicate information relating to the proceedings received from a person in the first column for the purpose for which he or she received that information.

Interpretation

4.1 In this Practice Direction -

'lay adviser' means a non-professional person who gives lay advice on behalf of an organisation in the lay advice sector; and

'McKenzie Friend' means any person permitted by the court or tribunal to sit beside an unrepresented litigant in court or in a tribunal to assist that litigant by prompting, taking notes and giving advice to that litigant.

PRACTICE DIRECTION 27A – FAMILY PROCEEDINGS: COURT BUNDLES (UNIVERSAL PRACTICE TO BE APPLIED IN THE HIGH COURT AND FAMILY COURT)

This Practice Direction supplements FPR Part 27

1.1 The President of the Family Division has issued this practice direction to achieve consistency across the country in the Family Court and the Family Division of the High Court in the preparation of court bundles and in respect of other related matters.

Application of the practice direction

2.1 Except as specified in paragraph 2.4, and subject to specific directions given in any particular case, the following practice applies to:

(a) all hearings before a judge sitting in the Family Division of the High Court wherever the court may be sitting; and
(b) all hearings in the Family Court.

2.2 'Hearing' includes all appearances before the court, whether with or without notice to other parties and whether for directions or for substantive relief.

2.3 This practice direction applies whether a bundle is being lodged for the first time or is being re-lodged for a further hearing (see paragraph 9.2).

2.4 This practice direction does not apply to the hearing of any urgent application if and to the extent that it is impossible to comply with it.

Responsibility for the preparation of the bundle

3.1 A bundle for the use of the court at the hearing shall be provided by the party in the position of applicant at the hearing (or, if there are cross-applications, by the party whose application was first in time) or, if that person is a litigant in person, by the first listed respondent who is not a litigant in person. Where all the parties are litigants in person none of them shall, unless the court otherwise directs, be obliged to provide a bundle, but any bundle which they choose to lodge must be prepared and lodged so as to comply with this practice direction.

3.2 The party preparing the bundle shall paginate it using Arabic numbering throughout. If possible the contents of the bundle shall be agreed by all parties.

Contents of the bundle

4.1 The bundle shall contain copies of only those documents which are relevant to the hearing and which it is necessary for the court to read or which will actually be referred to during the hearing. In particular, copies of the following classes of documents must not be included in the bundle unless specifically directed by the court:

(a) correspondence (including letters of instruction to experts);
(b) medical records (including hospital, GP and health visitor records);
(c) bank and credit card statements and other financial records;
(d) notes of contact visits;
(e) foster carer logs;
(f) social services files (with the exception of any assessment being relied on by any of the parties);
(g) police disclosure.

This does not prevent the inclusion in the bundle of specific documents which it is necessary for the court to read or which will actually be referred to during the hearing.

4.2 The documents in the bundle shall be arranged in chronological order from the front of the bundle, paginated individually and consecutively (starting with page 1 and using Arabic numbering throughout), indexed and divided into separate sections (each section being separately paginated) as follows:

(a) preliminary documents (see paragraph 4.3) and any other case management documents required by any other practice direction;
(b) applications and orders;
(c) statements and affidavits (which must be dated in the top right corner of the front page) but without exhibiting or duplicating documents referred to in para 4.1;
(d) care plans (where appropriate);
(e) experts' reports and other reports (including those of a guardian, children's guardian or litigation friend); and
(f) other documents, divided into further sections as may be appropriate.

All statements, affidavits, care plans, experts' reports and other reports included in the bundle must be copies of originals which have been signed and dated.

4.3 At the commencement of the bundle there shall be inserted the following documents (the preliminary documents):

(a) an up to date case summary of the background to the hearing confined to those matters which are relevant to the hearing and the management of the case and limited, if practicable, to four A4 pages;
(b) a statement of the issue or issues to be determined (1) at that hearing and (2) at the final hearing;
(c) a position statement by each party including a summary of the order or directions sought by that party (1) at that hearing and (2) at the final hearing;
(d) an up to date chronology, if it is a final hearing or if the summary under (i) is insufficient;
(e) skeleton arguments, if appropriate;
(f) a list of essential reading for that hearing; and
(g) the time estimate (see paragraph 10.1).

Copies of all authorities relied on must be contained in a separate composite bundle agreed between the advocates.

4.4 Each of the preliminary documents shall be as short and succinct as possible and shall state on the front page immediately below the heading the date when it was prepared and the date of the hearing for which it was prepared. Where proceedings relating to a child are being heard by magistrates the summary of the background shall be prepared in anonymised form, omitting the names and identifying information of every person referred to other than the parties' legal representatives, and stating the number of pages contained in the bundle. Identifying information can be contained in all other preliminary documents.

4.5 The summary of the background, statement of issues, chronology, position statement and any skeleton arguments shall be cross-referenced to the relevant pages of the bundle.

4.6 The summary of the background, statement of issues, chronology and reading list shall in the case of a final hearing, and shall so far as practicable in the case of any other hearing, each consist of a single document in a form agreed by all parties. Where the parties disagree as to the content the fact of their disagreement and their differing contentions shall be set out at the appropriate places in the document.

4.7 Where the nature of the hearing is such that a complete bundle of all documents is unnecessary, the bundle (which need not be repaginated) may comprise only those documents necessary for the hearing, but

(a) the summary of the background must commence with a statement that the bundle is limited or incomplete; and
(b) the bundle shall if reasonably practicable be in a form agreed by all parties.

4.8 Where the bundle is re-lodged in accordance with paragraph 9.2, before it is re-lodged:

(a) the bundle shall be updated as appropriate; and
(b) all superseded documents (and in particular all outdated summaries, statements of issues, chronologies, skeleton arguments and similar documents) shall be removed from the bundle.

Format of the bundle

5.1 Unless the court has specifically directed otherwise, being satisfied that such direction is necessary to enable the proceedings to be disposed of justly, the bundle shall be contained in one A4 size ring binder or lever arch file limited to no more than 350 sheets of A4 paper and 350 sides of text.

5.2 All documents in the bundle shall (a) be copied on one side of paper only, unless the court has specifically directed otherwise, and (b) be typed or printed in a font no smaller than 12 point and with 1½ or double spacing.

5.3 The ring binder or lever arch file shall have clearly marked on the front and the spine:

(a) the title and number of the case;
(b) the place where the case has been listed;
(c) the hearing date and time;
(d) if known, the name of the judge hearing the case; and
(e) where in accordance with a direction of the court there is more than one ring binder or lever arch file, a distinguishing letter (A, B, C etc).

Timetable for preparing and lodging the bundle

6.1 The party preparing the bundle shall, whether or not the bundle has been agreed, provide a paginated index to all other parties not less than 4 working days before the hearing.

6.2 Where counsel is to be instructed at any hearing, a paginated bundle shall (if not already in counsel's possession) be delivered to counsel by the person instructing that counsel not less than 3 working days before the hearing.

6.3 The bundle (with the exception of the preliminary documents if and insofar as they are not then available) shall be lodged with the court not less than 2 working days before the hearing, or at such other time as may be specified by the court.

6.4 The preliminary documents shall be lodged with the court no later than 11 am on the day before the hearing and, where the hearing is before a judge of the High Court and the name of the judge is known, shall (with the exception of the authorities, which are to be lodged in hard copy and not sent by email) at the same time be sent by email to the judge's clerk.

Lodging the bundle

7.1 The bundle shall be lodged at the appropriate office. If the bundle is lodged in the wrong place the court may:

(a) treat the bundle as having not been lodged; and
(b) take the steps referred to in paragraph 12.

7.2 Unless the court has given some other direction as to where the bundle in any particular case is to be lodged (for example a direction that the bundle is to be lodged with the judge's clerk) the bundle shall be lodged:

(a) for hearings at the RCJ, in the office of the Clerk of the Rules, 1st Mezzanine (Rm 1M), Queen's Building, Royal Courts of Justice, Strand, London WC2A 2LL (DX 44450 Strand);
(b) for hearings at any other place, at such place as may be designated by the designated family judge responsible for that place and in default of any such designation at the court office for the place where the hearing is to take place.

7.3 Any bundle sent to the court by post, DX or courier shall be clearly addressed to the appropriate office and shall show the date and place of the hearing on the outside of any packaging as well as on the bundle itself.

7.4 Unless the court has given some other direction or paragraph 7.5 applies only one copy of the bundle shall be lodged with the court but the party who is responsible for lodging the bundle shall bring to court at each hearing at which oral evidence may be called a copy of the bundle for use by the witnesses.

7.5 In the case of a hearing listed before a bench of magistrates four copies of the bundle shall be lodged with the court.

7.6 In the case of hearings at the RCJ or at any other place where the designated family judge responsible for that place has directed that this paragraph shall apply, parties shall:

(a) if the bundle or preliminary documents are delivered personally, ensure that they obtain a receipt from the clerk accepting it or them; and
(b) if the bundle or preliminary documents are sent by post or DX, ensure that they obtain proof of posting or despatch.

The receipt (or proof of posting or despatch, as the case may be) shall be brought to court on the day of the hearing and must be produced to the court if requested. If the receipt (or proof of posting or despatch) cannot be produced to the court the judge may: (a) treat the bundle as having not been lodged; and (b) take the steps referred to in paragraph 12.

Lodging the bundle – additional requirements for Family Division or Family Court cases being heard at the RCJ

8.1 Bundles or preliminary documents delivered after 11 am on the day before the hearing may not be accepted by the Clerk of the Rules and if not shall be delivered:

(a) in a case where the hearing is before a judge of the High Court, directly to the clerk of the judge hearing the case;
(b) in a case where the hearing is before any other judge, to such place as may be specified by the Clerk of the Rules.

8.2 Upon learning before which judge a hearing is to take place, the clerk to counsel, or other advocate, representing the party in the position of applicant shall no later than 3 pm the day before the hearing:

(a) in a case where the hearing is before a judge of the High Court, telephone the clerk of the judge hearing the case;
(b) in a case where the hearing is before any other judge email the Clerk of the Rules at RCJ.familyhighcourt@hmcts.gsi.gov.uk;

to ascertain whether the judge has received the bundle (including the preliminary documents) and, if not, shall organise prompt delivery by the applicant's solicitor.

Removing and re-lodging the bundle

9.1 Unless either the court wishes to retain the bundle or specific alternative arrangements have been agreed with the court, the party responsible for the bundle shall, following completion of the hearing, retrieve the bundle from the court immediately or, if that is not practicable, collect it from the court within 5 working days. Bundles which are not collected in due time are liable to be destroyed without further notice.

9.2 The bundle shall be re-lodged for the next and any further hearings in accordance with the provisions of this practice direction and in a form which complies with para 4.7.

Time estimates

10.1 In every case a time estimate (which shall be inserted at the front of the bundle) shall be prepared which shall so far as practicable be agreed by all parties and shall:

(a) specify separately: (i) the time estimated to be required for judicial pre-reading; and (ii) the time required for hearing all evidence and submissions; and (iii) the time estimated to be required for preparing and delivering judgment;
(b) be prepared on the basis that before they give evidence all witnesses will have read all relevant filed statements and reports; and
(c) take appropriate account of any additional time likely to be incurred by the use of interpreters or intermediaries.

10.2 Once a case has been listed, any change in time estimates shall be notified immediately by telephone (and then immediately confirmed in writing):

(a) in the case of hearings in the RCJ, to the Clerk of the Rules; and
(b) in the case of hearings elsewhere, to the relevant listing officer.

Taking cases out of the list

11.1 As soon as it becomes known that a hearing will no longer be effective, whether as a result of the parties reaching agreement or for any other reason, the parties and their representatives shall immediately notify the court by telephone and email which shall be confirmed by letter. The letter, which shall wherever possible be a joint letter sent on behalf of all parties with their signatures applied or appended, shall include:

(a) a short background summary of the case;

(b) the written consent of each party who consents and, where a party does not consent, details of the steps which have been taken to obtain that party's consent and, where known, an explanation of why that consent has not been given;
(c) a draft of the order being sought; and
(d) enough information to enable the court to decide (i) whether to take the case out of the list and (ii) whether to make the proposed order.

Penalties for failure to comply with the practice direction

12.1 Failure to comply with any part of this practice direction may result in the judge removing the case from the list or putting the case further back in the list and may also result in a 'wasted costs' order or some other adverse costs order.

Commencement of the practice direction and application of other practice directions

13.1 Subject to paragraph 13.2 this practice direction shall have effect from 22 April 2014.

13.2 Sub-paragraphs (a)–(c) and (e)–(g) of paragraph 4.1 and paragraphs 5.1 and 5.3(e) shall have effect from 31 July 2014. In the meantime paragraphs 5.1 and 5.3(e) shall have effect as if:

(a) paragraph 5.1 read 'The bundle shall be contained in one or more A4 size ring binders or lever arch files (each lever arch file being limited to no more than 350 pages).'; and
(b) in paragraph 5.3(e) the words 'in accordance with a direction of the court' were omitted.

14.1 This practice direction should where appropriate be read in conjunction with the Public Law Outline 2014 (PD 12A) and the Child Arrangements Programme 2014 (PD 12B). In particular, nothing in this practice direction is to be read as removing or altering any obligation to comply with the requirements of the Public Law Outline 2014 and the Child Arrangements Programme 2014.

PRACTICE GUIDANCE 12 JULY 2010 – MCKENZIE FRIENDS (CIVIL AND FAMILY COURTS)

1 This Guidance applies to civil and family proceedings in the Court of Appeal (Civil Division), the High Court of Justice, the County Courts and the Family Proceedings Court in the Magistrates' Courts.[1] It is issued as guidance (**not** as a Practice Direction) by the Master of the Rolls, as Head of Civil Justice, and the President of the Family Division, as Head of Family Justice. It is intended to remind courts and litigants of the principles set out in the authorities and supersedes the guidance contained in *Practice Note (Family Courts: McKenzie Friends) (No 2)* [2008] 1 WLR 2757, which is now withdrawn.[2] It is issued in light of the increase in litigants-in-person (litigants) in all levels of the civil and family courts.

The Right to Reasonable Assistance

2 Litigants have the right to have reasonable assistance from a layperson, sometimes called a McKenzie Friend (MF). Litigants assisted by MFs remain litigants-in-person. MFs have no independent right to provide assistance. They have no right to act as advocates or to carry out the conduct of litigation.

What McKenzie Friends may do

3 MFs may: i) provide moral support for litigants; ii) take notes; iii) help with case papers; iv) quietly give advice on any aspect of the conduct of the case.

What McKenzie Friends may not do

4 MFs may not: i) act as the litigants' agent in relation to the proceedings; ii) manage litigants' cases outside court, for example by signing court documents; or iii) address the court, make oral submissions or examine witnesses.

Exercising the Right to Reasonable Assistance

5 While litigants ordinarily have a right to receive reasonable assistance from MFs the court retains the power to refuse to permit such assistance. The court may do so where it is satisfied that, in that case, the interests of justice and fairness do not require the litigant to receive such assistance.

6 A litigant who wishes to exercise this right should inform the judge as soon as possible indicating who the MF will be. The proposed MF should produce a short curriculum vitae or other statement setting out relevant experience, confirming that he or she has no interest in the case and understands the MF's role and the duty of confidentiality.

7 If the court considers that there might be grounds for circumscribing the right to receive such assistance, or a party objects to the presence of, or assistance given by a MF, it is not for the litigant to justify the exercise of the right. It is for the court or the objecting party to provide sufficient reasons why the litigant should not receive such assistance.

8 When considering whether to circumscribe the right to assistance or refuse a MF permission to attend the right to a fair trial is engaged. The matter should be considered carefully. The litigant

should be given a reasonable opportunity to argue the point. The proposed MF should not be excluded from that hearing and should normally be allowed to help the litigant.

9 Where proceedings are in *closed court*, i.e. the hearing is in chambers, is in private, or the proceedings relate to a child, the litigant is required to justify the MF's presence in court. The presumption in favour of permitting a MF to attend such hearings, and thereby enable litigants to exercise the right to assistance, is a strong one.

10 The court may refuse to allow a litigant to exercise the right to receive assistance at the start of a hearing. The court can also circumscribe the right during the course of a hearing. It may be refused at the start of a hearing or later circumscribed where the court forms the view that a MF may give, has given, or is giving, assistance which impedes the efficient administration of justice. However, the court should also consider whether a firm and unequivocal warning to the litigant and/or MF might suffice in the first instance.

11 A decision by the court not to curtail assistance from a MF should be regarded as final, save on the ground of subsequent misconduct by the MF or on the ground that the MF's continuing presence will impede the efficient administration of justice. In such event the court should give a short judgment setting out the reasons why it has curtailed the right to assistance. Litigants may appeal such decisions. MFs have no standing to do so.

12 The following factors should not be taken to justify the court refusing to permit a litigant receiving such assistance:

- (i) The case or application is simple or straightforward, or is, for instance, a directions or case management hearing;
- (ii) The litigant appears capable of conducting the case without assistance;
- (iii) The litigant is unrepresented through choice;
- (iv) The other party is not represented;
- (v) The proposed MF belongs to an organisation that promotes a particular cause;
- (vi) The proceedings are confidential and the court papers contain sensitive information relating to a family's affairs.

13 A litigant may be denied the assistance of a MF because its provision might undermine or has undermined the efficient administration of justice. Examples of circumstances where this might arise are: i) the assistance is being provided for an improper purpose; ii) the assistance is unreasonable in nature or degree; iii) the MF is subject to a civil proceedings order or a civil restraint order; iv) the MF is using the litigant as a puppet; v) the MF is directly or indirectly conducting the litigation; vi) the court is not satisfied that the MF fully understands the duty of confidentiality.

14 Where a litigant is receiving assistance from a MF in care proceedings, the court should consider the MF's attendance at any advocates' meetings directed by the court, and, with regard to cases commenced after 1.4.08, consider directions in accordance with paragraph 13.2 of the Practice Direction Guide to Case Management in Public Law Proceedings.

15 Litigants are permitted to communicate any information, including filed evidence, relating to the proceedings to MFs for the purpose of obtaining advice or assistance in relation to the proceedings.

16 Legal representatives should ensure that documents are served on litigants in good time to enable them to seek assistance regarding their content from MFs in advance of any hearing or advocates' meeting.

17 The High Court can, under its inherent jurisdiction, impose a civil restraint order on MFs who repeatedly act in ways that undermine the efficient administration of justice.

Rights of audience and rights to conduct litigation

18 MFs do **not** have a right of audience or a right to conduct litigation. It is a criminal offence to exercise rights of audience or to conduct litigation unless properly qualified and authorised to do so by an appropriate regulatory body or, in the case of an otherwise unqualified or unauthorised individual (i.e., a lay individual including a MF), the court grants such rights on a case-by-case basis.[3]

19 Courts should be slow to grant any application from a litigant for a right of audience or a right to conduct litigation to any lay person, including a MF. This is because a person exercising such rights must ordinarily be properly trained, be under professional discipline (including an obligation to insure against liability for negligence) and be subject to an overriding duty to the court. These requirements are necessary for the protection of all parties to litigation and are essential to the proper administration of justice.

20 Any application for a right of audience or a right to conduct litigation to be granted to any lay person should therefore be considered very carefully. The court should only be prepared to grant such rights where there is good reason to do so taking into account all the circumstances of the case, which are likely to vary greatly. Such grants should not be extended to lay persons automatically or without due consideration. They should not be granted for mere convenience.

21 Examples of the type of special circumstances which have been held to justify the grant of a right of audience to a lay person, including a MF, are: i) that person is a close relative of the litigant; ii) health problems preclude the litigant from addressing the court, or conducting litigation, and the litigant cannot afford to pay for a qualified legal representative; iii) the litigant is relatively inarticulate and prompting by that person may unnecessarily prolong the proceedings.

22 It is for the litigant to persuade the court that the circumstances of the case are such that it is in the interests of justice for the court to grant a lay person a right of audience or a right to conduct litigation.

23 The grant of a right of audience or a right to conduct litigation to lay persons who hold themselves out as professional advocates or professional MFs or who seek to exercise such rights on a regular basis, whether for reward or not, will however only be granted in exceptional circumstances. To do otherwise would tend to subvert the will of Parliament.

24 If a litigant wants a lay person to be granted a right of audience, an application must be made at the start of the hearing. If a right to conduct litigation is sought such an application must be made at the earliest possible time and must be made, in any event, before the lay person does anything which amounts to the conduct of litigation. It is for litigants to persuade the court, on a case-by-case basis, that the grant of such rights is justified.

25 Rights of audience and the right to conduct litigation are separate rights. The grant of one right to a lay person does not mean that a grant of the other right has been made. If both rights are sought their grant must be applied for individually and justified separately.

26 Having granted either a right of audience or a right to conduct litigation, the court has the power to remove either right. The grant of such rights in one set of proceedings cannot be relied on as a precedent supporting their grant in future proceedings.

Remuneration

27 Litigants can enter into lawful agreements to pay fees to MFs for the provision of reasonable assistance in court or out of court by, for instance, carrying out clerical or mechanical activities, such as photocopying documents, preparing bundles, delivering documents to opposing parties or the court, or the provision of legal advice in connection with court proceedings. Such fees cannot be lawfully recovered from the opposing party.

28 Fees said to be incurred by MFs for carrying out the conduct of litigation, where the court has not granted such a right, cannot lawfully be recovered from either the litigant for whom they carry out such work or the opposing party.

29 Fees said to be incurred by MFs for carrying out the conduct of litigation after the court has granted such a right are in principle recoverable from the litigant for whom the work is carried out. Such fees cannot be lawfully recovered from the opposing party.

30 Fees said to be incurred by MFs for exercising a right of audience following the grant of such a right by the court are in principle recoverable from the litigant on whose behalf the right is exercised. Such fees are also recoverable, in principle, from the opposing party as a recoverable disbursement: CPR 48.6(2) and 48(6)(3)(ii).

Personal Support Unit & Citizen's Advice Bureau

31 Litigants should also be aware of the services provided by local Personal Support Units and Citizens' Advice Bureaux. The PSU at the Royal Courts of Justice in London can be contacted on 020 7947 7701, by email at cbps@bello.co.uk or at the enquiry desk. The CAB at the Royal Courts of Justice in London can be contacted on 020 7947 6564 or at the enquiry desk.

Lord Neuberger of Abbotsbury
Master of the Rolls

Sir Nicholas Wall
President of the Family Division

PRACTICE GUIDANCE 16 JANUARY 2014 – TRANSPARENCY IN THE FAMILY COURTS: PUBLICATION OF JUDGMENTS

The purpose of this Guidance

1 This Guidance (together with similar Guidance issued at the same time for the Court of Protection) is intended to bring about an immediate and significant change in practice in relation to the publication of judgments in family courts and the Court of Protection.

2 In both courts there is a need for greater transparency in order to improve public understanding of the court process and confidence in the court system. At present too few judgments are made available to the public, which has a legitimate interest in being able to read what is being done by the judges in its name. The Guidance will have the effect of increasing the number of judgments available for publication (even if they will often need to be published in appropriately anonymised form).

3 In July 2011 Sir Nicholas Wall P issued, jointly with Bob Satchwell, Executive Director of the Society of Editors, a paper, *The Family Courts: Media Access & Reporting* (Media Access & Reporting), setting out a statement of the current state of the law. In their preface they recognised that the debate on increased transparency and public confidence in the family courts would move forward and that future consideration of this difficult and sensitive area would need to include the questions of access to and reporting of proceedings by the media, whilst maintaining the privacy of the families involved. The paper is to be found at:

http://www.judiciary.gov.uk/Resources/JCO/Documents/Guidance/family-courts¬media-july2011.pdf

4 In April 2013 I issued a statement, *View from the President's Chambers: the Process of Reform*, [2013] Fam Law 548, in which I identified transparency as one of the three strands in the reforms which the family justice system is currently undergoing. I said:

> 'I am determined to take steps to improve access to and reporting of family proceedings. I am determined that the new Family Court should not be saddled, as the family courts are at present, with the charge that we are a system of secret and unaccountable justice. Work, commenced by my predecessor, is well underway. I hope to be in a position to make important announcements in the near future.'

5 That applies just as much to the issue of transparency in the Court of Protection.

6 Very similar issues arise in both the Family Court (as it will be from April 2014) and the Court of Protection in relation to the need to protect the personal privacy of children and vulnerable adults. The applicable rules differ, however, and this is something that needs attention. My starting point is that so far as possible the same rules and principles should apply in both the family courts (in due course the Family Court) and the Court of Protection.

7 I propose to adopt an incremental approach. Initially I am issuing this Guidance. This will be followed by further Guidance and in due course more formal Practice Directions and changes to

the Rules (the Court of Protection Rules 2007 and the Family Procedure Rules 2010). Changes to primary legislation are unlikely in the near future.

8 As provided in paragraph 14 below, this Guidance applies only to judgments delivered by certain judges. In due course, following the introduction of the Family Court, consideration will be given to extending it to judgments delivered by other judges (including lay justices).

The legal framework

9 The effect of section 12 of the Administration of Justice Act 1960 is that it is a contempt of court to publish a judgment in a family court case involving children unless either the judgment has been delivered in public or, where delivered in private, the judge has authorised publication. In the latter case, the judge normally gives permission for the judgment to be published on condition that the published version protects the anonymity of the children and members of their family.

10 In every case the terms on which publication is permitted are a matter for the judge and will be set out by the judge in a rubric at the start of the judgment.

11 The normal terms as described in paragraph 9 may be appropriate in a case where no-one wishes to discuss the proceedings otherwise than anonymously. But they may be inappropriate, for example, where parents who have been exonerated in care proceedings wish to discuss their experiences in public, identifying themselves and making use of the judgment. Equally, they may be inappropriate in cases where findings have been made against a person and someone else contends and/or the judge concludes that it is in the public interest for that person to be identified in any published version of the judgment.

12 If any party wishes to identify himself or herself, or any other party or person, as being a person referred to in any published version of the judgment, their remedy is to seek an order of the court and a suitable modification of the rubric: Media Access & Reporting, para 82; *Re RB (Adult) (No 4)* [2011] EWHC 3017 (Fam), [2012] 1 FLR 466, paras [17], [19].

13 Nothing in this Guidance affects the exercise by the judge in any particular case of whatever powers would otherwise be available to regulate the publication of material relating to the proceedings. For example, where a judgment is likely to be used in a way that would defeat the purpose of any anonymisation, it is open to the judge to refuse to publish the judgment or to make an order restricting its use.

Guidance

14 This Guidance takes effect from 3 February 2014. It applies

- (i) in the family courts (and in due course in the Family Court), to judgments delivered by Circuit Judges, High Court Judges and persons sitting as judges of the High Court; and
- (ii) to all judgments delivered by High Court Judges (and persons sitting as judges of the High Court) exercising the inherent jurisdiction to make orders in respect of children and incapacitated or vulnerable adults.

15 The following paragraphs of this Guidance distinguish between two classes of judgment:

- (i) those that the judge *must* ordinarily allow to be published (paragraphs 16 and 17); and
- (ii) those that *may* be published (paragraph 18).

16 Permission to publish a judgment should always be given whenever the judge concludes that publication would be in the public interest and whether or not a request has been made by a party or the media.

17 Where a judgment relates to matters set out in Schedule 1 or 2 below and a written judgment already exists in a publishable form or the judge has already ordered that the judgment be transcribed, the starting point is that permission should be given for the judgment to be published unless there are compelling reasons why the judgment should not be published.

Schedule 1

In the family courts (and in due course in the Family Court), including in proceedings under the inherent jurisdiction of the High Court relating to children, judgments arising from:

(i) a substantial contested fact-finding hearing at which serious allegations, for example allegations of significant physical, emotional or sexual harm, have been determined;
(ii) the making or refusal of a final care order or supervision order under Part 4 of the Children Act 1989, or any order for the discharge of any such order, except where the order is made with the consent of all participating parties;
(iii) the making or refusal of a placement order or adoption order under the Adoption and Children Act 2002, or any order for the discharge of any such order, except where the order is made with the consent of all participating parties;
(iv) the making or refusal of any declaration or order authorising a deprivation of liberty, including an order for a secure accommodation order under section 25 of the Children Act 1989;
(v) any application for an order involving the giving or withholding of serious medical treatment;
(vi) any application for an order involving a restraint on publication of information relating to the proceedings.

Schedule 2

In proceedings under the inherent jurisdiction of the High Court relating to incapacitated or vulnerable adults, judgments arising from:

(i) any application for a declaration or order involving a deprivation or possible deprivation of liberty;
(ii) any application for an order involving the giving or withholding of serious medical treatment;
(iii) any application for an order that an incapacitated or vulnerable adult be moved into or out of a residential establishment or other institution;
(iv) any application for a declaration as to capacity to marry or to consent to sexual relations;
(v) any application for an order involving a restraint on publication of information relating to the proceedings.

18 In all other cases, the starting point is that permission may be given for the judgment to be published whenever a party or an accredited member of the media applies for an order permitting publication, and the judge concludes that permission for the judgment to be published should be given.

19 In deciding whether and if so when to publish a judgment, the judge shall have regard to all the circumstances, the rights arising under any relevant provision of the European Convention on Human Rights, including Articles 6 (right to a fair hearing), 8 (respect for private and family life) and 10 (freedom of expression), and the effect of publication upon any current or potential criminal proceedings.

20 In all cases where a judge gives permission for a judgment to be published:

(i) public authorities and expert witnesses should be named in the judgment approved for publication, unless there are compelling reasons why they should not be so named;

(ii) the children who are the subject of the proceedings in the family courts, and other members of their family, and the person who is the subject of proceedings under the inherent jurisdiction of the High Court relating to incapacitated or vulnerable adults, and other members of their family, should not normally be named in the judgment approved for publication unless the judge otherwise orders;

(iii) anonymity in the judgment as published should not normally extend beyond protecting the privacy of the children and adults who are the subject of the proceedings and other members of their families, unless there are compelling reasons to do so.

21 Unless the judgment is already in anonymised form or the judge otherwise orders, any necessary anonymisation of the judgment shall be carried out, in the case of judgments being published pursuant to paragraphs 16 and 17 above, by the solicitor for the applicant in the proceedings and, in the case of a judgment being published pursuant to paragraph 18 above, by the solicitor for the party or person applying for publication of the judgment. The anonymised version of the judgment must be submitted to the judge within a period specified by the judge for approval. The version approved for publication will contain such rubric as the judge specifies. Unless the rubric specified by the judge provides expressly to the contrary every published judgment shall be deemed to contain the following rubric:

> 'This judgment was delivered in private. The judge has given leave for this version of the judgment to be published on condition that (irrespective of what is contained in the judgment) in any published version of the judgment the anonymity of the children and members of their family must be strictly preserved. All persons, including representatives of the media, must ensure that this condition is strictly complied with. Failure to do so will be a contempt of court.'

22 The judge will need to consider who should be ordered to bear the cost of transcribing the judgment. Unless the judge otherwise orders:

(i) in cases falling under paragraph 16 the cost of transcribing the judgment is to be at public expense;

(ii) subject to (i), in cases falling under paragraph 17 the cost of transcribing the judgment shall be borne equally by the parties to the proceedings;

(iii) in cases falling under paragraph 18, the cost of transcribing the judgment shall be borne by the party or person applying for publication of the judgment.

23 In all cases where permission is given for a judgment to be published, the version of the judgment approved for publication shall be made available, upon payment of any appropriate charge that may be required, to any person who requests a copy. Where a judgment to which paragraph 16 or 17 applies is approved for publication, it shall as soon as reasonably practicable be placed by the court on the BAILII website. Where a judgment to which paragraph 18 applies is approved for publication, the judge shall consider whether it should be placed on the BAILII website and, if so, it shall as soon as reasonably practicable be placed by the court on the BAILII website.

Sir James Munby
President of the Family Division

PRACTICE GUIDANCE 18 JANUARY 2017 – FAMILY COURT – DURATION OF EX PARTE (WITHOUT NOTICE) ORDERS

This Guidance was originally issued on 13 October 2014. This revised Guidance, issued on 18 January 2017, supersedes the previous Guidance.

1 The Magistrates' Association and the National Bench Chairs' Forum have raised with me the question of whether it is proper to grant an ex parte non-molestation injunction for an unlimited period. They suggest that practice varies. They express the view that to grant such an order for an unlimited time is wrong in principle.

2 In expressing that view, the Magistrates' Association and the National Bench Chairs' Forum are entirely correct. To grant an ex parte (without notice) injunction for an unlimited time is wrong in principle. The practice of granting such orders for an unlimited time, if this is still occurring, must stop.

3 Subject only to paragraph 8, the same principles, as set out below, apply to all ex parte (without notice) injunctive orders made by the Family Court or by the Family Division, irrespective of the subject matter of the proceedings or the terms of the order.

4 The law is to be found in *Horgan v Horgan* [2002] EWCA Civ 1371, paras 5-6 (Ward LJ), *R (Casey) v Restormel Borough Council* [2007] EWHC 2554 (Admin), paras 37-41 (Munby J), *In re C (A Child) (Family Proceedings: Practice)* [2013] EWCA Civ 1412, [2014] 1 WLR 2182, [2014] 1 FLR 1239, para 15 (Ryder LJ), and *Re A (A Child)* [2016] EWCA Civ 572, [2016] 4 WLR 111, paras 49-61, esp paras 59-61 (Munby P).

5 The relevant principles, compliance with which is essential, are as follows:

(i) An ex parte (without notice) injunctive order must never be made without limit of time. There must be a fixed end date. It is not sufficient merely to specify a return day. The order must specify on its face and in clear terms precisely when it expires (eg, 12 noon on 20 March 2017).

(ii) The order must also fix a return day. The order must specify the date, time and place of the hearing on the return day. The return day should normally be no more than 14 days after the date when the order was made. How long the hearing on the return day should be listed for must be a matter for the discretion of the judge. However, having regard to paragraph 6, often a very short listing may well be appropriate.

(iii) Careful consideration needs to be given to the duration of any order made ex parte (without notice). Many orders will be of short duration, typically no more than 14 days. But in appropriate cases involving personal protection, such as non-molestation injunctions granted in accordance with Part IV of the Family Law Act 1996, the order itself can be for a longer period, such as 6 or even 12 months, provided that the order specifies a return day within no more than 14 days. This must be a matter for the discretion of the judge, but a period longer than 6 months is likely to be appropriate only where the allegation is of long term abuse or where some other good reason is shown. Conversely, a period shorter than 6 months may be appropriate in a case where there appears to be a one-off problem that may subside in weeks rather than months.

(iv) The order must make it clear that (a) it was made in the absence of the respondent and that the court has considered only the evidence of the applicant and (b) the court has made no finding of fact. Where the evidence is written, it must be identified in the order. Where, exceptionally, the court has received oral or other evidence (eg, a photograph) that evidence should be recorded on the face of the order or reduced to writing and served with the order.

(v) Where the order has been made in accordance with Part IV of the Family Law Act 1996 it must recite that the court has had regard to sections 45(1) and (2) of the Act.

(vi) The order (see FPR 18.10(3)) 'must contain a statement of the right to make an application to set aside or vary the order under rule 18.11.' The phrase 'liberty to apply' is not sufficient for this purpose. The order must spell out that the respondent is entitled, without waiting for the return day, to apply to set aside or vary the order.

(vii) If the respondent does apply to set aside or vary the order the court must list the application as a matter of urgency, within a matter of days at most.

6 Experience suggests that in certain types of case, for example, non-molestation or other orders granted in accordance with Part IV of the Family Law Act 1996, the respondent frequently neither applies to set aside or vary the order nor attends the hearing on the return day.

(i) When, in such cases, there is no attendance by the respondent and the order, having been served, does not require amendment there is no need for re-service. The order made on the return should however record that the respondent, although afforded the opportunity to be heard, has neither attended nor sought to be heard.

(ii) If, however, variation of the original order is sought by the applicant (eg by extending the ambit or the duration of the order) then:

   (a) Paragraphs 5(i), (iii)-(v) must be complied with in relation to the new order and the new order will need to be served.

   (b) Unless, before the return day, the respondent was given proper notice of the proposed amendments, either in the application or in the initial order, (a) the new order must specify a new return day, and (b) paragraph 5(ii) must be complied with in relation to the new order.

7 I remind all practitioners and judges of the principle, which applies to all ex parte (without notice) injunctive orders made by the Family Court or by the Family Division, irrespective of the subject matter of the proceedings or the terms of the order, that a without notice application will normally be appropriate only if:

(a) there is an emergency or other great urgency, so that it is impossible to give any notice, however short or informal, or

(b) there is a real risk that, if alerted to what is proposed, if 'tipped off', the respondent will take steps in advance of the hearing to thwart the court's order or otherwise to defeat the ends of justice. In an appropriate case this can justify the grant of a non-molestation injunction without notice, lest the respondent, having been served with an application, further molests his (or her) victim or exerts pressure on her (him) to abandon the proceedings.

8 Nothing in this Guidance derogates from, or otherwise modifies, the principles and safeguards to be observed on an application for an ex parte (without notice) freezing or search order: see *L v K (Freezing Orders: Principles and Safeguards)* [2013] EWHC 1735 (Fam), [2014] Fam 35.

Sir James Munby
President of the Family Division

PART III

KEY CASES

CATEGORISED BY TOPIC

APPLICATIONS FOR LEAVE

Re G; Re Z (Children: Sperm Donors: Leave to Apply for Children Act Orders) [2013] 1 FLR 1334

Re M (Care: Contact: Grandmother's Application for Leave) [1995] 2 FLR 86

Re S (Contact: Application by Sibling) [1998] 2 FLR 897

Re W (Care Proceedings: Leave to Apply) [2005] 2 FLR 468

APPLICATIONS FOR LEAVE ON NOTICE

Re F and R (Section 8 Order: Grandparent's Application) [1995] 1 FLR 524

Re M (Prohibited Steps Order: Application for Leave) [1993] 1 FLR 275

Re W (Contact Application: Procedure) [2000] 1 FLR 263

ARBITRATION

AI v MT (alternative dispute resolution) [2013] 2 FLR 371

S v S (Financial Remedies: Arbitral Award) [2014] 1 FLR 1257

BANKRUPTCY

Hill v Haines [2008] 1 FLR 1192

Paulin v Paulin [2009] 2 FLR 354, CA

CAPITALISATION AND VARIATION OF PERIODICAL PAYMENTS

Duxbury v Duxbury [1987] 1 FLR 7, CA

Hvorostovsky v Hvorostovsky [2009] 2 FLR 1574

Lauder [2007] 2 FLR 802

Pearce v Pearce [2003] 2 FLR 1144 (CA)

Vaughan v Vaughan [2010] 2 FLR 242

VB v JP [2008] 1 FLR 742

CHILD ARRANGEMENTS ORDERS (CONTACT)

Determining with whom a child lives

Re H (Contact: Adverse Finding of Fact) [2011] 2 FLR 1201

Domestic abuse

H (Contact: Domestic Violence) [2000] 2 FLR 334

Re H (Interim Contact: Domestic Violence Allegations) [2014] 1 FLR 41

Re L (Contact: Domestic Violence); Re v (Contact: Domestic Violence); Re M (Contact: Domestic Violence); Re H (Contact: Domestic Violence) [2000] 2 FLR 334

Re W (Children: Domestic Violence) [2014] 1 FLR 260

Duty on parents to work together

Re H-B (Contact) [2015] EWCA Civ 389

Re J and K [2015] 1 FLR 86

Re W (Contact: Permission to Appeal) [2013] 1 FLR 609

Re W (Direct Contact) [2013] 1 FLR 494

Grandparents

Re A (Section 8 Order: Grandparent Application) [1995] 2 FLR 153

Re W (Contact: Application by Grandparent) [1997] 1 FLR 793

Importance of biological parentage

Re A (A Child: Joint Residence: Parental Responsibility) [2008] 2 FLR 1593

A v B and C (Lesbian Co-parents: Role of Father) [2012] 2 FLR 607

Re B (A Child) [2010] 1 FLR 551

DB v AB and CB [2014] 2 FLR 1197

Re G (Shared Residence Order: Biological Mother of Donor Egg) [2014] 2 FLR 897

Re H (A Child) [2012] 2 FLR 627

H v S (Surrogacy Agreement) [2016] 1 FLR 723

Step-parents

Re H (A Minor) (Contact) [1994] 2 FLR 776

CHILD ARRANGEMENTS ORDERS (LIVING ARRANGEMENTS)

Importance of biological parentage

Re E-R (A Child) [2016] 1 FLR 521

Re B (A Child) [2010] 1 FLR 551

Re G (Children) [2006] 2 FLR 629, HL

Re G (Shared Residence Order: Biological Mother of Donor Egg) [2014] 2 FLR 897

H v S (Surrogacy Agreement) [2016] 1 FLR 723

COMPANIES – TREATMENT

A v A [2006] 2 FLR 115

R v R (Financial Relief: Company Valuation) [2005] 2 FLR 365

V v V (Financial Relief) [2005] 2 FLR 697

COMPANIES – VALUATION

Charman v Charman (No 2) [2007] 1 FLR 593

G v G (Financial Provision: Equal Division) [2002] 2 FLR 1143

H v H [2008] 2 FLR 2092

Irvine v Irvine [2006] EWHC 583 (Ch)

NA v MA [2007] 1 FLR 1760

P v P (Financial Relief: Illiquid Assets) [2005] 1 FLR 548

Re C (Divorce: Financial Relief) [2008] 1 FLR 625

Re Bird Precision Bellows Ltd [1984] 1 Ch 419, CA

COMPANIES – CORPORATE VEIL

Ben Hashem v Al Shayif [2009] 1 FLR 115

Gowers v Gowers [2012] 1 FLR 1040

M v M and Others [2014] 1 FLR 439

Prest v Petrodel Resources Ltd & Others [2013] 2 FLR 732

COMPENSATION

H v H [2014] 2 FLR 1338

Hvorostovsky v Hvorostovsky [2009] 2 FLR 1574

Lauder v Lauder [2007] 2 FLR 802

RP v RP [2007] 1 FLR 2105

CONDUCT

FZ v SZ and Others (Ancillary Relief: Conduct: Valuations) [2011] 1 FLR 64

H v H (Financial Relief: Attempted Murder as Conduct) [2006] 1 FLR 990

M v M (Third Party Subpoena: Financial Conduct) [2006] 2 FLR 1253

Miller v Miller; McFarlane v McFarlane [2006] 1 FLR 1186

S v S (Non-matrimonial Property: Conduct) [2007] 1 FLR 1496

WF v NF [2007] EWHC 3050 (Fam)

CONSENT ORDERS

Edgar v Edgar (1981) 2 FLR 19

Rose v Rose [2002] 1 FLR 978

TW v PL (Agreement) [2014] 2 FLR 106

X v X (Y and Z intervening) [2002] 1 FLR 508

Xydhias v Xydhias [1999] 1 FLR 683

CONTRIBUTIONS

Charman v Charman (No 4) [2007] 1 FLR 1246, CA

G v G (Financial Provision: Equal Division) [2002] 2 FLR 1143

H v H [2010] 1 FLR 1864

Lauder v Lauder [2007] 2 FLR 802

Sorrell v Sorell [2006] 1 FLR 497

White v White [2000] 2 FLR 981

COSTS

Children proceedings

HH v BLW (Appeal: Cost: Proportionality) [2013] 1 FLR 420

Re G (Contact Proceedings: Cost) [2014] 1 FLR 517

MG and JG v JF (Child Maintenance: Costs Allowance) [2016] 1 FLR 424

R v R (Costs: Child Case) [1997] 2 FLR 95

Financial

Baker v Rowe [2010] 1 FLR 761

Judge v Judge [2009] 1 FLR 1287

Joy v Joy-Morancho [2016] 1 FLR 815

General

Calderbank v Calderbank (1975) FLR Rep 113, CA

Gojkovic v Gojkovic (No 2) [1991] 2 FLR 233

Sears Tooth (a firm) v Payne Hicks Beach (a firm) and others [1997] 2 FLR 116

COST ALLOWANCES – SCHEDULE 1, CHILDREN ACT 1989

CF v KM [2011] 1 FLR 208

Currey v Currey (No 2) [2007] 1 FLR 946

G v G (Child Maintenance: Interim Costs Provision) [2010] 2 FLR 1264

M-T v T [2007] 2 FLR 925

R v F (Schedule One: Child Maintenance: Mother's Costs of Contact Proceedings) [2011] 2 FLR 991

Re PG and TW (No 1) (Child: Financial Provision: Legal Funding) [2014] 1 FLR 508

COSTS ORDERS – SCHEDULE 1, CHILDREN ACT 1989

KS v ND (Schedule 1: Appeal: Costs) [2013] 2 FLR 698

DECLARATION OF MARITAL STATUS

Abbassi v Abbassi and Another [2006] 2 FLR 415

Galloway v Goldstein [2012] 1 FLR 1254

Solovyev v Solovyeva [2015] 1 FLR 734

DEPARTURE FROM CAFCASS REPORT

Re J (Children) (Residence: Expert Evidence) [2001] 2 FCR 44

Re P (Custody of Children: Split Custody Order) [1991] 1 FLR 337

Re R (Residence Order) [2010] 1 FLR 509

Re V (Residence: Review) [1995] 2 FLR 1010

DISCLOSURE

Gohil v Gohil [2015] 2 FLR 1289

Imerman v Tchenguiz [2010] 2 FLR 814

Sharland v Sharland [2015] 2 FLR 1367

Tchenguiz-Imerman v Imerman [2014] 1 FLR 232

Young v Young [2014] 2 FLR 786

DISCLOSURE – CHILDREN PROCEEDINGS

Re A and B (Minors) (No 2) [1995] 1 FLR 351

Re D (Minors) (Conciliation: Disclosure of Information) [1993] 1 FLR 932

DURATION OF THE MARRIAGE/CIVIL PARTNERSHIP

CO v CO (Ancillary Relief: Pre-marriage cohabitation) [2004] 1 FLR 1095

GW v RW (Financial Provision: Departure from Equality) [2003] 2 FLR 108

Miller v Miller; McFarlane v McFarlane [2006] 1 FLR 1186

ENFORCEMENT OF CHILD ARRANGEMENTS ORDERS

Re A (Intractable Contact Dispute: Human Rights Violations) [2014] 1 FLR 1185

Re L-W (Enforcement and Committal: Contact); CPL v CH-W and Others) [2011] 1 FLR 1095

EXPERT EVIDENCE

Re C (A Child) (Procedural Requirements of a Part 25 Application) [2016] 1 FLR 707

Daniels v Walker (Practice Note) [2000] 1 WLR 1382

EXPERT EVIDENCE – CHILDREN PROCEEDINGS

JG (A Child) v Legal Services Commission and Others [2013] 2 FLR 1174

Re H-L (Expert Evidence: Test for Permission) [2013] 2 FLR 1434

FACT FINDING

AA v NA and KAB [2010] 2 FLR 1173

Re H (Interim Contact: Domestic Violence Allegations) [2014] 1 FLR 41

Re R (Fact-Finding Hearing) [2009] 2 FLR 83

FINANCIAL COMPENSATION ORDER

Re L-W (Enforcement and Committal: Contact); CPL v CH-W and Others [2011] 1 FLR 1095

HABITUAL RESIDENCE

Re A (Jurisdiction: Return of Child) [2014] 1 FLR 111

Mercredi v Chaffe [2011] 2 FLR 515

Re G (Abduction: Withdrawal of proceedings) [2008] 2 FLR 351

Re KL (A Child) [2014] 1 FLR 772

Re LC (Reunite: International Child Abduction Centre Intervening) [2014] 1 FLR 1486

HUMAN RIGHTS

Elsholz v Germany [2000] 2 FLR 486

Re C (Direct Contact: Suspension) [2011] 2 FLR 912

S and G v Italy [2000] 2 FLR 771

INJUNCTIONS

Finance

KY v DD (Injunctions) [2012] 2 FLR 200

Mareva Cia Naviera SA v International Bulk carriers SA [1980] 1 All ER 213, CA

ND v KP (Freezing Order: Ex Parte Application) [2011] 2 FLR 662

Shipman v Shipman [1991] 1 FLR 250

UL v BK (Freezing Orders: Safeguards: Standard Examples) [2013] EWHC 1735 (Fam)

Anti suit (*Hemain*)

Bloch v Bloch [2003] 1 FLR 1

Hemain v Hemain [1988] 2 FLR 388, CA

R v R (Divorce: Hemain Injunction) [2005] 1 FLR 386

S v S (Hemain Injunction) [2010] 2 FLR 502

T v T (Hemain Injunction) [2014] 1 FLR 96

INTRACTABLE CONTACT

Re A (Intractable Contact Dispute: Human Rights Violations) [2014] 1 FLR 1185

Re G (*Intractable Contact Dispute)* [2014] Fam Law 23

Re H-B (Contact) [2015] EWCA Civ 389

Re M (Intractable Contact Dispute: Interim Care Order) [2003] 2 FLR 636

JURISDICTION – FORUM CONVENIENS

Chai v Peng (Estoppel: Foreign Judgment) (No 1) [2015] 2 FLR 412 and *Chai v Peng (Jurisdiction: Forum Conveniens) (No 2)* [2015] 2 FLR 424

JKN v JCN (Divorce: Forum) [2011] 1 FLR 826

Mittal v Mittal [2014] 1 FLR 1514

Owusu v Jackson (Case C-281/02) [2005] QB 801

T v P (Jurisdiction: Lugano Convention and forum conveniens) [2013] 1 FLR 478

LEGAL SERVICES ORDERS

Chai v Peng (No 2) [2015] 1 FLR 637

AM v SS [2014] EWHC 4380 (Fam)

BN v MA [2013] EWHC 4250 (Fam)

Makarskaya v Korthagin [2013] EWHC 4393 (Fam)

MET v HAT (No 2) [2015] 1 FLR 576

Rubin v Rubin [2014] 2 FLR 1018

LIQUID V ILLIQUID ASSETS

P v P (Financial Relief: Illiquid Assets) [2005] 1 FLR 548

Wells v Wells [2002] 2 FLR 97

LUMP SUMS

Banyard v Banyard [1984] FLR 643

Hamilton v Hamilton [2014] 1 FLR 55

Masefield v Alexander (Lump Sum: Extension of Time) [1995] 1 FLR 100

Milton v Milton [2009] 1 FLR 661

MAINTENANCE PENDING SUIT AND INTERIM COSTS (ALSO SEE LEGAL SERVICE ORDERS ABOVE)

A v A (maintenance pending suit: payment of legal fees) [2001] 1 FLR 377

Chai v Peng [2014] 2 FLR 1189

M v M (Maintenance Pending Suit: Enforcement on Dismissal of Suit) [2009] 1 FLR 790

Moore v Moore [2010] 1 FLR 1413

TL v ML and others (Ancillary Relief: Claim against Assets of Extended Family) [2006] 1 FLR 1263

MARITAL AGREEMENTS

AH v PH (Scandinavian Marriage Settlement) [2014] 2 FLR 251

B v S (Financial Remedy: Marital Property Regime) [2012] 2 FLR 502

F v F (Pre-nuptial Agreement) [2010] 1 FLR 1743

Luckwell v Limata [2014] 2 FLR 168

Radmacher v Granatino [2010] 2 FLR 1900

V v V (Pre-Nuptial Agreement) [2012] 1 FLR 1315

Z v Z (No 2) (Financial Remedy: Marriage Contract) [2012] 1 FLR 1315

NON-MARRIAGE

Dukali v Lamrani [2012] 2 FLR 1099

Galloway v Goldstein [2012] 1 FLR 1254

Sharbatly v Shagroon [2013] 1 FLR 1493

NON-MOLESTATION AND OCCUPATION ORDERS

C v C (Non-molestation Order: Jurisdiction) [1998] 1 FLR 554

Chalmers v Johns [1999] 1 FLR 392

JM v CZ [2015] 1 FLR 559

Johnson v Walton [1990] 1 FLR 350

M v W (Non-molestation order: Duration) [2000] 1 FLR 107

Yemshaw v Hounslow London Borough Council [2011] 1 FLR 1614

PARENTAL RESPONSIBILITY

M v M (Parental Responsibility) [1999] 2 FLR 737

Re C and V (Minors) (Contact: Parental Responsibility Order) [1998] 1 FLR 392

Re D (Contact and parental responsibility: Lesbian mothers and known father) (No 2) [2006] EWHC 2 (Fam)

Re H (Parental Responsibility) [1998] 1 FLR 855

Re M (Parental Responsibility Order) [2014] 1 FLR 339

Re S (Parental Responsibility) [1995] 2 FLR 648

PARENTAL RESPONSIBILITY – TERMINATION

P v D, X, Y, Z [2014] EWHC 2355 (Fam)

CW v SG [2013] 2 FLR 655

Re D (A Child) [2015] 1 FLR 166

Re P (Terminating Parental Responsibility) [1995] 1 FLR 1048

PART III MFPA 1984

Abuchian v Khojah [2015] 2 FLR 153

MA v SK [2016] 1 FLR 310

Agbaje v Agbaje [2010] 1 FLR 1813

M v W [2015] 1 FLR 465

Traversa v Freddi [2011] 2 FLR 272

Z v A [2012] 2 FLR 667

PENSIONS

Behzadi v Behzadi [2009] 2 FLR 649

H v H (Financial Relief: Pensions) [2010] 2 FLR 173

Martin Dye v Martin Dye [2006] 2 FLR 901

Vaughan v Vaughan [2008] 1 FLR 1108

PERIODICAL PAYMENTS – CHILD

T v T (Financial provision: Private Education) [2006] 1 FLR 903

PERIODICAL PAYMENTS – SPOUSAL

Wright v Wright [2015] EWCA Civ 201

SS v NS [2015] 2 FLR 1124

H v H [2015] 2 FLR 447

C v C (Financial Relief: Short Marriage) [1997] 2 FLR 26

Flavell v Flavell [1997] 1 FLR 353

G v G [2012] 2 FLR 48

Miller v Miller; McFarlane v McFarlane [2006] 1 FLR 1186, HL

POST SEPARATION ACCRUALS

B v B (Ancillary Relief: Post-Separation Income) [2010] 2 FLR 1214

Evans v Evans [2013] 2 FLR 999

Gordon (formerly Stefanou) v Stefanou [2011] 1 FLR 1582

H v H [2010] 1 FLR 1864

H v W (Cap on Wife's Share of Bonus Payments) [2015] 1 FLR 75

H v W (Cap on Wife's Share of Bonus Payments)(No 2) [2015] 2 FLR 161

S v S (Ancillary Relief after Lengthy Separation) [2007] 1 FLR 2120

SK v WL (Ancillary Relief: Post-Separation Accrual) [2011] 1 FLR 1471

Cooper-Hohn v Hohn [2015] 1 FLR 745

POWER TO MAKE AN ORDER OF COURT'S OWN INITIATIVE

Gloucestershire County Council v P [1999] 2 FLR 61

Re C (Children) [2013] 1 FLR 1089

PRE-MARITAL/INHERITED WEALTH

C v C [2009] 1 FLR 8

Jones v Jones [2011] 1 FLR 1723

K v L (Non-Matrimonial Property: Special Contribution) [2011] 2 FLR 980

N v F (Financial Orders: Pre-Acquired Wealth) [2011] 2 FLR 533

JL v SL [2015] 2 FLR 1202

PROHIBITED STEPS ORDERS

Croydon London Borough Council v A (No 1) [1992] 2 FLR 341

F v R (Contact: Justices' Reasons) [1995] 1 FLR 227

R v Leicestershire Education Authority ex parte C [1991] Fam Law 302

Re H (Prohibited Steps Order) [1995] 1 FLR 638

Re L (A Child) [2013] 1 FLR 430

Re N (A Child: Religion: Jehovah's Witness) [2012] 2 FLR 917

Re PC (Change of Surname) [1997] 2 FLR 730

S v B and Newport City Council; Re K [2007] 1 FLR 1116

SH v MM and RM (Prohibited Steps Order: Abduction) [2012] 1 FLR 837

C v K [2015] 2 FLR 791

PROPERTY ORDERS

Birch v Birch [2016] 2 FLR 467

Curran v Collins [2016] 1 FLR 505

Arif v Anwar and Rehan [2016] 1 FLR 359

Carson v Carson (1981) 2 FLR 352

Dinch v Dinch [1987] 2 FLR 162

Mesher v Mesher and Hall [1980] 1 All ER 126, CA

Prest v Petrodel Resources Ltd and Others [2013] 2 FLR 732

Sandford v Sandford [1986] 1 FLR 412

Wicks v Wicks [1998] 1 FLR 470

PUBLICITY

Birmingham City Council v Sarfraz Riaz and Others [2015] EWHC 1857 (Fam)

Re C (Publication of Judgment) [2015] EWCA Civ 500

City and County of Swansea v XZ and Others [2014] EWHC 212 (Fam)

Re J (A Child) [2014] 1 FLR 523

Re P (Enforced Caesarean: Reporting Restrictions) [2014] 2 FLR 410

Re S (Identification: Restrictions on Publication) [2005] 1 FLR 591

RELOCATION

Re R (A Child: Relocation) [2015] EWHC 456 (Fam)

H v F (Relocation) [2014] EWFC 11

K v K (Relocation: Shared Care Arrangement) [2012] 2 FLR 880

Payne v Payne [2001] 1 FLR 1052

SCHEDULE 1, CHILDREN ACT APPLICATIONS

Carer's allowance

Re PG and TW (No 2) (Child: Financial Provision) [2014] 1 FLR 923

Scope

Morgan v Hill [2007] 1 FLR 1480

N v C [2013] EWHC 399 (Fam)

PK v BC (Financial Remedies: Schedule 1) [2012] 2 FLR 1426

Re S (Child: Financial Provision) [2005] 2 FLR 94

Dickson v Rennie [2015] 2 FLR 978

Re A (A Child) [2015] 2 FLR 625

Gap years

A v A (A minor: Financial Provision) [1994] 1 FLR 657

Phillips v Peace [1996] 2 FLR 230

Re N (Payments for Benefit of Child) [2009] 1 FLR 1442

Standard of living

F v G (Child: Financial Provision) [2005] 1 FLR 261

H v C [2009] 2 FLR 1540

J v C [1999] 1 FLR 152

MT v OT (Financial Provision: Costs) [2008] 2 FLR 1311

N v D [2008] 1 FLR 1629

Re P [2003] 2 FLR 865

Separate representation for child

Re S (Unmarried Parent: Financial Provision) [2006] 2 FLR 950

SEARCH ORDERS (ANTON PILLER)

Anton Piller KG v Manufacturing Processes Ltd [1976] Ch 55

Burgess v Burgess [1996] 2 FLR 34

Imerman v Tchenguiz [2010] 2 FLR 814

UL v BK (Freezing Orders: Safeguards: Standard Examples) [2014] 1 FLR 1239

SECTION 7 REPORTS

Re W (Welfare Reports) [1995] 2 FLR 142

SECTION 91(14) ORDERS

Re C (Litigant in Person: s 91(14) Order) [2009] 2 FLR 1461

Re M (Parental Responsibility Order) [2014] 1 FLR 339

Re P (Section 91(14) Guidelines) (Residence and Religious Heritage) [1999] 2 FLR 573

SHARED CARE (PRIOR TO CHILD ARRANGEMENTS ORDERS)

D v D (Shared Residence Order) [2001] 1 FLR 495

Re A (Joint Residence/Parental Responsibility) [2008] 2 FLR 1593

Re W (Shared Residence Order) [2009] 2 FLR 436

SPECIFIC ISSUE ORDERS

Dawson v Wearmouth [1997] 2 FLR 629

M v M (Specific Issue: Choice of School) [2007] 1 FLR 251

Re C (HIV Test) [1999] 2 FLR 1004

Re C (Welfare of Child: Immunisation) [2003] 2 FLR 1054

Re F (Internal Relocation) [2011] 1 FLR 1382

Re HG (Specific Issue Order: Sterilisation) [1993] 1 FLR 587

Re J (Specific Issue Orders: Child's Religious Upbringing and Circumcision) [2000] 1 FLR 571

Re PC (Change of Surname) [1997] 2 FLR 730

SPECIFIC ISSUE ORDERS – JURISDICTION

EY v RZ [2013] EWHC 4403 (Fam)

Re D (A Minor) (Child: Removal from Jurisdiction) [1992] 1 FLR 637

Re R (Children: Temporary Leave to Remove from Jurisdiction) [2014] 2 FLR 1402

STANDARD OF LIVING

G v G (Financial Remedies: Short Marriage: Trust Assets) [2012] 2 FLR 48

S v S [2008] 2 FLR 113

TIMETABLING

B v B (Minors) (Interviews and Listing Arrangements) [1994] 2 FLR 489, CA

Re A and B (Minors) (No 2) [1995] 1 FLR 351

Re H (Minors) (Welfare Reports) [1990] 2 FLR 172, CA

TOLATA 1996 APPLICATIONS

Jones v Kernott [2012] 1 FLR 45

Oxley v Hiscock [2004] 2 FLR 669

Smith v Bottomley [2014] 1 FLR 626

Stack v Dowden [2007] 1 FLR 1858

Thompson v Hurst [2014] 1 FLR 238

Bagum v Hafiz & Anor [2016] 2 FLR 337

O'Kelly v Davies [2015] 2 FLR 1311

TRANSFERRING RESIDENCE IN LIGHT OF REPEATED BREACHES OF ORDERS (PRIOR TO CHILD ARRANGEMENTS ORDERS)

Re A (Residence Order) [2010] 1 FLR 1083

Re C (Residence Order) [2008] 1 FLR 211

Re S (Transfer of Residence) [2011] 1 FLR 1789

TRUSTS

A v A [2007] 2 FLR 467

B v B (Ancillary Relief) [2010] 2 FLR 887

C v C (Ancillary Relief: Trust Fund) [2010] 1 FLR 337

De Bruyne v De Bruyne [2010] 2 FLR 1240

SR v CR (Ancillary Relief: Family Trusts) [2009] 2 FLR

Whaley v Whaley [2012] 1 FLR 735

WISHES AND FEELINGS

M v M (Removal from Jurisdiction) [1993] 1 FCR 5

R (A Child) [2010] 1 FLR 509

Re H (A Child) [2014] EWCA Civ 271

WITHOUT NOTICE APPLICATIONS

C (A Child) & Anor v KH [2014] 1 FLR 1239

Croydon LBC v A (No 3) [1992] 2 FLR 350

KY v DD [2012] 2 FLR 200

Re S (Ex Parte Orders) [2001] 1 FLR 308

Re W (Ex Parte Orders) [2000] 2 FLR 927

PART IV

2017–18 TABLES

INCOME TAX AND NATIONAL INSURANCE CONTRIBUTIONS

INCOME TAX ALLOWANCES 2017/18

Personal allowance	£11,500
Income limit for personal allowance	£100,000
Income limit for married couple's allowance	£28,000
Minimum amount of married couple's allowance	£3,260
Blind person's allowance	£2,320
Personal savings allowance for basic rate taxpayers	£1,000
Personal savings allowance for higher rate taxpayers	£500

INCOME TAX BANDS 2017/18

Basic rate	20%	£0 – £33,500
Higher rate	40%	£33,501 – £150,000
Additional rate	45%	Over £150,000

NATIONAL INSURANCE CONTRIBUTIONS: 2009–18

Limits	Year								
	17–18	16-17	15–16	14–15	13–14	12–13	11–12	10–11	09–10
Lower earnings limit, primary class 1	£113	£112	£112	£111	£109	£107	£102	£97	£95
Upper earnings limit, primary class 1	£866	£827	£815	£805	£797	£817	£817	£844	£844
Primary threshold	£157	£155	£155	£153	£149	£146	£139	£110	£110
Secondary threshold	£157	£156	£156	£153	£148	£144	£136	£110	£110
Class 2 rate	£2.85	£2.80	£2.80	£2.75	£2.70	£2.65	£2.50	£2.40	£2.40
Class 2 small earnings exception	N/A	N/A	N/A	£5,885	£5,725	£5,595	£5,315	£5,075	£5,075
Class 2 small profits threshold	£6,025	£5,965	£5,965						
Class 3 rate	£14.25	£14.10	£14.10	£13.90	£13.55	£13.25	£12.60	£12.05	£12.05
Class 4 lower profits limit	£8,164	£8,060	£8,060	£7,956	£7,755	£7,605	£7,225	£5,715	£5,715
Class 4 upper profit limit	45,000	43,000	42,385	41,865	41,450	42,475	42,475	43,875	43,875
Class 4 rate between lower profit limit and upper profits limit	9%	9%	9%	9%	9%	9%	9%	8%	8%

OTHER TAX RATES, LIMITS AND RELIEFS

CAPITAL GAINS TAX

Capital gains rate of tax 2017/18

Rates of tax	
Standard rate	10%/18%*
Higher rate	20%/28%*
Entrepreneurs' relief rate	10%

* CGT rates of 10% and 20% introduced for disposals on or after 6 April 2016 do not apply to transactions involving residential property or carried interest. Rates for these transactions remain at 18% and 28%.

Capital gains annual allowance 2017/18

Individuals	£11,300
Trusts	£5,650

INHERITANCE TAX

Inheritance tax rates

		2017/18
Nil band		£325,000
Death tax	40%	Excess
Lifetime tax	20%	Excess

Taper relief

Where tax is charged on death on any gift made within 7 years of death, taper relief may apply as follows:

Years before death	0–3	3–4	4–5	5–6	6–7
Percentage taxable on death	100	80	60	40	20

STAMP DUTY LAND TAX RATES AND THRESHOLDS

Stamp Duty Land Tax (SDLT) is charged on land and property transactions in the UK. The tax is charged at different rates and has different thresholds for different types of property and different values of transaction.

The tax rate and payment threshold can vary according to whether the property is residential or non-residential, and whether it is a freehold or leasehold. SDLT relief is available for certain kinds of property or transaction.

SDLT rates for residential property

The table below applies for all freehold residential purchases and transfers and the premium paid for a new lease or the assignment of an existing lease. (If the property will be used for both residential and non-residential purposes the rates differ).

New leasehold sales and transfers

If the total rent over the life the lease (known as the 'net present value') is more than £125,000, an additional SDLT charge of 1% on the portion over £125,000 will be payable. This can be worked out using HMRC's online calculator.

Residential land or property SDLT rates and thresholds

Purchase price/lease premium or transfer value	SDLT rate
Up to £125,000	Zero
Over £125,000 to £250,000	2%
Over £250,000 to £925,000	5%
Over £925,000 to £1.5 million	10%
Over £1.5 million	12%

FOSTERING ALLOWANCES

Minimum allowances for fostering are now set nationally by the Government. Current and historical figures are set out below.

Recommended fostering allowance per week

2017–2018: Minimum allowances rates

Weekly Rates	Babies	Pre-primary	Primary	11–15	16–17
London	£144	£147	£165	£187	£219
South East	£138	£142	£158	£179	£211
Rest of UK	£125	£128	£141	£161	£188

2015–2016/2016-2017: Minimum allowances rates

Weekly Rates	Babies	Pre-primary	Primary	11–15	16–17
London	£142	£145	£163	£184	£216
South East	£136	£140	£156	£177	£208
Rest of UK	£123	£126	£139	£159	£185

2014–2015: Minimum allowances rates

Weekly Rates	Babies	Pre-primary	Primary	11–15	16–17
London	£137	£140	£157	£178	£209
South East	£131	£135	£151	£171	£201
Rest of UK	£119	£122	£134	£154	£179

2013–2014: Minimum allowances rates

Weekly Rates	Babies	Pre-primary	Primary	11–15	16–17
London	£135	£140	£157	£178	£209
South East	£129	£133	£142	£167	£197
Rest of UK	£116	£119	£126	£151	£175

Tax-free earnings

A tax free exemption of up to £10,000 per year (less for a shorter period), shared equally among foster carers in the sane household, is available.

This means that you do not pay tax on the first £10,000 income (after expenses) you make from fostering.

Tax relief

In addition tax relief is available on earnings over £10,000:

Age of child	Tax relief
Under 11	£200 per child per week
Over 11	£250 per child per week

SOCIAL SECURITY BENEFITS

INTRODUCTION

The information below is intended to give a brief overview of the main benefits and tax credits in the state social security system, and to allow you to check benefit rates over the last five years.

News in brief

- Many benefit rates – especially means-tested ones – are still frozen this year at 2015–16 rates. A few amounts have crept up by a matter of pence. This year Bereavement Support Payment replaces all three existing bereavement benefits in relation to a death occurring from 6 April 2017 onwards. The two new benefits introduced in 2013–2014, Personal Independence Payment and Universal Credit, are now in their fifth year. PIP is replacing Disability Living Allowance for disabled claimants aged 16+ and under 65; no new DLA claims can be made except for children under 16, and existing 16+ DLA claimants are being invited to re-claim under PIP; many fail the new test so appeal rates are high. UC is replacing Income Support, income-based Jobseeker's Allowance, income-related Employment and Support Allowance, Housing Benefit and Tax Credits. UC is being piloted in a growing number of areas for increasing categories of claimant. For some claimants, especially those on income-related Employment and Support Allowance, it continues to remain in the background. Conversion of existing cases to UC has yet to begin in earnest. The conversion of old Incapacity Benefit claims to Employment and Support Allowance is almost complete however. Claimants of both ESA and PIP are experiencing considerable upheaval in terms of proving their level of disability, with some delay a familiar part of the claim process. Nevertheless, the speed of processing claims has dramatically improved now.
- The £29.05 work-related activity component in Employment and Support Allowance has now been abolished for new claims since 6 April 2017. This means people with limited capability for work who are not in the support group mostly just get a basic £73.10pw, the same as those on Jobseeker's Allowance.
- Council Tax Benefit was replaced from 1 April 2013 by local Council Tax reduction schemes designed and operated independently by each local authority, subject to national minimum standards.
- In 2014 the definition of a couple who are not married or civil partners changed in most social security law to '*living together as a married couple*'.
- The benefits cap operates for those on Housing Benefit or Universal Credit. It means that total benefit income (as defined) cannot exceed a given weekly amount (monthly amount in the case of UC).

Provisos

Note the following provisos and points:

- Information on each benefit is meant as a simplified summary of the key qualifying conditions; the wording we use does not always correspond precisely to the legislative wording.
- You should be cautious about advising clients to make benefit claims, or lodge appeals, based on the information in this section and, if in doubt, check a reliable and current reference book

such as Child Poverty Action Group's *Welfare Benefits and Tax Credits Handbook*, read the wording of the legislation, and preferably refer your client to a benefits specialist.

- It is in the nature of social security legislation that *nearly all* statements as to qualifying conditions have one or more exceptions; often there are exceptions to the exceptions as well – these are omitted here for the sake of brevity.
- All rates given are weekly amounts, except Tax Credits, which are annual figures, and Universal Credit and Bereavement Support Payment which are monthly amounts.
- For means-tested benefits and tax credits the weekly, monthly or annual rates of benefit are not the whole story: they should be used as part of the whole calculation which will often produce different results because of the effect of income on the final entitlement figures.
- The term 'overlapping benefit' refers to a rule which prevents the duplication of certain benefits in cases where a claimant is on the face of it entitled to more than one. For example, it would not be possible to claim full Carer's Allowance at the same time as a state pension. Where one exceeds the other in value, then the excess value may be added to the lower-value of the two available benefits. Note that further, more complex overlapping rules apply when a client has an entitlement to a war disablement pension or war widow's pension.

Disclaimer: this information is intended as a quick reference aid and should not be regarded as a substitute for proper reference books. Do look up the full details of any question that arises when advising about a real-life benefits situation. Most advisers will need to use CPAG's *Welfare Benefits & Tax Credits Handbook*. If there are mistakes, we apologise, and ask you to let us know, but we cannot accept any responsibility for the consequences of any such errors.

MEANS-TESTED BENEFITS

Universal Credit

A new umbrella benefit to replace means-tested benefits and tax credits for those of working age. Its introduction is still running very slowly. It is capped at £1666.66pcm for couples (£1916.66 in London) and those with children and £1116.66pcm (£1284.16 in London) for single people without children.

Standard allowances						
	2012–13	2013–14 £ per month	2014–15 £ per month	2015–16 £ per month	2016–17 £ per month	2017–18 £ per month
Single under 25		£246.81	£249.80	£251.77	£251.77	£251.77
Single 25+		£311.55	£314.67	£317.82	£317.82	£317.82
Couple both under 25		£387.42	£391.29	£395.90	£395.20	£395.20
Couple one or both 25+		£489.06	£493.95	£498.89	£498.89	£498.89
Elements						
First child		£272.08	£274.58	£277.08	£277.08	£277.08
Each other child		£226.67	£229.17	£231.67	£231.67	£231.67

Disabled child (lower rate)		£123.62	£124.86	£126.11	£126.11	£126.11
Disabled child (higher rate)		£352.92	£362.92	£367.92	£367.92	£372.30
Limited capability for work		£123.62	£124.86	£126.11	£126.11	£126.11
Limited capability for work-related activity		£303.66	£311.86	£315.60	£315.60	£318.76
Carer		£144.70	£148.61	£150.39	£150.39	£151.89
Childcare costs – 1 child		up to £532.29	up to £532.29	up to £532.29	up to £646.35	up to £646.35
Childcare costs – 2+ children		up to £912.50	up to £912.50	up to £912.50	up to £1108.04	up to £1108.04

contributory?	**overlapping?**	**dependent additions?**	**means-tested?**	**counts as income for means-tested benefits?**	**counts as income for tax credits?**
no	no	yes	yes	not applicable	not applicable

Who gets it?

People under pensionable age, on low incomes who are in or out of work, whether unemployed, carers, those with limited capability for work, single parents or others.

Only certain categories of claimant, and in pilot areas only, are so far able to claim

Other conditions and points

Maximum monthly amounts are offset by income (with some disregards) to produce a monthly entitlement.

Mortgage interest and rent are covered (within limits)

Income Support and income-based Jobseeker's Allowance

For people who have not yet reached the qualifying age for pension credit, in certain eligible groups such as lone parents with a child under five years and carers (Income Support), or those who are out of work and meeting the 'labour-market conditions' by signing on and looking for work (income-based Jobseeker's Allowance); they must also have a low enough income to qualify, and must not exceed the capital limits.

Personal allowances						
	2012–13	2013–14	2014–15	2015–16	2016–17	2017–18
16–24	£56.25	£56.80	£57.35	£57.90	£57.90	£57.90
25+	£71.00	£71.70	£72.40	£73.10	£73.10	£73.10
Lone parent under-18 normal rate	£56.25	£56.80	£57.35	£57.90	£57.90	£57.90
lone parent 18+	£71.00	£71.70	£72.40	£73.10	£73.10	£73.10
couple 18+	£111.45	£112.55	£113.70	£114.85	£114.85	£114.85
child under 20	£64.99*	£65.62*	£66.33*	£66.90*	£66.90*	£66.90*

* only in 'old scheme' Income Support claims – made before 6 April 2004, with no Child Tax Credit

Premiums						
	2012–13	**2013–14**	**2014–15**	**2015–16**	**2016–17**	**2017–18**
Carer	£32.60	£33.30	£34.20	£34.60	£34.60	£34.95
Disability – single	£30.35**	£31.00**	£31.85**	£32.25**	£32.25**	£32.55**
Disability – couple	£43.25**	£44.20**	£45.40**	£45.95**	£45.95**	£46.40**
Enhanced Disability – single	£14.80	£15.15	£15.55	£15.75	£15.75	£15.90
Enhanced Disability – couple	£21.30	£21.75	£22.35	£22.60	£22.60	£22.85
Severe Disability – per qualifying person	£58.20	£59.50	£61.10	£61.85	£61.85	£62.45
Family	£17.40*	£17.40*	£17.45*	£17.45*	£17.45*	£17.45*
Disabled child	£56.63*	£57.89*	£59.50*	£60.06*	£60.06*	£60.90*
Enhanced Disability – child	£22.89*	£23.45*	£24.08*	£24.43*	£24.43*	£24.78*

* only in 'old scheme' Income Support claims – made before 6 April 2004, with no Child Tax Credit
** now largely superseded by Employment and Support Allowance except for claimants getting DLA or PIP but capable of work

contributory?	**overlapping?**	**dependent additions?**	**means-tested?**	**counts as income for means-tested benefits?**	**counts as income for tax credits?**
no	no	yes	yes	no	no

Who gets IS?

- lone parents with a child under 5
- carers
- a few other eligible groups

Who gets income-based-Jobseeker's Allowance?

- unemployed people who can show they are available for, and actively seeking, work

Other conditions and points

Applicable amounts are determined according to the above figures but must then be offset by amounts of income received by the claimant and any partner – as prescribed.

IS and i-b-JSA will be absorbed into UC

State Pension Credit

For people on a low enough income to qualify, who have reached the qualifying age – ie, for women: their pensionable age; and, for men: the pensionable age of a woman born the same day as he was.

	2012–13	2013–14	2014–15	2015–16	2016–17	2017–18
Standard minimum guarantee – single	£142.70	£145.40	£148.35	£151.20	£155.60	£159.35
Standard minimum guarantee – couple	£217.90	£222.05	£226.50	£230.85	£237.55	£243.25
Carer	£32.60	£33.30	£34.20	£34.60	£34.60	£34.95
Severe disability – per qualifying person	£58.20	£59.50	£61.10	£61.85	£61.85	£62.45
Savings Credit threshold – single	£111.80	£115.30	£120.35	£126.50	£133.82	£137.35
Savings Credit threshold – couple	£178.35	£183.90	£192.00	£201.80	£212.97	£218.42
Savings Credit maximum – single	£18.54	£18.06	£16.80	£14.82	£13.07	£13.20
Savings Credit maximum – couple	£23.73	£22.89	£20.70	£17.43	£14.75	£14.90

contributory?	**overlapping?**	**dependent additions?**	**means-tested?**	**counts as income for means-tested benefits?**	**counts as income for tax credits?**
no	no	yes	yes	no	no

Who gets it?

- those who have reached the qualifying age for pension credit can get the Guarantee Credit component
- those aged 65 or more (men or women) can also get the Savings Credit component

Other conditions and points

The above figures give weekly rates and maximums but the full calculation is too complex for inclusion here.

State Pension Credit will not be absorbed into UC

Housing Benefit

For people paying rent whose income is low enough for them to qualify. Council Tax Benefit was abolished from April 2013 and is replaced by variable local Council Tax reduction schemes. HB is capped where a person's total benefit income (with some exceptions) exceeds £384.62pw (£442.31pw in London) for couples and those with children and £257.69pw for single people (£296.35 in London) without children.

Applicable Amounts						
	2012–13	2013–14	2014–15	2015–16	2016–17	2017–18
	Weekly applicable amounts are largely aligned exactly with Income Support (or, for people with limited capability for work, income-related Employment and Support Allowance) – with some exceptions. Amounts in respect of children (ie child personal allowances, disabled child premium and enhanced disability premium for a child – but no longer family premium) are included in all relevant cases and unlike in Income Support are not just for pre-2004 old-scheme cases.					

contributory?	overlapping?	dependent additions?	means-tested?	counts as income for other means-tested benefits?	counts as income for tax credits?
no	no	yes	yes	no	no

Who gets it?

- HB: anyone paying rent on the property they occupy whose income is low enough for them to qualify

Other conditions and points

Those on Income Support, the Guarantee Credit part of State Pension Credit, income-related ESA or income-based Jobseeker's Allowance are passported onto maximum HB.

For others, the amounts payable are determined by measuring excess income above the relevant applicable amounts, and requiring the claimant to pay 65% of this excess towards the eligible rent; HB then meets the remainder of the cost up to limits as follows.

In both passported and non-passported cases, eligible rent in the private sector is usually restricted to what is considered a reasonable market rent, as determined by the Valuation Office Agency. This is called Local Housing Allowance. In the social housing sector the amount of HB is further reduced by a fixed proportion if there are too many bedrooms. This is widely called the bedroom tax.

HB will be absorbed into UC.

Tax Credits

For people who have children and/or are in full-time work, whose income is low enough for them to qualify.

Child tax credit and working tax credit						
		2013–14	2014–15	2015–16	2016–17	2017–18
		Annual figures				
Child tax credit	Family element	£545	£545	£545	£545	£545
	Child element	£2,720	£2,750	£2,780	£2,780	£2,780
	Disability element (child)	£3,015	£3,100	£3,140	£3,140	£3,175
	Severe disability element (child)	£1,220	£1,255	£1,275	£1,275	£1,290
Working tax credit	Basic element	£1,920	£1,940	£1,960	£1,960	£1,960
	Couple or lone parent element	£1,970	£1,990	£2,010	£2,010	£2,010
	30-hours element	£790	£800	£810	£810	£810
	Disabled worker element	£2,855	£2,935	£2,970	£2,970	£3,000
	Severe disability element	£1,220	£1,255	£1,275	£1,275	£1,290

Contributory?	Overlapping?	Dependent additions?	Means-tested?	Counts as income for means-tested benefits?	Counts as income for tax credits?
no	no	yes	yes	no	no

Other conditions and points

- the amount of annual entitlement is determined by adding together the appropriate elements and reducing this total by 41% of excess income (if any) above the income threshold of £6,420 (all cases involving working tax credit) or £16,105 (cases involving child tax credit only).
- Tax credits will be absorbed into UC

BENEFITS FOR INCAPACITY OR LIMITED CAPABILITY FOR WORK

Statutory Sick Pay

For employees earning more than earnings threshold who are incapable of work for at least four days.

	2013–14	2014–15	2015–16	2016–17	2017–18
Weekly SSP	£86.70	£87.55	£88.45	£88.45	£89.35
Earnings threshold pw:	£109.00	£111.00	£112.00	£112.00	£113.00
contributory?	**overlapping?**	**dependent additions?**	**means-tested?**	**counts as income for means-tested benefits?**	**counts as income for tax credits?**
no	no	no	no	yes	yes

Who gets it?

- people who are in paid employment and
- are not in an 'excluded employees' group
- are off sick
- age 16+ and under qualifying age for pension credit
- for up to 28 weeks

Other conditions and points

Paid by and paid for by the employer.

Not available if an excluded employee.

Not for self-employed.

Example

Jim is a bar-worker at a large pub. He's worked there three years, full time. He goes off sick with a bad back, gets a doctor's note, and the brewery have to pay him SSP, even if his back problem lasts up to 28 weeks. His employer can ask him to keep supplying doctor's notes. He can't automatically be dismissed.

Typical client problems with this benefit

Very few problems.

Employers' reluctance to pay:

My employer just refuses to pay. He says I haven't been with him long enough and that there is a three-month qualifying period.

(Note that these objections to paying would not be correct.)

Employment and Support Allowance

ESA is paid to those with limited capability for work. Since October 2008, it replaces Incapacity Benefit and Income Support paid on grounds of disability. It has two versions, contributory and income-related. In either case, a claimant may be in the work-related activity group or the support group. That affects the components they receive and whether they have to do work-related activity.

	2012–13	2013–14	2014–15	2015–16	2016–17	2017–18
basic amounts	largely as for Income Support					
premiums	largely as for Income Support, except no disability premium					
work-related activity component	£28.15	£28.45	£28.75	£29.05	£29.05	£29.05*
support component	£34.05	£34.80	£35.75	£36.20	£36.20	£36.55

* pre-6 April 2017 claims only

contributory?	**overlapping?**	**dependent additions?**	**means-tested?**	**counts as income for means-tested benefits?**	**counts as income for tax credits?**
yes (contributory version); no (income-related version)	yes (contributory version); no (income-related version)	yes	no (contributory version); yes (income-related version)	n/a	yes (contributory version); no (income-related version)

Who gets it?

- people who satisfy the Limited Capability for Work Assessment
- income-related Employment and Support Allowance will be absorbed into UC
- the contributory version of Employment and Support Allowance for those in the work-related activity group is only paid for one year

Other conditions and points

Subject to sometimes frequent medical examinations to apply the work capability assessment

May also be subject to attendance at work-focused interview and work-related activity

Typical client problems with this benefit

Employment and Support Allowance withdrawals:

'I had been on ESA happily for 2 years due to my lumbago, then I had to go to a medical. The paramedic doing it was hurried and not very sympathetic, and hardly asked any relevant questions. Now only days later I've had a letter saying I'm fit enough to work and I must go and sign on.'

Incapacity Benefit

No new claims: do not advise clients to claim this if they are not already on it.

Previously paid to people incapable of work who had paid sufficient NI contributions. It was paid at short-term lower rate for the first 28 weeks, short-term higher rate weeks 29–52, long-term rate week 53 onward. Now abolished and replaced – for new claims – by Employment and Support Allowance from 27 October 2008. Existing claims should switch to ESA soon.

	2012–13	**2013–14**	**2014–15**	**2015–16**	**2016–17**	**2017–18**
short-term: lower	£74.80	£76.45	£78.50	£79.45	£79.45	£80.25
short-term: higher	£88.55	£90.50	£92.95	£94.05	£94.05	£95.00
long-term	£99.15	£101.35	£104.10	£105.35	£105.35	£106.40
Age additions						
to be added when the claimant's incapacity started at ages ...	**2012–13**	**2013–14**	**2014–15**	**2015–16**	**2016–17**	**2017–18**
under 35	£11.70	£10.70	£11.00	£11.15	£11.15	£11.25
35–44	£5.90	£6.00	£6.15	£6.20	£6.20	£6.25

contributory?	**overlapping?**	**dependent additions?**	**Means-tested?**	**counts as income for means-tested benefits?**	**counts as income for tax credits?**
yes	yes	yes	No	yes	yes (except for short-term lower rate IB)

Who gets it?

- people who are incapable of work under the Personal Capability Assessment and
- who have paid sufficient NI contributions

Severe Disablement Allowance

No new claims: do not advise clients to claim this. It is very unusual to find still-extant SDA claims.

For those who claimed before April 2001, who are incapable of work, at least 80% disabled, and did not pay enough National Insurance contributions to be entitled to Incapacity Benefit.

	2012–13	2013–14	2014–15	2015–16	2016–17	2017–18
Weekly SDA	£69.00	£71.80	£73.75	£74.65	£74.65	£75.40
Age additions						
to be added when the claimant's incapacity started at ages ...	**2011–12**	**2012–13**	**2013–14**	**2014–15**	**2015–16**	**2017–18**
under 40	£11.70	£10.70	£11.00	£11.15	£11.15	£11.25
40–59	£5.90	£6.00	£6.15	£6.20	£6.20	£6.25

contributory?	**overlapping?**	**dependent additions?**	**means-tested?**	**counts as income for means-tested benefits?**	**counts as income for tax credits?**
no	yes	yes	yes	yes	no

Who gets it?

- those who were on SDA as of April 2001

Other conditions and points

Abolished for new claims from April 2001: now only payable to those already in receipt as of April 2001. Existing claims have mostly switched to ESA (or UC) by now.

Typical client problems with this benefit

Few issues arise now, since its abolition.

BENEFITS FOR SEVERE DISABILITY AND CARERS

Personal Independence Payment: mobility component

For people 16+ and under 65 with disabilities, who have significant mobility problems.

		2013–14	2014–15	2015–16	2016–17	2017–18
enhanced rate		£55.25	£56.75	£57.45	£57.45	£58.00
standard rate		£21.00	£21.55	£21.80	£21.80	£22.00

contributory?	**overlapping?**	**dependent additions?**	**means-tested?**	**counts as income for means-tested benefits?**	**counts as income for tax credits?**
no	no	no	no	no	no

Who gets it?

People aged 16+ and under 65 who score enough points on the schedule as to mobilising range and ability. You need 8+ points to get standard rate or 12+ points for enhanced rate. Points are scored for planning and following a journey and for standing and moving around.

Personal Independence Payment: daily living component

For people 16+ and under 65, who have significant care needs.

		2013–14	2014–15	2015–16	2016–17	2017–18
enhanced rate		£79.15	£81.30	£82.30	£82.30	£83.10
standard rate		£53.00	£54.45	£55.10	£55.10	£55.65

contributory?	**overlapping?**	**dependent additions?**	**means-tested?**	**counts as income for means-tested benefits?**	**counts as income for tax credits?**
no	no	no	no	no	no

Who gets it?

People who can score enough points on the schedule of points for daily living activities. You need 8+ points to get standard rate or 12+ points for enhanced rate. Points are scored for things like washing, dressing, communicating, budgeting and engaging with other people.

Disability Living Allowance: mobility component

No new claims for those aged 16 or more: do not advise clients aged 16 or more to claim this.

	2012–13	2013–14	2014–15	2015–16	2016–17	2017–18
higher rate	£54.05	£55.25	£56.75	£57.45	£57.45	£58.00
lower rate	£20.55	£21.00	£21.55	£21.80	£21.80	£22.00

contributory?	**overlapping?**	**dependent additions?**	**means-tested?**	**counts as income for means-tested benefits?**	**counts as income for tax credits?**
no	no	no	no	no	no

Who gets it?

- people aged 3+ (lower rate 5+) and under 65 who

Higher rate:

- unable or virtually unable to walk, because of a physical problem, or
- the exertion of walking could endanger health, or
- severe visual impairment, or
- severely mentally impaired

Lower rate:

- can walk but need supervision or guidance in order to make progress out of doors in an unfamiliar place

Other conditions and points

For lower rate children must need more supervision/guidance than normal.

Three months pre-qualifying and six months post-qualifying periods.

For higher rate based on inability or virtual inability to walk, disability must be a physical one.

Example

Esther is 42 and has severe arthritis in all parts of her body. She can get about her flat, but only very slowly, with great pain mostly, and only holding onto things such as furniture as she goes. Out of doors she uses a walking frame, but can get 30m along the road on some days. This takes her about four–six minutes each way.

Typical client problems with this benefit

Form too long and confusing.

DWP underestimation of level of care needs.

Clients' exaggeration of their abilities.

Misunderstanding of distances.

Is the problem physical or non-physical?

Fluctuating conditions.

The disabling role of pain/discomfort.

'I filled in the form with lots of detail about how far I can get, but it seems that because I was honest and said that some days I can make it to the post office they have penalised me and said I am able to walk. Yet most days I couldn't possibly manage that distance, and when I rarely do, it leaves me unable to do anything at all for a good 48 hours...'

Disability Living Allowance: care component

For people with disabilities aged under 65 when they first claim, who have significant care needs. No new claims for those aged 16 or more: do not advise clients aged 16 or more to claim this.

	2012–13	2013–14	2014–15	2015–16	2016–17	2017–18
highest rate	£77.45	£79.15	£81.30	£82.30	£82.30	£83.10
middle rate	£51.85	£53.00	£54.45	£55.10	£55.10	£55.65
lowest rate	£20.55	£21.00	£21.55	£21.80	£21.80	£22.00

contributory?	overlapping?	dependent additions?	means-tested?	counts as income for means-tested benefits?	counts as income for tax credits?
no	no	no	no	no	no

Who gets it?

Middle or highest rates:

- people over three months and under 65 who
- need frequent attention throughout the day, or
- prolonged or repeated attention at night, in connection with bodily functions; or
- who need continual daytime supervision to avoid danger
- or someone watching over them at night to avoid danger

Lowest rate:

- people unable to prepare a cooked main meal or
- who need attention in connection with bodily functions for a substantial portion of the day

Other conditions and points

Middle rate applies where care is needed night or day.

Highest rate applies where care needed night *and* day.

Typical client problems with this benefit

Does the care required have to be given by somebody else?

What is day and what is night?

What is a bodily function?

How frequent is frequent?

How dangerous is the danger?

What about mental health conditions?

Attendance Allowance

For people with disabilities aged 65 or more when they first claim, who have significant care needs.

	2012–13	2013–14	2014–15	2015–16	2016–17	2017–18
higher rate	£77.45	£79.15	£81.30	£82.30	£82.30	£83.10
lower rate	£51.85	£53.00	£54.45	£55.10	£55.10	£55.65

contributory?	**overlapping?**	**dependent additions?**	**means-tested?**	**counts as income for means-tested benefits?**	**counts as income for tax credits?**
no	no	no	no	no	no

Who gets it?
people 65 or more who

- need frequent attention throughout the day, or
- prolonged or repeated attention at night, in connection with bodily functions; or
- who need continual daytime supervision to avoid danger,
- or someone watching over them at night to avoid danger

Other conditions and points

Lower rate applies where care is needed night or day.

Higher rate applies where care is needed night *and* day.

Six months pre-qualifying period.

No upper age limit.

Example

Violet is 89, suffers from severe short-term memory problems and lapses of awareness; and now needs someone around nearly all the time by day in her sheltered flat. This is in order to help her out of bed, get dressed, get washed, help her use the toilet, eat and take her pills; and also to make sure she is safe. At night she sleeps soundly and can call the warden with her emergency cord if necessary (she hardly ever has to).

Typical client problems with this benefit

See above under DLA Care Component.

'Why can't I get anything for mobility problems just because I'm so old?'

Carer's Allowance

For carers of someone getting PIP Daily Living Component (either rate), DLA Care Component (middle or highest rates), or Attendance Allowance, who do not work full time and who give regular and substantial amounts of caring.

	2012–13	2013–14	2014–15	2015–16	2016–17	2017–18
Weekly rate	£58.45	£59.75	£61.35	£62.10	£62.10	£62.70

contributory?	overlapping?	dependent additions?	means-tested?	counts as income for means-tested benefits?	counts as income for tax credits?
no	yes	yes	no	Yes	yes

Who gets it?

- people aged 16+
- looking after someone getting DLA Care Component Highest/Middle rate, PIP Daily Living Component or Attendance Allowance,
- giving 35 hours a week care, and
- not earning more than the earnings threshold (currently £110pw) and
- not in full-time education

Other conditions and points

Breaks in caring of up to four weeks in any six-month period are allowed.

Example

Janet Tregear is 58 and spends most days looking after her elderly mother, Violet. Some days she shares the caring responsibility with her brother Derek. Janet does not do any paid work, though her husband Rod does.

Typical client problems with this benefit

Impact of the earnings rule.

Disabled person comes off PIP (DL component), DLA Care or AA, or DLA Care goes down to lowest rate: CA ends.

Disabled person dies: CA ends after 8 weeks

Two carers both doing at least 35 hours' care pw for one person and both wanting to claim CA (only one of them may).

'My earnings in a shop went over the limit for about 2 months during the Christmas period when work was very busy. I didn't tell the DWP and now they have found out. They want to go back over my last 5 years' wageslips to see if there were other times I should have told them. I'm really worried it's going to land me with a bill for thousands of pounds.'

OTHER BENEFITS

Industrial Injuries Disablement Benefit

For those who have a disablement of at least 14% through an industrial injury or disease.

depending on percentage disablement sliding scale up to	**2012–13**	**2013–14**	**2014–15**	**2015–16**	**2016–17**	**2017–18**
lowest level (14% disablement)	£31.62	£32.32	£33.20	£33.60	£33.60	£33.94
highest level (100% disablement)	£158.10	£161.60	£166.00	£168.00	£168.00	£169.70

contributory?	**overlapping?**	**dependent additions?**	**means-tested?**	**counts as income for means-tested benefits?**	**counts as income for tax credits?**
no	no	no	no	yes	no

Who gets it?

- people with an industrial injury or
- prescribed industrial disease
- with long-term disablement of at least 14%

Other conditions and points

There are a number of obsolete additions to IIDB, such as reduced earnings allowance, which some people still get due to transitional protection.

You must have been an employed earner.

If an industrial disease it must correspond with the prescribed list; so must the job that the claimant was in when disease was contracted.

Under-18s get lower rates.

Example

Serkan worked in a financial organisation inputting data into a computer using a keyboard. Because of the way staff workstations were set up, Serkan ended up with severe repetition strain injuries in both his wrists. As his loss of faculty is classed as 19%, he is entitled to the minimum £33.94 rate of IIDB.

Typical client problems with this benefit

Too low a percentage assessment: '*I have been assessed as 13% disabled by my industrial hearing loss. This means I don't qualify for IIDB at all. What can I do about this?*'

Wrong job: '*I incurred hearing loss after working 20 years on oil rig engines. The DWP say this doesn't count as a "ship's engine room" so they won't pay me IIDB.*'

Contribution-based Jobseeker's Allowance

For people who become unemployed having recently paid National Insurance contributions.

aged	2012–13	2013–14	2014–15	2015–16	2016–17	2017–18
under 25	£56.25	£56.80	£57.35	£57.90	£57.90	£57.90
25+	£71.00	£71.70	£72.40	£73.10	£73.10	£73.10

contributory?	overlapping?	dependent additions?	means-tested?	counts as income for means-tested benefits?	counts as income for tax credits?
yes	yes	no	no	yes	yes

Who gets it?
people who are

- unemployed
- available for work and
- actively seeking work, and
- who have paid enough National Insurance contributions

Other conditions and points

Amount received is less any part-time earnings, and pensions.

Paid for 6 months only.

Example

Lou Shook Ching is a solicitor who has just been made redundant. She is unemployed to start with, following her loss of work. She has worked full time for the last seven years at the same firm. She should get 26 weeks' JSA.

Typical client problems with this benefit

Failure to take up a job offer, or to job seek sufficiently – leading to very heavy sanctions.

Satisfying the labour market conditions.

Jobcentre imposes over-stringent jobseeking requirements.

Low take-up among well-off groups.

Additional DWP pressure to find work after 13 weeks' unemployment.

'There's no way I can afford a season ticket to get to Chippenham every day out of the wages I'm being offered, yet the Jobcentre Plus say that if I don't take the job they'll sanction me **and** *prevent me getting benefit on a fresh claim as well.'*

Child Benefit

For people who have children with whom they live and for whom they are responsible.

	2012–13	2013–14	2014–15	2015–16	2016–17	2017–18
first child	£20.30	£20.30	£20.50	£20.70	£20.70	£20.70
each other child	£13.40	£13.40	£13.55	£13.70	£13.70	£13.70

contributory?	overlapping?	dependent additions?	means-tested?	counts as income for income support?	counts as income for tax credits?
no	No	no	no	no (in 'new scheme' Income Support); yes (for 'old-scheme' IS)	no

Example

Leslie and Pete have two children. They get one higher rate award and one lower rate award of Child Benefit, payable to Leslie. Later they split up; the children both live with Leslie, so she carries on receiving both lots of Child Benefit

Typical client problems with this benefit

Competing claims: *'Since my wife and I split up our children spend half the time with her and half the time with me. But she still gets the child benefit for both of them. This isn't fair because it stops me getting income support as a lone parent.'*

Coming from abroad: *'as we're subject to immigration control they say I can't get any Child Benefit yet.'*

For people with income of £50,000 or more in a tax year, although CB is paid as normal, income tax is adjusted so as to reduce or eliminate the value of the CB as income rises to £60,000.

Statutory Maternity Pay, Statutory Paternity Pay and Statutory Adoption Pay, Statutory Shared Parental Pay

For women employees on at least £112 per week who are in the SMP-payable maternity period (39 weeks), men in the paternity period (two weeks and further extended period after mother returns to work), or those who are adopting.

	2012–13	2013–14	2014–15	2015–16	2016–17	2017–18
SMP for 6 weeks	90% earnings	90% earnings	90% earnings	90% earnings	90% earnings	90% earnings
then SMP for 33 weeks	£135.45	£136.78	£138.18	£139.58	£139.58	£140.98
SPP SAP	£135.45	£136.78	£138.18	£139.58	£139.58	£140.98

contributory?	**overlapping?**	**dependent additions?**	**means-tested?**	**counts as income for income support?**	**counts as income for tax credits?**
no	no	no	no	yes	yes – excess over £100pw

Who gets SMP?

- women expecting a baby in the next 11 weeks or who have given birth and are still within an overall 39-week maternity period
- who worked in their present job for at least 26 weeks ending in the 15th week before the due date
- earning more than earnings threshold (£113pw)

Who gets SPP?

- those whose spouse, civil partner or partner recently gave birth or adopted
- available for 2 weeks
- additional SPP also now available for fathers taking time off when mother goes back to work within the maternity period

Who gets SAP?

those adopting a child

available for 26 weeks

Other conditions and points

Paid by the employer.

Example
Amina worked in her present job for the last 2 years. Now she is pregnant; her baby is due in three months' time. Once the expected week of birth is 11 weeks away, she can take maternity leave and claim SMP.

Typical client problems with this benefit
Not many problems.
Employer reluctance to pay: '*My employer says he isn't obliged to pay me SMP, and that he'll dismiss me if I take the matter further.*'

Maternity Allowance

For women during the maternity period who cannot get Statutory Maternity Pay.

	2012–13	2013–14	2014–15	2015–16	2016–17	2017–18
standard rate	£135.45	£136.78	£138.18	£139.58	£139.58	£140.98

contributory?	overlapping?	dependent additions?	means-tested?	counts as income for means-tested benefits?	counts as income for tax credits?
no	yes	yes	no	yes	No

Who gets it?
women with 11 weeks or less to go before the birth

- who worked for at least 26 weeks ...
- for at least £30pw in 13 of those weeks ...
- during the 66 weeks before the due date
- and who are not working during maternity period

Other conditions and points

Stays in payment for 39 weeks.

Example
Baljit has worked part time, earning between £50 and £150 pw, for the last three years, often changing jobs every few months. Now she is pregnant; her expected date of delivery is in 10 weeks' time. Baljit's current employer says she cannot get SMP from her because the job has only lasted three weeks so far.

Typical client problems with this benefit

Few problems arise.

Occasional difficulties working out qualifying work weeks: just use a calendar!

Bereavement Support Payment

A new benefit available for those who have been widowed and whose late spouse or civil partner paid enough National Insurance. The deceased must have died on or after 6 April 2017.

	2012–13	2013–14	2014–15	2015–16	2016–17	2017–18
For claimants **with children or pregnant:** initial lump sum						£3,500
...then monthly amount						£350 per month
For claimants **without children:** initial lump sum						£2,500
...then monthly amount						£100 per month

contributory?	**overlapping?**	**dependent additions?**	**means-tested?**	**counts as income for income support?**	**counts as income for tax credits?**
yes	yes	no	no	no	no

Who gets it?

- those widowed whilst under pensionable age
- and still under pensionable age
- whose late spouse/civil partner paid enough National Insurance contributions
- available for survivors in same-sex marriages just as in opposite-sex ones

- no lower age limit

Other conditions and points

Lasts for 18 months from death of spouse/civil partner.

Unmarried partners (or those not civil partners) don’t qualify.

Must claim within 3 months of the death (12 months for lump sum)

The lump sum counts as capital for means-tested benefits after one year

Bereavement Payment

A single payment for those who have been widowed before 6 April 2017; on or after that date – see Bereavement Support Payment above.

	2012–13	2013–14	2014–15	2015–16	2016–17	2017–18
	£2,000	£2,000	£2,000	£2,000	£2,000	£2,000

contributory?	overlapping?	dependent additions?	means-tested?	counts as capital for income support?	counts as income-generating capital for tax credits?
yes	no	no	no	yes	yes
					To be abolished from April 2018

Who gets it?

- those widowed whilst under 60
- whose late spouse or civil partner paid enough National Insurance contributions
- available for survivors in same-sex marriages just as in opposite-sex ones

Other conditions and points

NI conditions very easy to meet

Must be claimed within 12 months of the death.

Bereavement Allowance

For those who have been widowed, are still single, and whose late spouse or civil partner paid enough National Insurance. **Only payable in relation to a death before 6 April 2017**; on or after that date – see Bereavement Support Payment above.

	2012–13	2013–14	2014–15	2015–16	2016–17	2017–18
maximum rate, with sliding age-related reductions if under 55	£105.95	£108.30	£111.20	£112.55	£112.55	£113.70

contributory?	**overlapping?**	**dependent additions?**	**means-tested?**	**counts as income for income support?**	**counts as income for tax credits?**
yes	yes	yes	no	yes	yes

Who gets it?

- those widowed between age 45 and pensionable age
- and still under pensionable age
- whose late spouse/civil partner paid enough National Insurance contributions
- and who is still single
- available for survivors in same-sex marriages just as in opposite-sex ones

Other conditions and points

Lasts for 52 weeks from death of spouse/civil partner.

Unmarried partners don't qualify.

NI conditions waived if spouse/civil partner died from industrial injury or disease.

Ends if you remarry or re-civil-partner.

Suspended if you re-partner (not married or civil partners).

Widowed Parent's Allowance

For those who have been widowed, have children, are still single, and whose late spouse/civil partner paid enough National Insurance. **Only payable in relation to a death before 6 April 2017;** on or after that date – see Bereavement Support Payment above.

	2012–13	2013–14	2014–15	2015–16	2016–17	2017–18
	£105.95	£108.30	£111.20	£112.55	£112.55	£113.70

contributory?	overlapping?	dependent additions?	means-tested?	counts as income for income support?	counts as income for tax credits?
yes	yes	yes	no	yes	yes

Who gets it?

- those under pensionable age
- widowed whilst
- entitled to Child Benefit for, and living with, one or more children, or
- pregnant by late husband or
- living with spouse at time of death and pregnant by artificial insemination, and
- whose late spouse/civil partner paid enough National Insurance contributions
- available for survivors in same-sex marriages just as in opposite-sex ones

Other conditions and points

Ends if you remarry or enter a civil partnership.

Suspended if you re-partner other than marriage or civil partnership.

Retirement Pension

People reaching pension age from 6 April 2016 now get single-tier state pension based only on their own NI contributions. Those who reached pension age before that continue to get 'old-style' retirement pension.

	2012–13	2013–14	2014–15	2015–16	2016–17	2017–18
2016 version state pension ('single-tier')					£155.65	£159.55
old-style: main category A rate; category B for surviving spouse or civil partner	£107.45	£110.15	£113.10	£115.95	£119.30	£122.30
old-style: category B for spouses and civil partners; category D for over-80s	£64.40	£66.00	£67.80	£69.50	£65.70	£66.35

contributory?	**overlapping?**	**dependent additions?**	**means-tested?**	**counts as income for income support?**	**counts as income for tax credits?**
yes	yes	yes	no	yes	yes

Who gets it?

New single-tier state pension: for men and women who have reached pensionable age after 5 April 2016 who have paid sufficient National Insurance contributions.

Category A: men and women who reached pensionable age before 6 April 2016 who paid sufficient National Insurance contributions

Category B: married person or civil partner who reached pensionable age before 6 April 2016 whose spouse or civil partner is over pensionable age; also for some widows, widowers and surviving civil partners

Other conditions and points

Can be deferred in return for increase in its value or a lump sum.

Entitlement is regardless of whether working or not.

Pensionable age was 60 for women born before 6 April 1950, rising for those born after that; it is 65 for men. Women's pension age reaches 65 in November 2018. Pension age for men and women will then increase to 66 from December 2018 to October 2020.

Typical client problems with this benefit: very few problems arise.

Clients may need advice about deferring (don't advise yes or no, just give them the facts).

'What pension will I get if I divorce?'

'I'm a 56-year-old woman: do I need to carry on paying NI in order to get a full pension?'

'How do I claim my pension?'

'Can I claim in advance?'

RETAIL PRICE INDEX AND CONSUMER PRICE INDEX

RETAIL PRICE INDEX

Year	Jan	Feb	Mar	Apr	May	Jun	Jul	Aug	Sep	Oct	Nov	Dec
1967	15.7	15.7	15.7	15.8	15.8	15.9	15.85	15.7	15.7	15.8	15.9	16.0
1968	16.1	16.2	16.2	16.5	16.5	16.6	16.6	16.6	16.6	16.7	16.8	17.0
1969	17.1	17.2	17.2	17.4	17.4	17.5	17.5	17.4	17.8	17.6	17.6	17.8
1970	17.9	18.0	18.1	18.4	18.4	18.5	18.6	18.6	18.7	18.9	19.0	19.2
1971	19.4	19.5	19.7	20.1	20.2	20.4	20.5	20.5	20.6	20.7	20.8	20.9
1972	21.0	21.1	21.2	21.3	21.5	21.6	21.7	21.9	22.0	22.3	22.4	22.5
1973	22.7	22.8	23.0	23.4	23.6	23.6	23.8	23.8	24.0	24.6	24.7	24.9
1974	25.6	25.8	26.0	26.9	27.3	27.6	27.8	27.8	28.1	28.7	29.2	29.7
1975	30.4	30.9	31.5	32.7	34.1	34.8	35.1	35.1	35.6	36.1	36.6	37.1
1976	37.5	38.0	38.2	38.9	39.3	39.5	39.6	40.1	40.7	41.4	42.0	42.6
1977	43.7	44.1	44.6	45.7	46.1	46.5	46.6	46.8	47.1	47.3	47.5	47.8
1978	48.0	48.3	48.6	49.3	49.6	50.0	50.2	50.6	50.8	51.0	51.3	51.8
1979	52.5	53.0	53.4	54.3	54.7	55.7	58.1	58.5	59.1	59.7	60.3	60.7
1980	62.2	63.1	63.9	66.1	66.7	67.3	67.9	68.1	68.5	68.9	69.5	69.9
1981	70.3	70.9	72.0	74.1	74.6	75.0	75.3	75.9	76.3	77.0	77.8	78.3
1982	78.7	78.8	79.4	81.0	81.6	81.9	81.9	81.9	81.9	82.3	82.7	82.5
1983	82.6	83.0	83.1	84.3	84.6	84.8	85.3	85.7	86.1	86.4	86.7	86.9
1984	86.8	87.2	87.5	88.6	89.0	89.2	89.1	89.9	90.1	90.7	91.0	90.9
1985	91.2	91.9	92.8	94.8	95.2	95.4	95.2	95.5	95.4	95.6	95.9	96.1
1986	96.3	96.6	96.7	97.7	97.9	97.8	97.5	97.8	98.3	98.5	99.3	99.6
1987	100.0	100.4	100.6	101.8	101.9	101.9	108.7	102.1	102.4	102.9	103.4	103.3
1988	103.3	103.7	104.1	105.8	106.2	106.6	106.7	107.9	108.4	109.5	110.0	110.3
1989	111.0	111.8	112.3	114.3	115.0	115.4	115.5	115.8	116.6	117.5	118.5	118.8
1990	119.5	120.2	121.4	125.1	126.2	126.7	126.8	128.1	129.3	130.3	130.0	129.9
1991	130.2	130.9	131.4	133.1	133.5	134.1	133.8	134.1	134.6	135.1	135.6	135.7
1992	135.6	136.3	136.7	138.8	139.3	139.3	138.8	138.9	139.4	139.9	139.7	139.2
1993	137.9	138.8	139.3	140.6	141.1	141.0	140.7	141.3	141.9	141.8	141.6	141.9
1994	141.3	142.1	142.5	144.2	144.7	144.7	144.0	144.7	145.0	145.2	145.3	146.0
1995	146.0	146.9	147.5	149.0	149.6	149.8	149.1	149.9	150.6	149.8	149.8	150.7
1996	150.2	150.9	151.5	152.6	152.9	153.0	152.4	153.1	153.8	153.8	153.9	154.4
1997	154.4	155.0	155.4	156.3	156.9	157.5	157.5	158.5	159.3	159.5	159.6	160.0
1998	159.5	160.3	160.8	162.6	163.5	163.4	163.0	163.7	164.4	164.5	164.4	164.4
1999	163.4	163.7	164.1	165.2	165.6	165.6	165.1	165.5	166.2	166.5	166.7	167.3
2000	166.6	167.5	168.4	170.1	170.7	171.1	170.5	170.5	171.7	171.6	172.1	172.2
2001	171.1	172.0	172.2	173.1	174.2	174.4	173.3	184.0	174.6	174.3	173.6	173.4
2002	173.3	173.8	174.5	175.7	176.2	176.2	175.9	176.4	177.6	177.9	178.2	178.5
2003	178.4	179.3	179.9	181.2	181.5	181.3	181.3	181.6	182.5	182.6	182.7	183.5
2004	183.1	183.8	184.6	185.7	186.5	186.8	186.8	187.4	188.1	188.6	189.0	189.9
2005	188.9	189.6	190.5	191.6	192.0	192.2	192.2	192.6	193.1	193.3	193.6	194.1

Year	Jan	Feb	Mar	Apr	May	Jun	Jul	Aug	Sep	Oct	Nov	Dec
2006	193.4	194.2	195	196.5	197.7	198.5	198.5	199.2	200.1	200.4	201.1	202.7
2007	201.6	203.1	204.4	205.4	206.2	207.3	206.1	207.3	208.0	208.9	209.7	210.9
2008	209.8	211.4	212.1	214.0	215.1	216.8	216.5	217.2	218.4	217.7	216.0	212.9
2009	210.1	211.4	211.3	211.5	212.8	213.4	213.4	214.4	215.3	216	216.6	218
2010	217.9	219.2	220.7	222.8	223.6	224.1	223.6	224.5	225.3	225.8	226.8	228.4
2011	229.0	231.3	232.5	234.4	235.2	235.5	234.7	236.1	237.9	238.0	238.5	239.4
2012	238.0	239.9	240.8	242.5	242.4	241.8	242.1	243.0	244.2	245.6	245.6	246.8
2013	245.8	247.6	248.7	249.5	250	249.7	249.7	251	251.9	251.9	252.1	253.4
2014	252.6	254.2	254.8	255.7	255.9	256.3	256.0	257.0	257.6	252.7	257.1	257.5
2015	255.4	256.7	257.1	258.0	258.5	258.9	258.6	259.8	259.6	259.5	259.8	260.6
2016	258.8	260.0	261.1	261.4	262.1	263.1	263.4	264.4	264.9	264.8	265.5	267.1
2017	265.5	268.4	269.3	270.6	271.7	272.3	272.9	274.7				

CONSUMER PRICE INDEX

Year	Jan	Feb	Mar	Apr	May	Jun	Jul	Aug	Sep	Oct	Nov	Dec
2017	101.4	102.1	102.5	102.9	103.3	103.3	103.2	104.0				
2016	99.5	99.8	100.2	100.2	100.4	100.6	100.6	100.9	101.1	101.2	101.4	101.9
2015	99.3**	99.5	99.7	99.9	100.1	100.2	100.0	100.3	100.2	100.3	100.3	100.3
2014	126.7	127.3	127.7	128.1	128	128.3	127.8	128.3	128.4	128.5	128.2	128.2
2013	124.4	125.2	125.6	125.9	126.1	125.9	125.8	126.3	126.8	126.9	127	127.5
2012	121.1	121.8	122.2	122.9	122.8	122.3	122.5	123.1	123.5	124.2	124.4	125
2011	116.9	117.8	118.1	119.3	119.5	119.4	119.4	120.1	120.9	121	121.2	121.7
2010	112.4	112.9	113.5	114.2	114.4	114.6	114.3	114.9	114.9	115.2	115.6	116.8
2009	108.7	109.6	109.8	110.1	110.7	111	110.9	111.4	111.5	111.7	112	112.6
2008	105.5	106.3	106.7	107.6	108.3	109	109	109.7	110.3	110	109.9	109.5
2007	103.2	103.7	104.2	104.5	104.8	105	104.4	104.7	104.8	105.3	105.6	106.2
2006	100.5	100.9	101.1	101.7	102.2	102.5	102.5	102.9	103	103.2	103.4	104
2005	98.6	98.8	99.3	99.7	100	100	100.1	100.4	100.6	100.7	100.7	101
2004	97	97.2	97.4	97.8	98.1	98.1	97.8	98.1	98.2	98.4	98.6	99.1

** CPI and CPIH indices re-referenced and published with 2015=100.

INTEREST RATES

BANK OF ENGLAND BASE RATES 1999–PRESENT

Date	Rate
7 Jan 99	6.00%
4 Feb 99	5.50%
3 Mar 99	5.50%
8 April 99	5.25%
6 May 99	5.25%
10 Jun 99	5.00%
8 Jul 99	5.00%
5 Aug 99	5.00%
8 Sep 99	5.25%
7 Oct 99	5.25%
4 Nov 99	5.50%
9 Dec 99	5.50%
13 Jan 00	5.75%
10 Feb 00	6.00%
9 Mar 00	6.00%
6 Apr 00	6.00%
4 May 00	6.00%
7 Jun 00	6.00%
6 Jul 00	6.00%
3 Aug 00	6.00%
7 Sept 00	6.00%
5 Oct 00	6.00%
9 Nov 00	6.00%
7 Dec 00	6.00%
11 Jan 01	6.00%
8 Feb 01	5.75%
8 Mar 01	5.75%
5 Apr 01	5.50%
10 May 01	5.25%
6 Jun 01	5.25%
5 Jul 01	5.25%
2 Aug 01	5.00%
6 Sep 01	5.00%
18 Sep 01	4.75%
4 Oct 01	4.50%
7 Nov 01	4.00%

Date	Rate
5 Dec 01	4.00%
10 Jan 02	4.00%
7 Feb 02	4.00%
7 Mar 02	4.00%
4 Apr 02	4.00%
9 May 02	4.00%
21 Dec 02	4.50%
6 Jun 02	4.00%
4 Jul 02	4.00%
1 Aug 02	4.00%
5 Sep 02	4.00%
10 Oct 02	4.00%
7 Nov 02	4.00%
5 Dec 02	4.00%
9 Jan 03	4.00%
6 Feb 03	3.75%
6 Mar 03	3.75%
10 Apr 03	3.75%
8 May 03	3.75%
5 Jun 03	3.75%
10 Jul 03	3.50%
7 Aug 03	3.50%
4 Sep 03	3.50%
9 Oct 03	3.50%
6 Nov 03	3.75%
4 Dec 03	3.75%
8 Jan 04	3.75%
5 Feb 04	4.00%
4 Mar 04	4.00%
8 Apr 04	4.00%
6 May 04	4.25%
10 Jun 04	4.50%
8 Jul 04	4.50%
5 Aug 04	4.75%
9 Sep 04	4.75%
7 Oct 04	4.75%
4 Nov 04	4.75%
9 Dec 04	4.75%
13 Jan 05	4.75%
10 Feb 05	4.75%
10 Mar 05	4.75%
7 Apr 05	4.75%
9 May 05	4.75%
9 Jun 05	4.75%
7 Jul 05	4.75%

Date	Rate
4 Aug 05	4.50%
8 Sep 05	4.50%
6 Oct 05	4.50%
10 Nov 05	4.50%
8 Dec 05	4.50%
12 Jan 06	4.50%
9 Feb 06	4.5%
9 Mar 06	4.5%
6 Apr 06	4.5%
4 May 06	4.5%
4 Jun 06	4.5%
6 Jul 06	4.5%
3 Aug 06	4.75%
7 Sep 06	4.75%
5 Oct 06	4.75%
9 Nov 06	5.00%
7 Dec 06	5.00%
11 Jan 07	5.25%
8 Feb 07	5.25%
8 Mar 07	5.25%
5 Apr 07	5.25%
10 May 07	5.5%
7 Jun 07	5.5%
5 Jul 07	5.75%
2 Aug 07	5.75%
6 Sep 07	5.75%
4 Oct 07	5.75%
8 Nov 07	5.75%
6 Dec 07	5.5%
10 Jan 08	5.5%
07 Feb 08	5.25%
06 Mar 08	5.25%
10 Apr 08	5.00%
8 May 08	5.00%
5 Jun 08	5.00%
10 Jul 08	5.00%
7 Aug 08	5.00%
4 Sep 08	5.00%
8 Oct 08	4.50%
6 Nov 08	3.00%
14 Dec 08	2.00%
8 Jan 09	1.50%
5 Feb 09	1.00%
5 Mar 09	0.50%
9 Apr 09	0.50%

Date	Rate
7 May 09	0.50%
4 Jun 09	0.50%
9 Jul 09	0.50%
6 Aug 09	0.50%
10 Sep 09	0.50%
8 Oct 09	0.50%
5 Nov 09	0.50%
10 Dec 09	0.50%
7 Jan 10	0.50%
4 Feb 10	0.50%
4 Mar 10	0.50%
8 Apr 10	0.50%
10 May 10	0.50%
10 Jun 10	0.50%
08 Jul 10	0.50%
05 Aug 10	0.50%
09 Sep 10	0.50%
07 Oct 10	0.50%
04 Nov 10	0.50%
09 Dec 10	0.50%
13 Jan 11	0.50%
10 Feb 11	0.50%
10 Mar 11	0.50%
7 Apr 11	0.50%
5 May 11	0.50%
9 Jun 11	0.50%
7 Jul 11	0.50%
4 Aug 11	0.50%
8 Sep 11	0.50%
6 Oct 11	0.50%
10 Nov 11	0.50%
8 Dec 11	0.50%
12 Jan 12	0.50%
9 Feb 12	0.50%
8 Mar 12	0.50%
5 Apr 12	0.50%
10 May 12	0.50%
7 Jun 12	0.50%
5 Jul 12	0.50%
2 Aug 12	0.50%
5 Jul 12	0.50%
2 Aug 12	0.50%
6 Sep 12	0.50%
4 Oct 12	0.50%
8 Nov 12	0.50%

Date	Rate
6 Dec 12	0.50%
10 Jan 13	0.50%
7 Feb 13	0.50%
7 Mar 13	0.50%
4 Apr 13	0.50%
9 May 13	0.50%
13 Jun 13	0.50%
13 Jul 13	0.50%
13 Aug 13	0.50%
5 Sept 13	0.50%
10 Oct 13	0.50%
7 Nov 13	0.50%
5 Dec 13	0.50%
9 Jan 14	0.50%
6 Feb 14	0.50%
6 Mar 14	0.50%
10 Apr 14	0.50%
8 May 14	0.50%
5 Jun 14	0.50%
10 Jul 14	0.50%
7 Aug 14	0.50%
4 Sept 14	0.50%
9 Oct 14	0.50%
6 Nov 14	0.50%
4 Dec 14	0.50%
8 Jan 15	0.50%
5 Feb 15	0.50%
5 Mar 15	0.50%
9 April 15	0.50%
11 May 15	0.50%
4 Jun 15	0.50%
9 Jul 15	0.50%
6 Aug 15	0.50%
10 Sept 15	0.50%
8 Oct 15	0.50%
5 Nov 15	0.50%
10 Dec 15	0.50%
04 Jan 16	0.50%
04 Feb 16	0.50%
17 Mar 16	0.50%
14 Apr 16	0.50%
12 May 16	0.50%
16 Jun 16	0.50%
14 Jul 16	0.50%
4 Aug 16	0.25%

Date	Rate
15 Sept 16	0.25%
3 Nov 16	0.25%
15 Dec 16	0.25%
2 Feb 17	0.25%
16 Mar 17	0.25%
11 May 17	0.25%
15 Jun 17	0.25%
3 Aug 17	0.25%
14 Sept 17	0.25%